Race, Community, and Conflict

D0264370

Race, Community, and Conflict

A STUDY OF SPARKBROOK

JOHN REX and ROBERT MOORE

with the assistance of

ALAN SHUTTLEWORTH
JENNIFER WILLIAMS

Published for the
Institute of Race Relations, London
OXFORD UNIVERSITY PRESS
LONDON   NEW YORK

Oxford University Press, Ely House, London W.1

GLASGOW NEW YORK TORONTO MELBOURNE WELLINGTON
CAPE TOWN IBADAN NAIROBI DAR ES SALAAM LUSAKA ADDIS ABABA
DELHI BOMBAY CALCUTTA MADRAS KARACHI LAHORE DACCA
KUALA LUMPUR SINGAPORE HONG KONG TOKYO

ISBN 0 19 218162 9

First published 1967
Reprinted 1969 (with corrections), 1971, and 1974

The Survey of Race Relations in Britain

The Survey of Race Relations in Britain, a five-year project which was started in 1963 on a grant from the Nuffield Foundation, is concerned with the implications for British society of the presence of a substantial number of Commonwealth immigrants. It has commissioned a number of full-scale inquiries in cities with large immigrant settlements, within the immigrant communities themselves and in industry. From these studies and the basic information that is being assembled the Survey will produce its own findings and will advance proposals.

The Survey is being conducted under the auspices of the Institute of Race Relations, an unofficial and non-political body, founded in England in 1958 to encourage and facilitate the study of the relations between races everywhere. The Institute is precluded by the Memorandum and Articles of its incorporation from expressing a corporate view. The opinions expressed in this work are those of the authors.

PRINTED IN GREAT BRITAIN BY
HAZELL WATSON AND VINEY LTD
AYLESBURY, BUCKS

Foreword

E. J. B. Rose

Director, Survey of Race Relations in Britain

The city is a crucible into which we pour the most disparate elements in our modern industrial society, vaguely expecting that given time they will one day fuse into an acceptable amalgam. But it is becoming increasingly clear that the prevailing shortage of housing and the selective measures taken to meet this shortage are turning the city into a breeding ground for tensions which may disturb the balance of this society.

This book is a study of a decaying area in a city which except for post-war London has attracted a greater number of migrants than any other in England. The importance of the study is to be found on many different levels. As an analysis of the housing policies of a great municipal authority it should dispel many misconceptions which are widely held about the connexion between immigrants and housing shortages. As a study of a zone of transition where newcomers to a city have to make their lives, it is a contribution to urban sociology and to the literature of race relations.

Within a radius of a mile from the city centre, Birmingham, like many other industrial cities, contains an inner ring of houses built less than a hundred years ago as homes for the merchant classes but now abandoned by them as the size of families has declined. Taken over by landlords who split them into separate dwellings, they have fallen very rapidly into decay but because of the relative soundness of the housing fabric they are not considered decrepit enough to be condemned. They are areas which, in the words of the authors, have not yet reached the night of slumdom and are aptly called twilight zones, a term which has come to be applied not only to a certain type of housing but to a type of tenure, multi-occupation, which prevails within areas of immigrant settlement.

The inhabitants of these twilight zones are not there by choice. They are the newcomers to the city who have been forced to find accommodation by a society which denies them the opportunities of the market or the shelter of the welfare state. Where neither mortgages nor council housing are available to them the immigrant finds shelter with the middlemen who while they may exploit the situation are filling a yawning gap left by the system. These landlords, the authors point out, play an indispensable role; they are the safety net under the safety net of the welfare state.

It is one of the themes of this book that the twilight zone is produced and perpetuated by a policy of discrimination and that in abandoning their responsibility to this new class of landlord the authorities are creating racial tensions that could have been avoided. As most of the tenants and many of the landlords are immigrants, much of the blame which should attach to the city for its failure to solve its own housing problem is laid at the door of people of another race or culture. And a policy which denies the immigrant access to housing forces him into a kind of limbo mid-way between the culture which he has left behind and the somewhat dimly perceived culture of his hosts from which, apart from the contacts he may make at work, he is almost sealed off.

Sparkbrook was the twilight zone chosen for this study because it contained a thriving Community Association whose role in preserving the morale of a neighbourhood in decline is closely examined in this book. As the immigrants cluster together in colonies they confront the native citizens who, whether they have been unable to escape or have chosen to remain, resent the changes that have befallen their neighbourhood and are filled with nostalgia for the past. It is often thought that the aim of the voluntary association should be to involve the immigrant in the community but the authors show that it has an even more important role in preserving the morale of the native, for it provides an effective channel of action for people who might otherwise have found no outlet for their frustration except in some racialist organization.

Another good reason for the choice of Sparkbrook was the large proportion of the Irish who constitute more than half the immigrants in this area. There have been all too few studies of the Irish immigration and it is important that this book, one of the first studies of a twilight zone in this country, should be seen as a study of a situation which would exist even if there had been no coloured immigration.

This was the first research study to be supported by the Survey of Race Relations in Britain. We were indeed fortunate to find Professor Rex in Birmingham at the outset of our Survey eager to examine problems which confronted Birmingham and so many other cities. We were also fortunate that he was later joined by Robert Moore who shared with him a desire to approach these problems both as a sociologist and as a citizen. Professor Rex's leadership attracted a number of people within the University to contribute their time and talents to the study which we believe will illuminate one of the most urgent problems facing our society and, through its analysis of the causes, contribute towards a solution.

Contents

List of Illustrations

MAPS

PLATES

The photographs in this book were taken by students of the School of Photography, Birmingham College of Art and Design, during the course of their studies, and are reproduced by permission of the Principal, Meredith W. Hawes, A.R.I.C.A., A.R.W.S., F.R.S.A., N.R.D. (E.D.).

List of Tables

Preface and Acknowledgements

This book arose out of our concern with the immediate and practical problems of life in Birmingham in 1963. The immediate challenge to investigate these problems came when a Pakistani friend arrived in Birmingham to dissuade a fellow Pakistani from standing as an immigrant candidate for the Council in Sparkbrook. He also brought to our attention the important work being carried on by the Sparkbrook Association in a deteriorating urban area and, more generally, asked us to concern ourselves as sociologists with the problems which faced Pakistanis in Birmingham. That gave us a value standpoint from which to start.

Looking at problems from the point of view of Pakistanis or, more generally, of black Commonwealth immigrants meant that we were forced to look at the social constraints which were imposed upon their behaviour, and these we analysed in terms of theory derived from urban sociology and the sociology of race relations. At the most general level our theoretical perspective, however, was one which emphasized conflict within the urban social system rather than one which saw that system as a functionally integrated whole.

This perspective made it possible for us to say something not wholly unrealistic about policy. In subsequent years we have learned that policy-oriented research often involves a great deal of pretence. The researcher simply accepts the authorities' own definition of their goals and, without analysing these further, addresses himself to an empirical and technical problem. What we sought to do, however, and this was clearly stated in Chapter XI, was to look at the function which existing social structures subserved from a variety of points of view. In doing so we felt justified in suggesting that, given the long-term rather than short-term interest of those concerned with the welfare of Birmingham, policies discriminating against immigrants in the sphere of housing were damaging to the city.

We still hold this to be true, but, in the light of subsequent developments, it is important to ask whether men will always act only in terms of their short-term interests, and, if so, how? Our conclusion was that, while the imperatives which derived from the notion of a smoothly functioning urban social system or from the interests of the working class within Birmingham society pointed to policies which would eliminate racial discrimination, the actual behaviour of men in such circumstances was likely to be determined by a much wider socio-political context which shaped men's perceptions of their interests more directly.

This wider socio-political context was that of the relationship between the former colonial territories and the metropolitan countries and their working class. Thus, although this is a study of the effect on race relations of urban social processes, ultimately the overall pattern of race relations cannot be understood solely as an urban problem. This is a current American way of avoiding facing up to the race war and the Third World Revolution. We do not wish our work to be quoted in support of that kind of position. This is made clear in John Rex's later books, *Race Relations in Sociological Theory* and *Race, Colonialism and the City*.

In practical terms a number of crucial decisions were taken after this book was written which had the effect not of alleviating racial tension, but of intensifying it. Ten years after our study nothing has been done to interfere with the right of local authorities to operate systems of housing allocation which involve *de facto* discrimination. Successive Ministers of Housing notably failed to grasp this nettle. The most that was done was the appointment of the Cullingworth Committee on the allocation of council houses and the main recommendations of their Report have been ignored. The Birmingham Corporation Housing Act of 1965 which we criticized and which was subsequently criticized by the Housing Panel of the National Committee of Commonwealth Immigrants was not merely not repealed, but made national policy in its main essentials. It is little wonder then that the pattern of discrimination and suffering which we noted in Birmingham is as evident as it was in 1964. Moreover, this situation has been accompanied by a development of the kind of racist norm in political discussion which was unthinkable at the time of Mr. Peter Griffiths' election to Parliament. One cannot look back over the ten years since this research began without noting that the whole thrust of policy has been of a kind which intensifies racial conflict. So much is this the case that we feel it desirable to say at this time that we cannot recommend to any of our West Indian, or Pakistani, or Indian friends that they should trust any of the major political parties either at local or national level. The defence of their rights will depend on their own capacity to organize to defend themselves.

Since the book was written we have had reason to disagree with many of those who helped us at the time. For this very reason, however, we would wish to repeat that the survey could never have been undertaken without the close and friendly co-operation of Jim Rose and Nicholas Deakin of the Survey of Race Relations in Britain. Alan Shuttleworth and Jennifer Williams made contributions to the book itself through their research and writing. Edward Laing helped us with some participant observation in the West Indian community. Gillian Lee helped us with much of the more tedious and difficult work of data processing, and Gillian Lloyd provided us with much useful information while carrying on investigations for her undergraduate dissertation.

We would like to thank those Departments of the Birmingham Corporation which provided us with information, particularly the Departments of Rating and Valuation, Education, Housing Management, and Public Health, as well as the Central Statistical Office. We should also like to thank the Birmingham College of Art for allowing students of the School of Photography to produce our illustrations.

In the University of Birmingham we enjoyed the hospitality of the West Midlands Social and Political Research Unit through being allowed to locate our project there, and owe particular thanks to Professor François Lafitte, Dr. David Eversley, Mrs. Valerie Jackson, and Dr. Graham Lomas. We also gained the enthusiastic help of many voluntary interviewers amongst students, and are particularly grateful to the Indian and Pakistani Students' Societies for their help with translation. Other individuals who helped us with sorting and processing data were Elizabeth Wilson, John Burgess, Christine Roberts, and Margaret Moodie.

Lastly, we have to thank the people who put Sparkbrook on the map. First among these was the late Dr. Molly Barrow. Any words of tribute to Dr. Barrow would be inadequate and she would have brushed them aside as a waste of time which should have been devoted to solving people's problems. We cannot, however, forbear to say that she was quite simply one of the best human beings we have ever met. Sparkbrook and Birmingham could ill afford to lose her. As a result of her initiative other workers like Elizabeth Radford, Donald Curtis, Gene Pack, Lorna Webster, and Pamela Allen were able to carry on their work. We trust that someone other than ourselves will note the significant role of Elizabeth Radford in pioneering a new type of social work in Sparkbrook. It is hard to imagine a more happy choice for the job which had to be done there.

We would wish to acknowledge also the support which we received from the Sparkbrook Association Council and its Chairman, the Reverend Jack Reed, but more than this the friendship and hospitality offered to us by the many wonderful people whom we met in the course of our research in Sparkbrook. Some of those who lived there we know will have felt that writing a book about their area as a problem area might have amplified their problems. If this is the case, we apologize to them. For our part, however, whenever we visit Sparkbrook we still see the hardship and the suffering, but we see also a vigorous community life which makes living there far richer in human terms than it is in genteel suburbia.

Responsibility for the Introduction and Chapters I, VI, VIII, IX, XI, and XII belongs to John Rex, and for Chapters II, III, IV, V and VII to Robert Moore. Jennifer Williams wrote Chapter X. The typescript of the book was prepared in the University of Durham by Mrs. Sara Stubbs and Mrs. Joyce Nolan, who laboured long and hard to translate the manuscript and to produce the typescript on time.

October 1973
JOHN REX
University of Warwick

ROBERT MOORE
University of Aberdeen

Introduction

The problem of race relations which confronted and perplexed
the people of Birmingham in the early 1960s was one of immense practical political importance. What Birmingham does to
resolve it will have consequences not merely nationally but
internationally. It is important, therefore, that sociologists
studying it should report their findings not merely to an
academic audience, but to the widest possible audience of
citizens and practical men-of-affairs. For this reason we have
presented our findings in the pages which follow with the
minimum overt reference to sociological theories and concepts.
Yet we would wish to insist that this is a specifically sociological study, that the questions which we have attempted to
answer are sociological ones, and that what we have to say is of
some general significance for the study of race relations in an
urban context. We propose, therefore, in this introduction to discuss some of the methodological and theoretical issues involved
in our study and in a final chapter to point to some general
sociological conclusions.

A sociological study of race relations must, in the first place,
be distinguished from one which is purely historical and one
which is psychological in its approach. This is not by any means
to suggest that the historian and the psychologist do not have a
considerable contribution to make to the study of race relations.
It is to suggest, however, that neglect of the sociological dimensions of the problem could be disastrously misleading.

The inadequacy of historical explanation taken by itself rests
upon the historian's inability to make explicit the general
processes which his explanation assumes. Very few historians,
of course, confine themselves to reporting unique historical
sequences of events. In their use of conjunctions like 'because',
'so', and 'therefore', they refer implicitly to general psycho-

logical and sociological laws. And it is a mark of the good historian that the laws to which he does make reference are laws which are known to be empirically valid. None the less the prime virtue of the historian lies in the techniques which he has at his disposal for assessing the evidence as to what actually occurred. The explanatory laws to which he refers are for him a secondary matter. In the study of race relations his contribution will lie in his ability to record precisely what occurred in the situation of race contact. The interpretation of these occurrences in a task which falls to the generalizing, theoretical human sciences, above all to psychology and sociology.

But psychology alone cannot explain the kind of problem with which we are concerned. If, for example, we are concerned to explain prejudice and discriminatory behaviour, the psychologist could only hope to show either that there was some universal human tendency towards behaving in these ways or that there was a deviant minority who were prejudiced because of their disturbed personalities. In so far as he suggested that there were cultural factors or factors arising from a particular social system which caused the behaviour concerned, he would be passing into the realms of sociology.

In a recent review of race relation studies, Simpson and Yinger make this point when they say:

From our point of view, personality is best conceived not as a collection of traits, not as a static system . . . but as a process . . . the process of carrying out the functions of a shop steward in a union, superintendent of schools, or 'courteous customer' does not allow full individual variation to come into play. The roles themselves have some compulsions that influence which of the various tendencies the individual will express.[1]

It may be that amongst the people of Birmingham whom we studied some discriminatory behaviour was due to innate and universal tendencies. And it may be that some of it was the product of personality disturbance. But it is also the case that a great deal of it was sufficiently explained, once we knew something of Birmingham's social structure and conflicts, and the constellation of interests and roles which was built into Birming-

[1] R. Merton, L. Brook, and L. Cottrell, *Sociology Today*, New York, Basic Books, 1959, p. 379.

ham society. At the very least it must be said that the universal
factors and those having their roots in the individual personality
could only be known if the factors arising from the social,
economic, and cultural system were first sorted out.

This point was emphasized for us by the feeling which we and
many Birmingham people had about the race relations situation. This was the feeling that individuals were often acting in
contradiction of their own ideals and sometimes of their own
interests. They adopted discriminatory policies reluctantly,
regretfully, and sometimes guiltily because they felt compelled
to do so by circumstances beyond their control. Sometimes we
felt that they acted as men possessed by some evil demon. But
it is the task of sociologists to substitute causal explanation for
demonology and what we have tried to do is to show that that
which possessed them was not a demon, but the social system of
which they were part.

But our next task is to decide what the nature of this particular urban social system is. And in order to do so it is necessary
for us to resolve certain general questions about explanations in
terms of social systems and certain more particular questions
about urban society as a social system.

The theoretical approach of the sociologist to the explanation
of human behaviour which enjoys widespread popularity is
what is called 'functionalism'. The functionalist approach consists in explaining any recurrent aspect of human behaviour in
terms of the contribution which it makes to the maintenance of
a social system. So widespread, indeed, has this approach become that Kingsley Davis in his presidential address to the
American Sociological Association in 1959 suggested that all
sociology was functionalist.[1]

The criticism to which functionalism has been subject, however, is that, in emphasizing sociological determinism it allows
too little scope for human agency and appears to affirm that
what is, must necessarily be. This would seem to be particularly
true of the formulation of functionalist methodology by
Radcliffe-Brown,[2] who draws on the analogy between social
and organic systems and argues that a sociological explanation

---

[1] *American Sociological Review*, Vol. 24, No. 6, December 1959, pp. 757–72.
[2] A. Radcliffe-Brown, *Structure and Function in Primitive Society*, London, Cohen
and West, 1965.

must show the contribution which a recurrent activity makes to satisfying the needs of the social structure, just as a biological explanation shows the contribution made by an organic activity to maintaining the organic structure.

Yet even Radcliffe-Brown realizes that this analogy is imperfect in one crucial respect. For whereas organic systems cease to exist when crucial functions are not performed (i.e., organisms die), social systems may continue to exist but change their type. Thus any adequate formulation of the functionalist methodology must take account of this fact. Robert Merton[1] has suggested that this more adequate formulation can be attained by revising certain of the basic functionalist assumptions. These are: the postulate that everything has a function; the postulate of functional integration (i.e., of some sort of natural harmony of human activities); and the postulate of functional indispensability. Instead of these assumptions Merton proposes that it should be recognized that some activities occur which have no function or are even 'dysfunctional', that what is functional from the point of view of maintaining one partial structure may be dysfunctional from the point of view of maintaining another, and that, for any particular social function, there may be more than one feasible activity.

Merton, however, implicitly takes over the language of the organic analogy and it is not always clear what the partial structures are in terms of whose maintenance activities are being explained. The real problems involved in functionalist explanation only become apparent when they are set out not in terms of an analogical language, but in a language appropriate to the study of social action and interaction.

What we have assumed is that the determinants of an ongoing social system are to be found in the varied and sometimes conflicting interests of the typical actors in that system. For the achievement of their goals each of these actors ideally requires certain forms of behaviour of those around him, that is to say he requires the existence of certain structures of social relations. It is in this context that we can see clearly that what is functional from the one point of view is dysfunctional from the point of view of another. Thus, to take the central problem of our text

[1] R. Merton, *Social Theory and Social Structure*, Free Press of Glencoe, 1957, Chapter 1.

as an example, in a situation of housing shortage it will be functional from the point of view of the established residents that they should enjoy privileges in the allocation of housing. But this is highly dysfunctional from the point of view of new immigrants.

This approach to sociological explanation is one which we owe above all to Max Weber, Karl Mannheim, and Gunnar Myrdal. To Weber we owe the perception, which functionalist theory has too often obscured, that social phenomena can be investigated from many points of view according to their 'relevance for value' (i.e., their relevance for achieving various desired states of social affairs).[1] To Mannheim we owe the recognition that what is necessary from the point of view of one class may not be necessary from the point of view of another.[2] And to Myrdal we owe the combination of these perceptions so well applied in his own study of the American racial situation and explicitly set out in his appendixes to *An American Dilemma*. As he says there:

If a thing has a function it is good or at least essential. The term function can have a meaning only in terms of an assumed purpose; if that purpose is left undefined or implied to be the 'interest of society' which is not further defined, a considerable leeway for arbitrariness in practical implication is allowed.[3]

It should not be thought, however, that this rejection of the sort of determinism which argues tautologically that the *status quo* is necessary because it is the *status quo*, implies a retreat into a utopianism in which any goal at all may be regarded as realizable. What Myrdal's approach does imply is that having looked at a particular activity from several different perspectives it is possible to plan more realistically for the attainment of the goals of any one of them, knowing full well what obstacles lie in the way. Moreover, if we have no value-standpoint ourselves, we can attempt to predict the outcome of a social situation as the resultant of a number of conflicting forces.

To quote Myrdal again:

---

[1] M. Weber, *The Methodology of Social Science*, Free Press of Glencoe, 1949.
[2] K. Mannheim, *Ideology and Utopia*, London, Routledge and Kegan Paul, 1960.
[3] G. Myrdal, *An American Dilemma*, New York, Harper and Row, 1962, p. 1056.

In a scientific treatment of the practical aspect of social problems, the alternative sets of hypothetical value premises should not be chosen arbitrarily. The principle of selection should be their relevance. Relevance is determined by the interests and ideals of actual persons and groups of persons. There is thus no need of introducing value premises which are not held by anybody.

Within the circle of relevance so determined a still more narrow circle of significance may be taken to denote valuations which are held by substantial groups of people or by small groups with substantial social power. Realistic research on practical problems will have to concentrate its attention upon value premises corresponding to valuations which have high social significance. On the other hand, it is certainly not necessary to adopt only those value premises which are held by a majority of the population or a politically dominant group.[1]

We have attempted to apply these ideas in the pages which follow. We do not speak of the interests of Birmingham as such, nor do we adopt as our starting-point the value premises of the majority or the politically dominant group. Rather we begin by considering the goals of typical actors representing the various host and immigrant groups, the various politico-economic classes and more specifically what we have called 'housing classes'. We also refer to groups distinguished by more subtle criteria. It is out of the clash of interests, the conflicts and the truces between these groups that Birmingham society emerges.

It is important to emphasize, however, that the existence of conflicting group interests does not mean that there is a perpetual war of all against all, or of class against class, in Birmingham. If there were, Birmingham society would indeed cease to exist. What happens in such a situation is that the various groups mobilize what power they can to enforce compliance with their wishes, but that a point is reached in the power struggle where a realistic adjustment of interests is arrived at, at least temporarily, or organizational means are established for peaceful bargaining about which aims of which group shall be realized. Thus it is possible, even while adopting an approach not unlike Myrdal's to the study of race relations, to recognize the existence of some overall social system, consisting of those 'institutions of the truce' or those organizational means through

---

[1] Ibid., p. 1060.

which conflicts and tensions are managed. While we reject the conservative teleology of old-fashioned functionalism, we do not feel that there is any necessity to go to the other extreme and to posit limitless conflict.

There is another kind of integrative mechanism which serves to blur and modify conflict, of which we were profoundly aware in our study. This is that while various groups did have conflicting interests, they were also to some extent recognized as forming a status hierarchy, so that members of 'lower' groups aspired to membership of the higher. Moreover, it was the case, and usually is the case, that the associations and organizations through which the struggle of interests was fought out had historically inherited forms which modified the purposes of those who sought to use them to attain their own goals. Thus associational and communal life was organized in such a way as to blunt some of the conflicts inherent in the situation.

Our sociological perspective, then, does draw upon some of the insights of functionalism. Even though we do recognize and, indeed, emphasize conflict we recognize some kind of overall system within which behaviour has to be explained. Thus we reject the utopianism which assumes that any desired course of action can be pursued, because we recognize that actions have unintended consequences of a systematic kind, and because we recognize the existence of conflicting social pressures. And we also reject the empiricism of those who, having abandoned the perspective of the interconnectedness of social structure, concentrate on the analysis of single and isolated links in the causal chain.

So far, however, we have talked about theoretical approaches to sociology in general. We must now see how these ideas apply specifically within the field of urban sociology. We shall discuss the significance of what has gone before in relation to two sets of theoretical ideas about the city. The first of these is associated with the names of Park, Burgess, and Mackenzie[1] and the second with those of Tönnies,[2] Redfield,[3] and Wirth.[4]

---

[1] R. Park, E. Burgess, and R. MacKenzie, *The City*, Chicago, University of Chicago Press, 1923.
[2] F. Tönnies, *Fundamental Concepts of Sociology (Gemeinschaft und Gesellschaft)*, trans. C. P. Lomis, New York, Harper Torchbooks, 1963.
[3] R. Redfield, *The Little Community*, Chicago, University of Chicago Press, 1955.
[4] L. Wirth, *On Cities and Social Life*, Chicago, University of Chicago Press, 1964.

The most important contribution of Park and his colleagues, from our point of view, was their differentiation of the various residential zones of the city. It does not seem to us to matter very much whether these are to be regarded as forming concentric zones or as being arranged in sectors. What does matter is that Burgess indicates the existence within the city of several important sub-communities and it is these sub-communities— that of the lodging-house zone, that of the zone of working men's homes, that of the middle-class areas, and that of the commuters' suburbs—which we take as our own starting-point.

The weakness of the Chicago theory, to our mind, lies in its failure to investigate sufficiently the relationship between the culture and society of one sub-community and those of another. In fact, they seem to suggest two quite contradictory things about these sub-communities. One is that they are all to be understood in terms of an overall competition for land-use; the other that in each zone a relatively self-sufficient and internally integrated sub-community, lives a life segregated from that of the rest of the city.

We wish to modify the theory as follows: firstly, we suggest that in the initial settlement of the city, three different groups, differentially placed with regard to the possession of property, become segregated from one another and work out their own community style of life. The three groups involved here are: (a) the upper middle class characterized by their possession of property and capable of living without communal and neighbourly support; (b) the working class, which finds security in communal, collective and neighbourly institutions fashioned in the course of a struggle against economic adversity; and (c) a lower middle-class group aspiring to the way of life of the upper-middle classes, but enjoying only relatively inferior social facilities including housing.

Secondly, we, envisage a further stage of development characterized above all by the emergence of suburbia. This occurs when the lower middle classes, including white-collar people and some better-off artisans, forsake the centre of the city for a way of life in which, with the aid of credit facilities, they may more closely approximate to the life of the upper middle classes. Their deserted homes then pass to a motley population consisting on the one hand of the city's social rejects and on the other of newcomers who lack the defensive communal institutions of the working class, but who defend themselves and seek security within some sort of colony structure.

Already implicit in what we have said is the notion that these groups are not entirely culturally distinct from one another. All participate in a socio-cultural system in which the middle-class way of life enjoys high prestige and in which the move to the suburbs is a built-in aspiration. Not surprisingly, therefore, we have to take note of the third element in the situation, namely the use by the working class of the political power given to them by collective action to achieve their own version of the suburban move. Thus we get a new public suburbia paralleling the private suburbia which already exists.

Finally, we have to take note that this move by the working classes intensifies the disadvantaged position of the inhabitants of the lodging-house area. Burgess was quite correct in focusing so much of the attention of his colleagues on this zone. What he did not see was that the inhabitants of this zone did not simply enjoy a happy segregated community life of their own, but had their total situation defined by an urban value system in which they were at the back of a queue to move to the most desired style-of-life in the suburbs. Necessarily then, community life in this zone means something different from what it means in the redbrick working-class areas or the suburbs. It is a transitional life only and the communal institutions which it evolves are to be regarded as a means of fighting discrimination and providing temporary security until some kind of outward move can be made. Moreover, any attempt to segregate the inhabitants of this area permanently is bound to involve conflict. The long-term destiny of a city which frustrates the desire to improve their status by segregationist policies is some sort of urban riot. This follows from the fact that the city does to some extent share a unitary status-value system.

This view of the relationship between the various sub-communities of the city also helps us to throw some light on the controversy which goes on about the ideas of Tönnies, Redfield, and Wirth. All of these have laid emphasis upon the distinction between a communal peasant society and the society of the city.

The one is seen as characterized by what Parsons[1] calls affective, diffuse, particularistic and ascriptive relations maintained by informal social controls and rewards, the other as implying social relations which are affectively neutral, specific, universalistic and achievement-oriented, maintained by formal bureaucratic controls and rewards.

The study of newcomers to the city, however, has led a number of writers to question this distinction. Oscar Lewis, for example, directing his criticism mainly at Redfield and Wirth, writes:

[My] findings suggested that lower-class residents of Mexico City showed much less of the personal anonymity and isolation of the individual which has been postulated by Wirth as characteristic of urbanism as a way of life. The *vencidad* and the neighbourhood tended to break up the city into small communities that acted as cohesive and factors. . . . Life-time friendships and daily face-to-face relations with the same people were common and resembled a village situation. Most marriages also occurred within the colonia or adjoining colonies.[2]

This may well be true, but it does not alter the substance of Redfield's and Wirth's argument. Two things need to be distinguished. The first is the existence within the city of public agencies concerned with welfare and social control. The second is the social network of kin and neighbourhood which may vary independently of whether or not there are public services available for the meeting of human needs. We would expect that newcomers to the city would be precariously dependent for their emotional and personal security on the activation of such ties with kin and with fellow-villagers as are available. This is in no way inconsistent with the notion that the individual is also subject to and benefits from new formal agencies. But what happens to the individual who stays in the city is that he comes to be less and less dependent upon his colony and more and more dependent upon (a) the city's bureaucratic agencies and (b) his own conjugal family.

Thus the newcomer to the city living in the lodging-house area or its equivalent may be thought of as living in a tight-

---

[1] T. Parsons, *The Social System*, London, Tavistock Publications, 1952.
[2] P. M. Hauser and L. F. Schnore, *The Study of Urbanization*, New York, John Wiley, 1965.

knit community, perhaps one that is more tight-knit than any he knew in his village. But he is also launched into a larger society in which he has new rights and obligations as a citizen and in which in time he will be able to make his way, emotionally dependent only upon his own immediate family.

We suggested earlier that a functionalist approach which was applicable to the city should make explicit what interests and groups were to be the point of reference of functional explanations. We may now pause to indicate what these interests and groups are. Firstly, we should notice that the city's social organization demands that the individual should, so far as possible, be mobile and unencumbered by kinship ties. Secondly, the city's status system demands that all individuals should be motivated to compete to enter those sub-communities whose way of life is evaluated most highly. Thirdly, the same system demands that not all should succeed and, from the point of view of those about to enter the high-status sub-communities, it is important that others should be prevented from competing. Fourthly, from the point of view of the newcomer it is important that his own group should not suffer discrimination. Fifthly, from the point of view of the community at large and from that of the local community where the newcomers live, it is important that conflicts of interest should be managed and contained. And finally (though this is a psychological point), it is important to the individual that he should have group ties sufficient to guarantee him a minimum of emotional security. It is out of the balance between these various 'functional imperatives' that the actual structure of community life in the immigrant quarter must be formed.

In studying a zone of the city, then, our method is clear. We must find out who lives there, what primary community ties they have, what their housing situation, economic position and status aspirations are, what associations they form, how these associations interact and how far the various groups are incorporated into urban society as citizens. This is what we have sought to do in the chapters which follow.

Our aim, however, is to throw light on problems of race relations and it is now necessary to consider the relationship between the foregoing and the kind of study normally undertaken by students of race relations. Most such studies have proceeded on the basis of *ad hoc* theories and an *ad hoc* theoretical vocabulary. We must now show how race relations theory has to be assimilated to, and revised in terms of, the more general sociological theory we have been discussing. First, we consider the terms 'prejudice' and 'discrimination' and then a set of terms such as 'assimilation', 'accommodation', and 'integration', which refer to possible relations between ethnic groups.

A commonly held view is that prejudice is a psychological phenomenon and discrimination a sociological one. This approach to the study of prejudice has been greatly stimulated by the work of Adorno and his colleagues on the authoritarian personality. In their book they write:

Although personality is a product of the social environment of the past, it is not, once it has developed, a mere object of the contemporary environment. What has developed is a structure within the individual, something which is capable of self-initiated action upon the social environment and of selection with respect to impinging stimuli, something which although modifiable is frequently very resistant to fundamental change.[1]

Many students of prejudice have assumed that prejudiced beliefs about racial groups are to be explained in terms of this self-initiated action of the personality on the social environment; that is to say, they have argued that the prejudiced belief is to be explained in terms of the contribution which it makes to maintaining the dynamic equilibrium of the personality. Prejudice is thus held to be one aspect of the working of a disturbed authoritarian personality. It is a phenomenon to be found in a mentally disturbed minority.

This approach seemed to us to be inadequate because we were concerned to explain the behaviour, not of a minority, but of the majority of the host community. Moreover, we had to explain why people who had not in the past shown racial prejudice began to do so in a new social situation. We therefore thought it necessary to explain this prejudice not in terms of the personality system but in terms of the social system, that is, in terms of a structure of social relations.

When we speak of two people united by a social relation we mean that in the course of planning their action they have expectations of each other and are influenced in the course of their action by their expectations. When action takes place within a social context it is only rarely 'rational' in the sense that the actor uses the scientifically more efficient means of attaining his ends. More usually it is skewed from the rational by beliefs about and expectations with regard to other people.

Such non-rational (though not necessarily irrational) behaviour is to be explained by the part played by the beliefs, norms, and expectations which influence it in some larger system of social relations. Thus, for example, food taboos which appear to be irrational from a nutritional point of view may be based upon beliefs which are essential for ensuring group solidarity. False beliefs about an ethnic outgroup may serve to ensure that both an adherence to an ideal of social justice and a strong competitive position for one's group can be maintained. What we have to do is not merely to classify behaviour as prejudiced but to understand the part which customs, beliefs, norms, and expectations play in a larger social structure, be it the structure of an ethnic minority group or that of the overall urban society, marked as it is by diverse intergroup conflicts. Once we understand urban society as a structure of social interaction and conflict, prejudiced behaviour may be shown to fit naturally into or even to be required by that structure. Prejudice may be a social as well as a psychological phenomenon. Moreover, once it is so understood 'discrimination' in according rights to an outgroup might be seen to follow as a logical consequence, given the beliefs which are held.

Once we have grasped the idea of urban society as a number of overlapping and sometimes contradictory systems of social relations it soon becomes clear that the commonly used vocabulary of race relations which includes such words as 'assimilation', 'integration', and 'accommodation' is inadequate. Such vocabularies assume a 'host-immigrant' framework in which the culture and values of the host society are taken to be non-contradictory and static and in which the immigrant is seen as altering his own patterns of behaviour until they finally conform to those of the host society. The frame of reference is a cultural one and culture is seen as an independent variable which may change regardless of a man's position in the struc-

ture of social action and relations and regardless of the degree
to which he possesses property and power.

We believe that it is necessary to emphasize three points
which are confused once the host-immigrant framework is
adopted. Firstly, we have no unitary concept of the host society
but see it as compounded of groups in a state of conflict with
one another about property and about power, as well as of
groups with differing styles of life arranged in a status hierarchy.
Secondly, the relationship of a newcomer to the host-society
can vary along several axes other than those which refer to the
extent to which he has accepted the culture patterns of his host
and gained acceptance as a 'role-player' in the social system of
his host. And, thirdly, we see the immigrant, not simply as
moving from one culture to another, but as being cut off from
his native culture and groping for some kinds of cultural and
social signposts in a colony structure which belongs neither to
his homeland nor to the society of his hosts. What we have to
discover, therefore, is what kinds of primary community
immigrants form in order to obtain some sort of social and
cultural bearings in the new society and also what relationships
exist between their community structure as a whole and the
complex system of class conflict and status which we refer to as
'the host society'.

To begin with, we should notice the extreme type of situation in which the new immigrant might find himself. In this
situation he may be said to be cut off from effective contact
with his home culture, but not yet involved in the system of
social norms and interaction of the country to which he has
emigrated. This situation can, of course, never be complete
because there will always be some link with the home country
and at least a contractual tie with the world of employment in
the host society. But none the less we may speak of a minimum
situation when the immigrant is not in effective contact with
the society of his home country and when his ties with the
country of immigration are limited solely to the bond of
employment.

A second stage is reached when the individual still lacks more
than a contractual tie with the host society, but has built up a
primary community among his fellow-immigrants. Here he attempts to reproduce at least some of the social institutions of his

homeland and provides himself with a norm-governed home into which he can retreat from the world of the market-place. When this primary community becomes more extensive we may speak of his 'living in the colony'. The primary community or colony keeps him from falling into a state of complete demoralization and anomie.

Two further developments are then likely to occur. One is the incorporation of the immigrant into the society as a legal citizen having the social rights of a citizen. The other is the gradual extension of contractual ties with other groups and the modification of these contractual ties so that they come to be governed by new norms.

The body of rights which the immigrant may claim in modern Britain is fairly extensive. He can claim equal access to the courts. If he is a British subject he can vote and may in varying degrees claim social welfare benefits. As T. H. Marshall has pointed out,[1] this body of rights is sufficiently extensive to have made citizenship a more important focus of loyalty for the members of the working class than their class membership. Similarly, the immigrant undergoes some kind of incorporation into the host society as a citizen. Important though this is we should, however, notice its limitations for the immigrant. To have legal rights is not necessarily to be accepted completely into a society. In fact, the very necessity of the appeal to such rights shows that acceptance is not complete. And it is also true that the definition of a citizen sometimes excludes the immigrant and thus debars him from claiming particular rights (for instance, he has a long waiting period before he can be considered as having a claim to public housing).

In many areas of his life, however, the immigrant finds himself not simply enjoying his social rights as a citizen, but having to satisfy his needs in the market. This is particularly true with regard to finding a job and a home. Competition for and conflict over these facilities is, of course, to some extent regulated by law, but it is in the nature of a liberal capitalist society that it allows a degree of market freedom. Market freedom, moreover, means not merely that buyer may compete with buyer, seller with seller, and that individual buyer and

[1] T. H. Marshall, *Citizenship and Social Class*, London, Cambridge University Press, 1960.

individual seller may arrive at an agreed price by bargaining. It also means that groups of buyers and groups of sellers may unite and exercise some kind of monopoly power. The development of such power may easily spill over into the use of force and the market situation then becomes transformed into one which is based upon a balance of power.

The situation with which we have been concerned is clearly of this kind. Competition for the scarce resource of housing leads to the formation of groups very often on an ethnic basis and one group will attempt to restrict the opportunities of another by using whatever sanctions it can. In an extreme case this would mean the use of violence but more commonly resort may be had to the use of legitimate political power through legislation against the outgroup. But in any case, the conflict may well lead to a process of 'collective bargaining' of an informal kind in which each group tries to increase its own market opportunities to the maximum, but having done so arrives at some temporary agreement with the other side regarding relative shares of market opportunities.

When this kind of agreement based upon a balance of power is struck, it is all too easily confused with a situation in which cultural diversity is maintained after social acceptance and integration have been achieved by the minority group. And it is particularly likely that those who employ the host-immigrant framework, with its neglect of relations based on property, will make this confusion. We wish to emphasize that a variety of different inter-group power situations may exist between racial groups even where there is no overt conflict and violence. The main form of interest of a dynamic sociology of race relations should be to differentiate these and not to confuse them under such headings as 'accommodation' and 'pluralistic integration'.

We should also notice one special kind of collective bargain which is implicitly reached, namely that in which certain kinds of job, certain social and economic functions, or certain residential areas are recognized as belonging to a particular group. If such a situation develops and is peacefully maintained, the society could take on a caste-like character. But even where this extreme state is not reached it may be that there are certain social functions which are necessary and yet morally dubious in the eyes of the host society which come to be performed by a particular ethnic group. In mediaeval Europe the Jews formed a pariah group of this kind. On a smaller scale in urban society a pariah group of lodging-house landlords drawn from a particular group is always a likely possibility.

What we have said in the previous paragraphs is intended to emphasize elements of race relations in the city which have been neglected by race relations specialists. We feel that when the study of race relations is set in a context of urban sociology many of the problematic distinctions between inter-group situations are more readily understood. None the less, it is also true that the degree of commitment of individuals to their own group and its culture is to some extent an independent variable.

Several processes seem to operate. Firstly, class conflicts which are inherent in the situation because of shortage of facilities may cross-cut ethnic conflicts. Thus a tenant may come to see himself primarily as a tenant rather than as an Irishman or a West Indian. Or a landlord may come to put his economic interest as a landlord before his ethnic loyalty. Secondly, the children of a particular ethnic group may, through their school contacts, move into a different social world and so too may some adults. And, thirdly, since the available means of association (for instance, churches and political parties) are not historically geared to the existing conflict situation, membership of these organizations may serve to blur the lines of conflict.

Thus we see that there are a great many different situations which might easily be confused under the too-restricted terminology of the sociology of race relations. We would wish to distinguish at least two different variables: (1) the degree of involvement in the legal, social, and moral norms of the host society on the part of the immigrants; and (2) the degree of conflict between the various ethnic groups.

These are the variables which apply to the different groups. If we try a little artificially to put them in tabular form, our table might look something like this:

Degree of Involvement	*Degree of Intergroup Conflict*
(1) Anomie, lack of social orientation	(1) A free market situation between individuals competing for facilities
(2) 'Living in the colony'	(2) Mobilization of monopoly power by ethnic groups in a market situation

Degree of Involvement	*Degree of Intergroup Conflict*
(3) 'Living in the colony' but accepting formal rights in the host society	(3) Use of violence and/or mobilization of political power
(4) Acceptance of some social norms governing relations with strangers, apart from legal norms	(4) Collective bargaining and temporary contractual agreement
(5) Abandonment of the colony except for reasons of retrospective sentiment	

In addition to this one must note that the structure of the society in which all these processes take place may vary. It may be a relatively open society in which mobility between individuals from membership of one group to membership of another is possible, or it may not. And there will be considerable variation in the degrees to which in particular areas the institutional and associational structure blurs the lines of ethnic division.

What we have done in the chapters which follow is to employ some of the concepts which have been outlined in this chapter in order to analyse the social system of an urban ward when immigrant lodging-houses have emerged and are thought to constitute a social problem. We show the various social pressures which have operated to produce this situation and the kind of social interaction which has been produced on a community level. But we do this not because we wish to say that this outcome is inevitable in an expanding urban society. Rather, we hope that by drawing attention to some of the determinants of the situation we may make its rational control possible.

I. Race Relations and Housing
in Birmingham

The visitor to Birmingham in the early 1960s could not but be struck by the way in which racial problems dominated public discussion. It was hard to imagine, as one scanned the columns of the *Post*, the *Mail and Despatch*, the *Sunday Mercury*, and the *Planet*, that this was a city long famous for its radical and egalitarian tradition. Often the sentiments expressed by those who wrote to these newspapers or those who were reported in them, smacked more of the Deep South in the United States or of settler Africa than of the City of Reform.

Thus we find Councillor Collett, one of the leading advocates of immigration control, writing to the *Birmingham Evening Mail* in these terms:

How much longer have we Englishmen to tolerate the overt propaganda urging us to love the coloured immigrant who comes in peace and humility and ends by being the arrogant boss. For proof speak to or visit the white people living under a coloured landlord. On Monday a T.V. programme showed how a coloured man suffered when he came to live amongst us. He was expected to do the menial jobs and why shouldn't he? Few if any are capable of doing a skilled job and they could, of course, return home. But do they? Not on your life! Whether they be intellectual or not, they stay on, hoping to wear us down with the old theme 'love thy neighbour'. Only good coloured immigrants should be allowed to come here, good in morals and health, and they should be licensed so that their good behaviour and limitation is guaranteed.[1]

Perhaps Councillor Collett could be counted as an extremist on this issue and perhaps few people in Birmingham would have written in these terms. But the fact that such sentiments could be expressed at all indicates that there was widespread

[1] *Birmingham Evening Mail*, 25 September 1959.

disquiet amongst Birmingham people at the presence in their midst of over 50,000 coloured immigrants.

This disquiet did not arise principally from the employment situation, for Birmingham was one of the most affluent and fully employed cities in Britain. What did cause anxiety was the housing situation and in particular the fact that, at a time when there seemed little prospect of reducing the housing waiting-list of 30,000, large areas of the city, thought to be reasonably good residential areas, had become the homes of coloured immigrants and were deteriorating very rapidly. Almost invariably the question of colour was discussed in relation to housing problems and in relation to the so-called 'twilight zones', that is, areas where large, old houses, too good to be classified as slums, had become multi-occupied lodging-houses.[1]

Our own study of these problems in no way supported the conclusion that the influx of coloured immigrants had, through its sheer numbers, made Birmingham's housing situation worse. What we did observe was a process of discriminative and *de facto* segregation which compelled coloured people to live in certain typical conditions, and which of itself exacerbated racial ill-feeling. It was this process which provided the framework of the race relations problem in Birmingham and in order to understand it we must begin with an analysis of Birmingham's housing problem.

The deficiency of dwellings in relation to the number of families living in Birmingham in mid-1959 was about 30,000. It was estimated that even though about 52,000 houses would be built by public and private enterprise by 1971, the deficiency would increase to about 43,000. The shortage was still expected to exceed 30,000 by 1981.

In addition to this it is necessary to take account of other

---

[1] We have used the term 'lodging-house' as it is defined in the bye-laws of the City of Birmingham dated 5 February 1929. The definition given there is 'a house or part of a house intended or used for occupation by the working classes and let in lodgings or occupied by members of more than one family.' This appears to coincide with the definition of 'houses in multiple occupation' in the 1961 Housing Act which includes 'a house which, or part of which, is let in lodgings or which is occupied by members of more than one family'. In the context of Sparkbrook, we are referring to houses in which more than one household is to be found. Such houses are sharply differentiated from two types of houses in single-family occupation, namely, slums scheduled for demolition and structurally sound houses. The lodging-houses to which we refer are rarely scheduled slums and seldom in single-family occupation.

factors. A surplus of housing is necessary for mobility. This would raise the deficiency to 38,000 dwellings. And this figure tells us nothing of the shortage due to the existence of different kinds of demand. Nor does it say anything about the 'disguised shortage' among those forced to live in obsolescent housing which they would wish to leave. This is not merely incidental to our study, for such factors could mean that although 38,000 houses were built, the housing shortage would still be considerable.

How, then, are these surplus families housed and what kinds of housing are likely to become available to them? Obviously, as things stood in 1960, there must have been some 30,000 families who were either homeless, living in lodgings with relatives or with friends. That is to say, about 30,000 families at least would be living in conditions of multi-occupation. Moreover if each of these families resided in the home of another family not included in the 30,000, the number would be very much larger.

One way in which such people may be living, however, is in houses let in lodgings. The Chief Inspector of Birmingham's Public Health department, Mr. Wakelin, has estimated that about 12,000 families and 8,000 individuals live in Birmingham in this way. Before the 1961 Housing Act came into force, 3,752 lodging-houses were identified as requiring attention.

We must now see where these lodging-houses were and what prospects there were for the inhabitants to obtain other accommodation. In order to do this we must consider the kinds and quality of accommodation which are typically available.

Greve, in his pamphlet *The Housing Problem* gives the following table regarding the age and ownership of housing in Great Britain in 1958 (the numbers are given in millions).[1]

The table shows that 7·6 million houses were built before 1919, that 6·1 million of these were let by private landlords, and that, of all 15·5 million houses, 6·65 million were let by private landlords. This means that the proportion of private lettings is bound to decrease since slum-clearance will eliminate many of the pre-1919 houses. New housing is overwhelmingly local authority housing and in the future the tenants of privately let old houses must seek rehousing from this source. There is also

[1] J. Greve, *The Housing Problem*, London, Fabian Society, 1959.

TABLE 1: AGE AND OWNERSHIP OF HOUSING IN
GREAT BRITAIN (1958)

When Erected	No. of houses	Owner Occupied	Let by Private Landlords	Local Authorities Housing Associations
Before 1850	2·15 ⎫			
1850–1875	1·75 ⎪	1·5	6·1	0·1
1875–1900	2·0 ⎬			
1900–1919	1·7 ⎭			
1919–1945	4·6	2·7	0·6	1·3
1945–1958	3·3	0·8	0·05	2·45
TOTAL	15·5	5·0	6·75	3·85

evidence that an increasing proportion of the 6·1 million old
privately let houses are being sold for owner-occupation.

We do not know which houses will be scheduled for demolition as slums and the arbitrariness of the system whereby
houses were declared slums in the immediate post-war period
is notorious. But we do know that Birmingham scheduled
27,000 houses in five comprehensive redevelopment areas in
1947 and 25,000 houses in other parts in 1954. These houses
would all be of pre-1919 vintage and the loss of houses privately
let would therefore be enormous. The actual demolition of these
houses, of course, places a responsibility for rehousing the
tenants in council houses on the City Council, but for newcomers the possibility of obtaining privately rented housing
steadily decreases. The present situation is that immigrants are
scarcely moving into areas scheduled for demolition, since these
areas are already occupied by a relatively static British working
population and the house-type is generally too small for multi-
lodging occupation.

It must also be borne in mind that, although the area within
the City boundary actually decreased its population by about
7,000 in the period, the number of jobs within the city was
steadily increasing. Thus, what was happening was that the
former residents of the central area were moving outside the
city boundary, but had to continue to work in Birmingham
where they were joined by others for whom housing had to be
found.

The crucial questions, therefore, are how many local
authority-owned houses were being acquired or built and what
criteria operated in selecting tenants for them. When we have

understood these, we shall be able to turn to what for us is the crucial problem; namely, the types of housing available to the immigrant, and to others who did not qualify for local authority houses.

In 1963 a total of 5,339 houses were expected to become available to the Housing Management Committee, of which 3,221 were new houses in the city or in overspill areas and 2,991 were houses available for re-letting.

The planned allocations of these houses is shown in the following table:[1]

TABLE 2: PLANNED ALLOCATION OF COUNCIL HOUSES IN BIRMINGHAM (1963)

A.	Public Works Dept. (Road building, etc.)	472
	Key workers rehoused in overspill	50
	Special medical cases	170
B.	Slum clearance	1,984
	Demolitions and closing orders	490
	Dangerous dwellings	20
C.	Waiting-list allocations	1,303
D.	Homeless families	850
		5,339

In this table Category A merely shows the degree to which other social priorities emerge as direct demands on the available supply of houses. A total of 692 houses, or 12 per cent. of the total, were allocated to this category.

Category B reflects the rate at which the Council moves families from dwellings which they have defined as unfit for human habitation: 2,494 houses, or 47 per cent. of the total, were allocated to this category.

Category C consists of 1,303 dwellings allocated to the waiting list of 45,000. This took 24 per cent. of the total.

Category D contains 850 dwellings for homeless families. These are the families forced right out of the bottom of the housing system and on to the streets. The Council accepts the responsibility that 'no family must ever be without a roof over their heads through failure of the Housing Department to assist'. 16 per cent. of all houses were allotted to families in this category.

[1] Minutes of Birmingham City Council, February 1964.

The crucial categories from our point of view are categories C and D since newcomers are unlikely to be in a position to profit from the allocations under A and B. What are their chances of obtaining council houses and if they have none what other sources are open to them?

Houses in Category C are allocated on the basis of a points system. Points are awarded for housing need to applicants who have lived or worked in the city for at least five years. They are awarded for (1) bedroom deficiency; (2) shared accommodation; (3) lack of facilities; (4) lack of natural light; (5) broken families, or families forced to live apart; (6) general health; (7) period on the waiting list; and (8) war service.

It should be noted that the application form of the Housing Department contains no reference to the colour or country of origin of the inhabitant and in our talks with Council officials and Councillors we found a certain sense of pride in the formal justice of the scheme. As one leading Councillor put it, 'We see them only as numbers.' None the less, it is clear that the scheme as it stands uses formal criteria which exclude the vast body of immigrants.

This we found to be the crux of the immigrant housing problem in Birmingham. Whereas Birmingham people could go on to the Housing Register at any time and when they had acquired enough points obtain a council house, all immigrants, whether white or black, had a five-year waiting period before they could begin to qualify. Necessarily, therefore, there had to be some other form of housing for the large number of people for whom the Council refused to accept responsibility. This 'other form of housing' was provided by the lodging-houses in the so-called twilight zones of the city.

The other possibility of obtaining a house is under Category D and this would appear to be one possibility which is open to immigrants. But the applicant who applies on grounds of homelessness has formidable hurdles to overcome. In 1962–3, 1,259 families sought help from the Council on this ground. 438 either did not, in the opinion of the department, warrant help or rejected the accommodation offered. 286 dwellings were allocated to these families, mainly old houses awaiting demolition; 267 families were placed first in hostels and then in sub-standard dwellings. 195 were placed in hostels or found their own accommodation; 73 were still in hostels at the time of counting.

In dealing with homeless families the Council gives assistance 'according to the merits of the case'. Families who are high on the waiting-list and would in any case qualify for an offer in the foreseeable future are usually given an ordinary dwelling, though not one of the more desirable ones. Families who are not considered to have a sufficiently strong claim to warrant the allocation of a council-built house are usually placed initially in one of the city's 'patched' houses in a slum-clearance area. They are then usually rehoused again within six months. Families who are very recent arrivals in the city, who are considered to have no claim on council housing, are initially placed in a hostel. While there they are encouraged to find their own accommodation and about 30 per cent. do. The remainder are transferred to the poorest type of council house after a period in the hostel.

Hostel accommodation is required by the Council as a deterrent to those who might irresponsibly declare themselves homeless. We were repeatedly told by Councillors and officials that hostel accommodation is regarded as a valuable deterrent to those who might irresponsibly declare themselves to be homeless. This view was somewhat muted in the official Council minutes which stated in February 1964:

Action by the Health and other Committees on schemes for the improvement of housing conditions in Sparkbrook and other multi-occupation areas has led to an increase in the number of homeless families requiring assistance but the Housing Department is working closely with all the other departments concerned to keep a proper balance in the housing of families from slum-clearance, redevelopment, the waiting-list and other priority groups. Nevertheless your Committee consider it prudent to increase existing hostel accommodation. . . .[1]

Given the 'deterrent' theory, the appropriate conjunction in the last sentence should be 'therefore'. This was explicitly stated by a 'Birmingham Corporation spokesman' who was reported in the *Mail* as saying: 'Hostel accommodation for

[1] Minutes of Birmingham City Council, February 1964.

evicted people is deliberately made not too attractive, so as to make it not worthwhile being evicted.'[1]

Thus a possible weakness in the selection system is overcome. Very few find their way to council houses simply by way of homelessness. We must now examine, however, what happens to those who do qualify for Category C or Category D houses.

We have seen that there is a certain formal justice in the allocation system even though it discriminates against newcomers. But this formal justice of the bureaucrats is supplemented by an attempt on the part of the Housing Department to apply the substantive justice of social work. Each applicant is seen by a Housing Visitor and his or her circumstances are taken into account before it is decided what kind of house should be offered. The criteria according to which these decisions are reached are not, however, made public.

The trained Housing Visitor has a number of alternative offers which he may make. He may offer a low density pre-war council house, a post-war flat or house, a good house which has been taken into council ownership, a patched house awaiting demolition, or a house awaiting demolition which has not been patched. Any applicant who, for whatever reason, is regarded as undesirable as an occupant of the newer or better houses will be placed in slum property.

One obvious consequence of this policy is the concentration of people with low domestic standards in the slum-clearance area. During our stay in Birmingham this problem caused considerable protest in the Ladywood area. But more important from our point of view is the question of what happens to immigrants whom the Housing Visitor sees. Here we have been assured by councillors and officials of the Housing Department that no discrimination operates, but we cannot feel sure that this is the case in the light of our own observations.

It is clear, firstly, that there are very few coloured residents on the council house estates and most especially in the sought-after low density pre-war houses. Secondly, we found no case of a West Indian or other coloured applicant being offered a council-built house during our stay in Birmingham. Thirdly, we found a very strong conviction amongst West Indians that coloured applicants who qualified were always offered patched

[1] *Birmingham Evening Mail*, 19 July 1965.

houses and that the Council was, in fact, the largest slum land-lord in Birmingham. And, fourthly and crucially, we do not believe that the Housing Visitors are all so free of prejudice that a coloured skin is not taken to imply low domestic standards.

We do not by any means feel that we are able to prove that the Birmingham Council operates a discriminatory policy which keeps coloured people off its estates. What we do say is that it is quite possible under the present arrangements to discriminate without a policy of discrimination ever being publicly admitted.

We must now consider what happens to those who do not qualify for council houses in Birmingham. They must clearly become tenants or private landlords or owner-occupiers, in-cluding the possibility of becoming a tenant of lodgings in an owner-occupied house.

The inevitable consequences which flow from slum-clearance are (a) a decline in the number of small family cottages avail-able for letting and (b) a decline in the proportion of privately owned rented housing. It is thus inevitable that the housing of those for whom the Council cannot provide will fall more and more to the owners and owner-occupiers of large houses. Where there is both a slum-clearance programme and a long-unsatis-fied council waiting-list, the pressure for accommodation in large houses which are not slums is bound to grow.

If one looks at the housing map of Birmingham (p. 28) the location of these houses is very clear. Immediately around the centre of the city are five redevelopment areas which consisted almost entirely of very old small cottages. All those cottages falling within these areas were scheduled for demolition. With them will go much of Birmingham's former stock of rented housing. Beyond this ring is a more mixed area including not only cottages scheduled for demolition but a large number of other houses which are larger, younger, and structurally sounder. These houses were built in the period between 1860 and 1900, with a concentrated period of building in the 1880s. Their size, together with features such as servants' bells in their attics or basement, shows that they were originally intended for middle-class inhabitants. Such houses are grouped around the city in a rough secondary ring with two concentrations. In the north one finds them in the Soho, Handsworth, and Aston areas

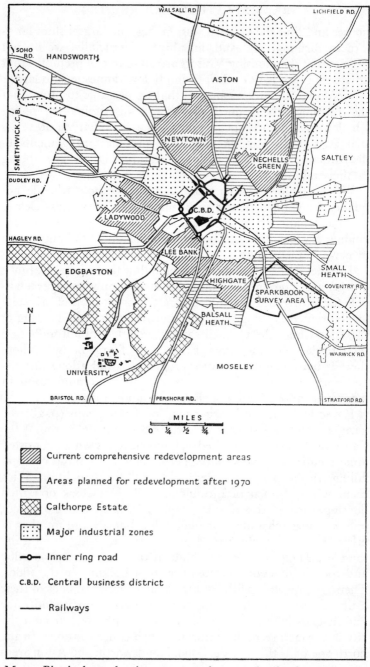

Map 1. Birmingham, showing current and proposed redevelopment areas.

and in the south in Edgbaston, Deritend, Moseley, Balsall Heath, Sparkbrook, and Small Heath. Because of the age of these houses the areas are known to the planners as 'twilight zones' implying that they are approaching, but have not yet reached, the night of slumdom.

It is difficult to discover when these various groups of houses first became let in lodgings. The directories of the early years of the century still show them to be occupied by professional people and shopkeepers. But there are memories in Sparkbrook of Welsh and Irish immigrants in lodgings there before the 1939–45 war and the process of conversion might have started then. It is clear, however, that this process was accelerated after the war and by the end of the 1950s multi-occupation was an evident fact because many of the tenants and a number of landlords were coloured.

It should be noted that in discussions of housing policy at the time there was much reference to under-used old houses which might be put to more intensive use so that house-owners who set up as lodging-house proprietors or sold their houses to be used as lodging-houses could claim to be doing their patriotic duty. But there were strong economic incentives also and the pace of conversion was bound in any case to quicken.

Firstly, there was the fact of sheer demand. The shortage of other possible rented housing either in the private or local authority sector meant that there were literally thousands of families who were looking for rented homes wherever they could be found and the twilight zones alone had the unused housing capacity. Secondly, however, the houses were not a sound proposition from the point of view of the owner-occupier looking for a home for his family. They only had short leases and were far too large for the average working-class or lower middle-class families of the 1950s. Those who wanted to stay, wanted to do so very largely for sentimental reasons. But even they would be liable to sell if a good price was offered and the threat that the whole area might lose status encouraged them to get out quickly.

The situation was one in which an entrepreneur of ability could make quick profits and in London this role was assumed by Perec Rachman. In Birmingham there was no landlord of Rachman's ability and the process of conversion went on piecemeal. The first landlords were, in fact, local residents, but they were quickly followed by immigrants who, in the process of housing themselves, could not but provide rented housing for others.

Some immigrants, particularly West Indians, had tried in the first place to obtain mortgages for the purchase of new houses in the suburbs. But even where there was no discrimination they were looked upon with suspicion by the building societies. Because of their crowded conditions they were suspected of intending to let suburban houses in lodgings and were refused mortgages on that ground. Others obtained mortgages but only after paying an estate agent a fee and sometimes by paying exorbitant rates of interest. In the late 1950s an estate agent was gaoled for fraudulently converting money left with him as house deposits by West Indians.

But mostly in fact the West Indian community were not interested in running lodging-houses. With a male/female ratio of 3/2 in 1961, they were on the whole looking for independent family life. A very different problem was presented by the Indian and Pakistani immigrants of the late 1950s and early 1960s, many of whom were single but who none the less wished to house themselves and their kinsmen and fellow villagers. There is virtually no provision in Birmingham for housing single men in hostels and no single man may be considered for rehousing.

In northern cities these immigrants found small back-to-back cottages for sale at £400 to £500. But there were no such houses in Birmingham. Virtually the only houses these immigrants could buy were the late Victorian and Edwardian terrace houses we have been discussing. They could not get mortgages but they could get bank loans if they produced £800 to £1,000 as a deposit and were able to convince the bank manager of their character and ability to pay. The bank loans were short term ones and the £800 to £1,000 could be raised only by borrowing from friends. Inevitably, therefore, the weekly charges which a house-purchaser had to meet were heavy, especially when one recognizes that the purchasers had very often to meet obligations to their wives and families at home. Buying a house of this kind was possible only if the owner proceeded to let rooms. Once he did this he found himself meeting a huge demand from other immigrants, black and white alike, from people who wanted accommodation with no questions asked, and from all those others who were at the back of the housing queue. There was profit in this and some landlords began to exploit their financial opportunities to the maximum. A room could be let to a family for £2 10s. 0d. to £3 per week and only minimal shared facilities were necessary to get this price. Moreover, since the owner had no long-term interest in the house, the building was bound to deteriorate very rapidly.

Once multi-occupation began in an area, it snowballed. In part the former owners left in panic because they feared a decline in house prices. In part, however, they left because they could get good prices for houses which were not much use to them. Very rapidly whole streets went over to multi-occupation. The map we have described tells only part of the story. The twilight zones became areas of multi-occupation but within them special blocks of streets were almost wholly converted to use as lodging-houses. What had been the smart streets of the twilight areas now became the centres of multi-occupation. 'Twilight zone' came to be a term applied not merely to a certain age of housing, but to an area of multi-occupation and an area of immigration.

But ideally suited though the twilight zones were to multi-occupation, the pressure was so great that other areas too were likely to go over to this new use and Birmingham had to develop a special planning and public health policy to control it. The crucial decision, perhaps, was taken when the City Council refused permission to a landlord to convert two houses in the residential suburb of Northfield to multi-occupation. The Ministry refused to sanction this action, but in 1963 the Corporation appealed successfully to the House of Lords and established its right to refuse planning permission to landlords who sought to establish new areas of multi-occupation.

But there could be no question of applying these powers throughout the city. The Manager of the City Housing Department, Mr. Macey, discussed this problem in an address reprinted in *Housing Review* for September/October 1962. Having said, 'We have grave misgivings that substantial numbers of additional slums are in the process of being created in the middle rings of houses built between 1890 and 1914', he went on:

So far as the cure is concerned, a 'blitz' on existing cases is out of the question as it would increase the number of homeless families by hundreds each year. At the same time, it would be likely to drive the evil from one district to another as yet unaffected by this disease. The worst of these houses are managed by very astute people and there is a great deal of profit involved. It seems that the cure must be applied gradually.[1]

This gradual cure was to be provided by the Public Health Department's powers of inspection of lodging-houses and prosecution of their proprietors under the 1961 Housing Act. The effects of these inspections and prosecutions are now being felt.

In fact, up to 1954 Birmingham had had considerable powers under its own bye-laws to register and inspect houses let in lodgings and upon the failure of the proprietor to conform with detailed standards to impose penalties. Surprisingly, these bye-laws were repealed at the time of the 1954 Housing Act and it was only in 1961 that a new Housing Act gave back to the local authority some of the powers that it had lost.

The 1961 Act gives the local authority power to make orders regarding any house which is let in lodgings or is occupied by more than one family. These orders are of three kinds. They may concern the management of common facilities (Section 13). They may concern the inadequate amenities of the house (Section 15). Or they may be concerned with overcrowding (Section 19). For convenience we refer to these three types of orders as management, amenity, and overcrowding orders.

The process whereby action may be taken by the Public Health Authorities against landlords offending under this section are slow and tedious and are clearly designed to protect the landlord against arbitrary action. First the local authority must give twenty-one days' notice of intention to serve an order and the landlord must be given time to make representations. Then it may serve an order, but again the landlord is entitled to appeal, this time to the magistrate's court. Only when this opportunity for appeal has passed may the local authority take further action.

In the cases of Sections 13 and 15 the local authority may do the necessary work itself and reclaim costs supported if neces-

---

[1] *Housing Review*, Vol. II, No. 5, Sept.–Oct. 1962, p. 155.

sary by the courts. But in the cases of Sections 13 and 19 they may bring the offending landlord before the magistrates' courts, where on the first offence he may be fined £20 and on the second offence fined £100 or imprisoned for three months, or both. Many prosecutions have now been made and the maximum penalties imposed on Birmingham landlords. These are discussed in detail in a later chapter.

There are, however, two important limitations on these powers. The first concerns overcrowding orders. The local authority is not given power to order a landlord to evict his tenants, and indeed might not welcome such a power, because it would then be compelled to treat the evicted tenants as 'homeless'. Instead, it simply orders the landlord not to take any new tenant if accepting that tenant would raise numbers above a named level. Thus the Act could not be expected to lead to an immediate abatement of overcrowding.

Secondly, the local authority is left to find out where the lodging-houses are. There is no requirement in the Act that someone setting up a lodging-house must seek permission and even the provision under Section 21 for the compiling of a register three years after the commencement of the Act does not require compulsory registration. This has led the Birmingham Corporation to initiate a Private Act of Parliament which is discussed below.

A further power is available to local authorities under the 1957 Housing Act. This is the power of compulsory purchase in order to carry out necessary repairs. This power, however, may be exercised only with the approval of the Ministry after a public inquiry. It has been very sparingly used in Birmingham and the Ministry's response has not been encouraging. In the case of fourteen houses in Sparkbrook, the Ministry first gave the landlords six months to do the necessary work and then agreed to only three houses being purchased by the Local Authority.

A Ministry circular also draws the attention of local authorities to their powers to encourage improvements and conversions and says: 'Where owners are willing to carry out conversions on this scale, local authorities should not hesitate to make grants and to accept any necessary rehousing of families who need alternative accommodation.'[1] However, in this case, as in

[1] Ministry of Housing Circular No. 16, 5 April 1962.

the case mentioned in the last paragraph, such action would mean that the local authorities were taking over some of the functions performed by the private landlord. The Birmingham Authority, fully extended in running its own housing programme, has showed no great willingness to take on further responsibilities of this kind.

There have, however, been two important legislative developments affecting Birmingham since the 1961 Act. One is the new power to make 'control orders' under the 1964 Act. The other is the Birmingham Corporation's Private Bill. 'Control orders' enable the local authority to assume the powers of the landlord for a period of five years, while giving due compensation to him. These orders had not yet been used at the time of writing, although we understand that it was the intention of the Birmingham local authority to use them.

The Birmingham Corporation Housing Act, however, is of the first importance. It is based upon the principle of compulsory registration. Under this Act no one is allowed to run a house let in lodgings without the permission of the City Council, and the Council may refuse permission on any one of several grounds. The main grounds are that the setting up of lodging-houses would detract from the amenities of a particular area, or that the landlord is not thought to be a fit person to operate a lodging-house.

The rationale behind the Birmingham Act is that the Council wishes to prevent landlords who have been prosecuted under the 1961 Act from moving on to other houses and areas where the orders do not apply, and to prevent areas of Birmingham which are not yet marked by extension of multi-occupation from becoming so marked. To some social workers in Sparkbrook it seemed that this Act failed to recognize the positive function performed by the lodging-houses and that there was a danger that, in confining multi-occupation to certain areas, the Council would be creating ghettoes. These points were raised at a public meeting called to discuss the Bill, but were little noticed and the amended Bill which finally emerged and gained Royal Assent in July 1965, in no way excluded the possibility that the Council would use its powers to concentrate the lodging-houses in the twilight zones.

Related to the discussion of this Bill is the question of what the

Council proposed to do about the twilight zones. For some time people in Sparkbrook, who inquired of the councillors on the Planning Department what Sparkbrook's future was, were told that plans were being worked out for its partial redevelopment, although sometimes it was suggested that a second group of comprehensive redevelopment areas was to be designated which would include Sparkbrook. Eventually a plan was put forward in July 1965. When this came before the Council, however, it was found that the number of houses proposed in the new scheme were far short of what would be necessary to re-house the population. As a member of the Public Works Committee put it, '600 immigrant families would have had to be rehoused.'[1] As a result the plan was rejected and the Council called for a special report on the problem of redeveloping the twilight zones. It is difficult, however, to see how any such report can get round the problem of rehousing which such redevelopment involves.

One other area of legislation which might affect the lodging-houses required mention. This concerns rent control in furnished lettings. We have not found that tenants of lodging-houses were prepared to take the risk of taking their cases to the rent tribunal even if they were aware of their rights. In this respect, the Labour Government's Prevention of Eviction Act provided something of a strengthening of the tenant's powers, but so long as the lodging-house landlords are in a mono-polistic position as suppliers of furnished rented accommodation, it was proving difficult to restrict their powers.

We have now described the system of housing, allocation, ownership, and control in Birmingham. We have done so not simply in order to make a judgement as to whether or not it is discriminatory, but in order to see what pattern of competing interests and what pattern of social relations are set up by this system. We believe that the system of housing allocation is one of the two main determinants of the structure of race relations in Birmingham. The other main determinant is differential access to employment, which must be the subject of other studies.

It is perhaps worth noting in passing that what we are doing here is of some significance for urban sociology. This field of

---

[1] *Birmingham Evening Mail*, 4 October 1965.

study is one in which there is a great need for a general hypothesis which, though it could not be expected to explain everything, would, none the less, provide a general framework within
which particular developments might be studied. On the most
general level we accept the hypothesis that in modern urban
industrial societies the structure of social relations is determined by a pattern of conflicting interests set up by the differential control by different groups of men of material facilities.
That much is agreed by two great traditions of sociological
theory, those of Marx and of Max Weber. But we agree with
Max Weber when, in his analysis of the formation of classes, he
gives equal consideration to ownership of domestic property
and ownership of the means of industrial production.[1] We do
not believe that an adequate sociology of the city could be
written without making this assumption. What then is the
social structure which is set up by the ownership and control of
housing in Birmingham?

In so far as the figures given earlier in this chapter may be
applied to Birmingham, there are clearly three classes of people
to be found in the city. Slightly less than one-third will be
owner-occupiers. Rather more than two-fifths will be tenants of
private landlords. The remainder, rather less than a quarter,
will be tenants of the Council. The owner-occupiers, however,
will include a small proportion who share their houses with
tenants and the tenants of private landlords a proportion who
do not rent a whole house. Thus we may say that there are five
classes produced by the system of house-ownership and allocation: (1) the outright owner-occupiers; (2) the council house
tenants; (3) the tenants of whole private houses; (4) the lodging-
house proprietors; and (5) the tenants of lodging-houses. Being
a member of one or other of these classes is of first importance
in determining a man's associations, his interests, his life-style,
and his position in the urban social structure; moreover, each
class has its own qualifications for entry.

Owner-occupiers must have certain qualifications as regards
capital, amount of income and type of income. They must also
qualify in advance in terms of their style of life. They must have
at least enough capital for a deposit to obtain a mortgage. Their

[1] See R. Bendix and S. M. Lipset, *Class Status and Power*, Free Press of Glencoe,
1953, p. 63.

income has to be sufficiently large to convince a building society that they can make their repayments and their employment has to be sufficiently secure and regular, for the same reason. They must be capable of convincing the building society that they will keep the property which is mortgaged in reasonable condition and they must not sub-let any part of the property.

A number of categories of people are excluded from the owner-occupier class by these criteria. Many casual and un-skilled workers, for example, are either unable to produce a deposit or have incomes which are too low or too irregular to make them good risks. So far as immigrants are concerned, access to the mutual aid system which operates in their own primary communities, together with their willingness to work overtime, makes it possible for some of them at least to obtain a deposit. But they are more than likely to be excluded on other grounds. The possibility of their return to their homelands and their greater vulnerability to redundancy mean that they cannot be counted as having stability of employment. And their style of life, which may involve low standards of furnishing and an obligation to house kinsmen, will exclude many others. As a consequence the number of immigrants who succeed in entering the class of owner-occupiers is small.

A council house tenancy is obtained as we have seen on grounds of need and on grounds of long residence. It also depends upon having a certain style of life and upon not having an obligation to take lodgers. Most immigrants are excluded on grounds of residence alone, but those who do qualify on these grounds are likely to be admitted only to the inferior council houses. The upper sub-class of council tenants in council-built flats and houses will include very few immigrants.

These two classes enjoy a considerable *de facto* security of tenure, even though the council tenants are in theory subject to eviction at short notice. This is not true of the remaining classes. Tenancies of whole houses owned by private landlords are increasingly difficult to obtain because of the demolition of old rented property. But even where such tenancies are available they are rarely advertised and friendship or kinship with the landlord or with neighbours may be an important criterion in the selection of these tenants. Moreover, unlike the council, private landlords do not choose their tenants on the basis of

formally defined standards. The private landlord has the power
to discriminate according to his own whims. Since nearly all
landlords who let whole-houses are English, the overwhelming
likelihood is that these tenancies will not be given to coloured
immigrants.

The fourth housing possibility is that of living in and owning
a lodging-house. To join this class the one requirement is that
an individual should control a relatively large amount of
capital and have a good prospect of a large income for a relatively short period. It is easier for an immigrant to obtain these
qualifications than to acquire those which are essential for any
of the three classes mentioned above. He can, by borrowing
from relatives and friends, accumulate fairly large amounts of
capital. He can usually give a character reference to the bank
or moneylender and he can point to the prospect of a large income from rents. But these qualifications are sufficient only if
the house concerned is one in which no one has a long-term
interest and if it has sufficient rooms to guarantee a good rent
income.

Finally, we have the housing class who need have no qualifications at all apart from their willingness to pay a high rent in
relation to housing space offered during an insecure tenancy.
This will include all those in employment who for one reason or
another cannot obtain accommodation elsewhere, and who
cannot obtain the capital to put down the deposit on a house.
It will include the immigrants, many people with irregular
forms of family life, and social deviants. Their relationship with
their landlord is likely to be simply a market relationship. This
has both advantages and disadvantages. The advantages lie
in the fact that he does offer accommodation and offers it 'with
no questions asked'—that is, without considering any other
criteria such as colour, style of life, and even security of income.
The disadvantages lie in overcrowding, high rent, lack of
privacy, and an absence of any choice as to who one's neighbours shall be.

This housing class is more diverse than any other and lacks
the capacity and perhaps the desire to organize itself as an
interest group. The discharged prisoner, the deserted wife, the
coloured immigrant, and the prostitute have little in common
except their housing conditions, and such groupings of tenants

as emerge are more likely to be ethnic or kin-groupings than groups of tenants as such. One should perhaps add that they are also joined by fellow-residents who are not simply tenants like themselves but friends and kin of the landlord, paying only a nominal rent.

It is possible to look on this classification by housing-classes in a somewhat different way as the result of the operation of three separate socio-economic systems. The first of these is a system of allocation of whole houses by means of the market modified by a credit system which gives the building societies a degree of bureaucratic control of selection. The second is a system of bureaucratic allocation in terms of formal criteria. The third is a free market in housing space.

The last of these, is certain where there is a sellers' market, to result in the intensive use of housing space by private landlords or in other words in overcrowding and the exploitation of tenants. Since it leads to living conditions which are at odds with the standards of the welfare state, it has to be subject to continuous control. But it also leads to a considerable amount of ideological confusion.

In debates about social policy in Britain two kinds of socio-economic system are advocated. One is that of the 'property-owning democracy'. In this system the individual is encouraged to own property and in particular to own his own house. The social mechanism whereby he obtains his property is the free market and the free market receives its ideological legitimation from the fact that it enables the individual to obtain security and independence for his family. The ideal man in this type of system is the 'owner-occupier'. The extension of credit facilities through the building societies makes it possible for more and more individuals to become owner-occupiers in this sense.

But since it is recognized that there will be many who cannot hope to achieve this position and this status, our society also provides for another system. This is the system of the 'welfare state', which is designed to ensure that any individual who is a citizen has certain minimum rights accorded to him, not on grounds of merit or ability to pay, but on grounds of need. These rights include such things as health and unemployment benefits. They also include, to some extent, the right to housing.

A great deal of the political debate which takes place in

Britain is about the rival merits of these two systems. The right-wing view is that we should aim to extend the 'property-owning democracy' as far as possible and that the welfare system should be tolerated simply as a 'safety net' for those who do not succeed in getting in to the property owning democracy. The left-wing view is that advantages of property should be undermined and that the welfare system be extended more and more. To achieve this, more and more resources should be devoted to local authority building so that 'housing becomes a social service'.

This debate, however, is utterly irrelevant to the justification of the third type of socio-economic and housing system which has grown up 'underneath the net of the welfare state'. For there is no net under the net and here the only answer which can be given to housing needs is to allow 'landlordism' to operate. Once it does operate there is a new ideological problem: that of determining how far it can be justified, or of identifying the causes of social evil.

Generally the two parties in the debate mentioned above are inclined to assimilate this problem to the quite different problems about which they are disagreed. The Left uses this manifest failure of private enterprise to provide minimum living conditions as an indictment of free enterprise. The Right blames the situation upon the restrictions which have been placed upon the private entrepreneur by concentration on local authority building and rent control. Both unite, however, in condemning the 'bad landlords' who operate the system, and also the tenants for their failure to obtain better housing.

Since the ideology of the free market does have some justification and does elsewhere in the city produce very satisfactory living conditions, the lodging-house entrepreneur stands condemned in terms of this ideology. He fails to provide minimum living conditions for his tenants. The declining class of private landlords of whole houses who subscribe to this ideology are not themselves inclined to go in for the lodging-house business. Yet someone has to be found to do this job, for neither the free market nor the welfare state provides adequately for housing the whole population. It is therefore necessary that a role should be performed which stands morally condemned in the eyes of the majority of the population. A pariah group of

Plate 1 Sparkbrook 1 —Lodging-houses

Plate 2 'Sparkbrook 1'—
Lodging-houses

Martin Evans

Plate 3 Sparkbrook 2 — Terraced Houses

Edward Pritchard

Plate 4 'Sparkbrook 3' — Barber Trust Housing

landlords is needed who will do an essential job and take the blame for doing it.

The blaming and the punishing of this group falls to the task of the local authority. It is charged with maintaining minimum public health standards and it must act punitively against those who undermine them. The attitudes of its agents are likely to be more bitterly hostile to the lodging-house proprietors only if they identify them with the evils of private enterprise. So the city, having failed to deal with its own housing problem, turns on those upon whom it relies to make alternative provision, and punishes them for its own failure.

Punishment, however, cannot go too far. For the consequence of driving the lodging-house landlords out of business would be to leave large numbers of the population to sleep in the parks and on the railway tracks. What has to be done, therefore, is to tolerate the lodging-houses within loosely defined limits in certain areas and 'to stop the evil from spreading' to other areas where the property-owning democracy and the welfare state may be preserved intact.

But one thing makes calm debate of this housing problem unlikely. Since most of the tenants and some of the landlords are immigrants, the cause of poor living conditions in the lodging-house areas can be attributed to their culture or race. In these circumstances 'stopping the cancer from spreading' becomes, consciously or unconsciously, a policy of creating ghetto areas for the immigrants. This, we believe, is where Birmingham's housing, planning, and public health policies have led, and from this point onwards we shall be concerned with a more detailed description of what this means for one of the partially segregated areas.

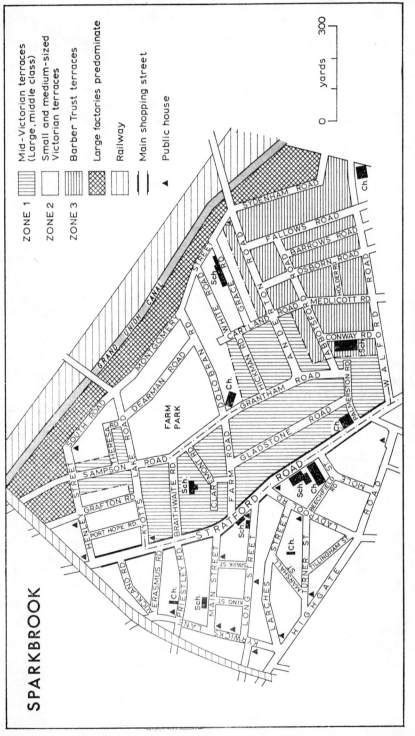

Map 2. The Three Sparkbrooks

II. The Three Sparkbrooks

Sparkbrook lies on the south-east side of Birmingham, a mile and a half from the city centre; its north-western border is the Great Western railway line, its north-eastern border the Grand Union Canal fronted by a series of medium-sized factories and warehouses. We took the Inner Ring road as the southern periphery of our research area as this was, in part, the ward boundary and the locally recognized limit of Sparkbrook. The Stratford Road, running immediately from the city centre to the suburbs of Hall Green and Acocks Green cuts Sparkbrook in half from north-west to south-east.

To the east of the Stratford Road is Farm Park, the one-time town seat of the Lloyd family; it was in the big house in Farm Park that Lloyds Bank was founded in 1765. The streets around the Park all bear names associated with the Lloyd family, being named after members of the family, their favourite politicians and places associated with their rural past. The houses in these streets were built for the professional and middle classes of the mid- and late nineteenth century; the houses are large, three-storey brick buildings, at one time richly ornamented and porched. The residents included headmistresses, doctors, businessmen and, at one time, the Town Clerk of Birmingham. The big houses all had servants and it is still possible to find local residents who were in service in the houses. The daughter of the Lloyds' last head gardener still lives in a cottage in the Park and clearly remembers the big dinner parties at the house at the turn of the century, when the coaches stood from the house door to the Park gates. Many of the residents regret the passing of the old days but others comment how glad they are that the days of plentiful cheap labour are past, when every house in Sampson Road was able to afford two maids.

Today this area—which we have called 'Sparkbrook 1'—is still deceptively rural. In summer the streets are green and leafy, and the houses stand back from the pavements; but the ornate façades are crumbling, the paint peeling, and in many blocks the front gardens are beaten into flat areas of hard earth, littered with broken bricks and glass, children's bicycles and dolls' prams battered beyond repair. Unfamiliar cooking smells and loud music issue from the windows and the street litter bins overflow with refuse. Forty years ago people put on their best suits to cross the Stratford Road into this area. Now they avoid coming over unless it is absolutely essential.

From the mid-1930s onwards the 'respectable' middle classes started moving out of Sparkbrook 1 to the by then more desirable suburbs. This middle-class emigration was accelerated by the war-time bombing; the nearby B.S.A. factory was a popular target and the Grand Union Canal the bombers' main route to the city centre. As the houses were vacated they were made over into lodging-houses; first with young English married couples and single Irishmen as tenants, later with European and then increasingly with Irish and coloured immigrants. To a casual observer today this area is a coloured quarter.

On the west of Stratford Road (where Joseph Priestley lived) there is a network of bare streets containing irregular blocks of houses built from 1830 onwards. The types of house vary from very small courtyard dwellings to a few almost like those in Sparkbrook 1, but in general these were good, red-brick artisans' dwellings of the mid- and late nineteenth century, many built straight on to the streets, with no front gardens. The inhabitants were, as one informant put it, 'working-class, but not rough labourers'. Life in this area seems to have followed a pattern similar to that in Bethnal Green described by Young and Willmott.[1] There was extensive neighbouring, the people all knew one another, and relied on kin and neighbours in finding a house; people in the street could be depended on to help in a crisis and the residents of various streets came together for Victory and Coronation parties. Today, this area—which we will call Sparkbrook 2—still looks more like an urban working-class zone than any other part of Sparkbrook. Women can be seen popping in and out of their neighbours' houses and in the warm evenings people sit on their front steps and call

[1] M. Young and P. Willmott, *Family and Kinship in East London*, London, Routledge and Kegan Paul, 1957.

across the road to one another. The figure of Mum, wearing an apron, arms folded, yelling up the road to her children, is a familiar sight.

There have been changes here too, however. Firstly, as a result of emigration, immigration, and deaths, and secondly because the Corporation has acquired some 50 per cent. of these houses for demolition and eventual redevelopment. Whole stretches of terraced houses have the familiar white 'death certificate' pasted beside their front doors. Meanwhile, the Corporation allocates tenancies in these houses according to its own priorities; they are used for slum-clearance families (from elsewhere in the city) judged unsuitable for new property, rather than for local young married couples at present sharing with in-laws. This is a source of considerable resentment against the Corporation in this area. The visual picture is, however, common to all such areas: mean, drab streets of terraced houses, small shops and corner pubs, indefinitely awaiting the bulldozer.

Sparkbrook 3, the ex-Barber Trust housing, constitutes another distinct zone within Sparkbrook although it runs into adjacent Sparkhill. These houses were built by a trust from the 1890s onwards on the land of Golden Hillock and Abbotsford Farms and over the Spark Brook from which the area takes its name. The streets were made very broad and planted with trees; all the houses were given small front gardens. The houses consist of two main sizes of neat, red-brick terraced dwellings, the larger having ten rooms and the smaller eight. The Barber Trust selected its tenants from among the 'better' working class, those with higher, more secure incomes, better job status, of good character and sober habits—a very necessary requirement, as the Trust built no public houses on their estates. Although the waiting time for a Barber Trust tenancy was short, it was a source of conflict for some people, and particular allocations created jealousies. These conflicts and jealousies are still commented on by older residents today.

In 1962 the Barber Trust attempted to sell the houses in lots of ten and twelve, over the heads of the sitting tenants. A residents' protest was organized, which resulted in the Corporation taking over the administration of the houses, although the Minister of Housing refused them permission to buy outright. Tenants were given the option of buying their houses or remaining council tenants and later becoming the tenants of another trust when one was found to take over the property in accordance with the Minister's wishes (which has not happened at the time of writing). Meanwhile, the Corporation has carried out many overdue repairs and continues to exercise its prerogative of selecting tenants when houses fall vacant, although disclaiming any *ultimate* responsibility for the property.

The local residents feel that their area is being used to rehouse large families or problem families. This they strongly resent, as they do not want their area to become a 'twilight zone', a term which they find extremely offensive when used in connexion with Sparkbrook. Sparkbrook 3 is by no means a twilight zone; its streets are very clean and quiet, its front gardens well kept, many of the tenants have considerably improved their houses by adding bathrooms, repainting, and decorating. Crucially, the houses in many cases are less than seventy years old and structurally in good condition, with long life-expectancy.

The Stratford Road has a mixture of large houses, commercial hotels, churches, and shops. The English shops improve in quality of goods sold as one moves from Sparkbrook to Sparkhill. There are second-hand furniture shops where the road borders Sparkbrook 1 but none at our southern border. Some of these shops have small workshops behind them, producing, among others, 'do-it-yourself' model-making kits and lampshades. There are about 100 factories and workshops in Sparkbrook, mainly in the Stratford Road and in the backyards and courts of Sparkbrook 2. The majority employ very small labour forces in which local people do not predominate.

Various provisions for the special needs of the population have been made on a commercial basis in the Stratford Road. Launderettes for those lacking adequate clothes-washing facilities; cafés which serve as dining-rooms for the bachelors in lodgings; small shops, staying open at all hours, as larders to the lodging-houses which lack suitable food storage provision. Immigrant-owned shops also flourish, notably the Bengal Supermarket and the New World Store. This latter not only sells Asiatic foods and spices but has a Muslim butcher, a barber, offices of a weekly Urdu newspaper, a travel agency exhibiting airline posters, a café, a nightclub, and twelve shower baths (the nearest public baths are in Sparkhill). Certain of the cafés are frequented by prostitutes. Thus, despite domestic poverty, practically every need felt by the migrant can be met by the commercial arrangements of the Stratford Road.

So far we have examined the historical differences in the three zones of Sparkbrook and the immediate visual variables in housing. We shall now consider their different social structures and styles of life, of which the outward appearances are but a hint.

Our basic reference point in seeking empirical data about Sparkbrook is the Registrar General's Decennial Census of 1961. This shows that there are two main Irish colonies in Birmingham. One is in Sparkbrook 1 and the other, three-quarters of a mile down the Stratford Road, is in Sparkhill: 32·5 per cent. and 27·37 per cent. of their populations respectively were Irish. The main centres of coloured population are elsewhere in the city, mainly to the north. The areas with more than 25 per cent. coloured immigrants were in parts of Edgbaston, Balsall Heath, Rotton Park, Market Hall, Sandwell, Moseley and King's Heath, and Soho. Of the population of Sparkbrook[1], 7·7 per cent. were coloured. The distribution of the population by country of birth was:

TABLE 3: POPULATION OF SPARKBROOK
BY NATIONALITY (1961)

Nationality	Male	Female	Total
English	5,233	5,465	10,698
Irish	1,528	1,066	2,594
West Indian	394	281	675
Pak./Indian	431	58	489
Others	376	203	579
			15,035

This population was not, and is not, evenly spread throughout Sparkbrook: 50 per cent. of all immigrants were to be found in the four central enumeration districts that constitute the

[1] Sparkbrook, as defined at the beginning of the chapter, consists of 18 out of the Registrar General's 30 enumeration districts, which cover a wider area, including north-east of the Grand Union Canal. All our figures refer to the 18 enumeration districts.

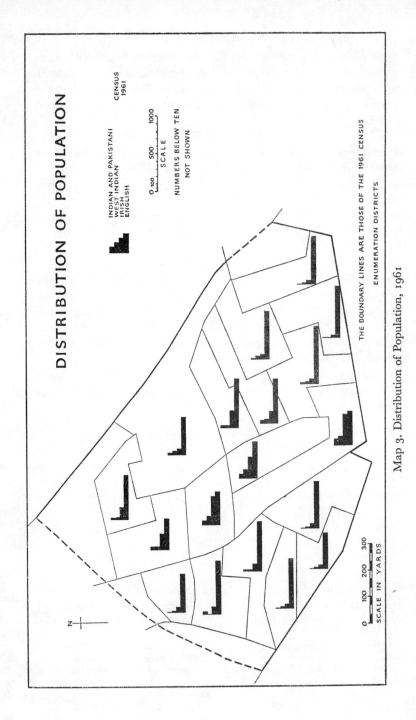

DISTRIBUTION OF POPULATION

INDIAN AND PAKISTANI
WEST INDIAN
IRISH
ENGLISH

CENSUS
1961

0 100   500   1000
SCALE

NUMBERS BELOW TEN
NOT SHOWN

THE BOUNDARY LINES ARE THOSE OF THE 1961 CENSUS
ENUMERATION DISTRICTS

0   100   200   300
SCALE IN YARDS

N

Map 3. Distribution of Population, 1961

major part of Sparkbrook 1. A few coloured immigrants appear in enumeration districts covering parts of Sparkbrook 3; but the enumeration districts (whose boundaries mainly run down the centres of roads) do not conform exactly to our Sparkbrooks 1, 2, and 3. In effect, there were no coloured immigrants in Sparkbrook 3. The Census also showed that dwelling-space and amenities were most heavily overloaded in these central enumeration districts.[1]

We believe the Census to have under-enumerated the immigrant population. Firstly, landlords who were overcrowding their houses sought to conceal the number of tenants in their houses. Secondly, many immigrants did not understand the Census. They either experienced language difficulties or believed the rumour then current that to fill in the Census form would ensure deportation. Thirdly, shift workers and men working very long hours were either never contacted by the enumerators or were totally oblivious of the Census. The enumerators found great difficulty in contacting tenants in houses which were more crowded in 1961 than at any time before or since and they also experienced language difficulties. One enumerator is

[1]DISTRIBUTION OF POPULATION (1961)

E.D. Number	Total Pop.	Eng.	Irish	W.I.	Ind./Pak.	Total Imm. Pop.
13	687	508	85	46	25	179
14	832	598	159	21	26	234
15	751	418	221	38	38	333
16	656	532	70	18	13	124
17	888	740	97	1	32	148
18	849	688	101	20	24	161
19	790	691	53	18	11	99
20	576	501	47	4	12	75
21	735	639	58	1	14	96
22	1,111	447	390	125	60	664
23	1,137	465	423	102	85	672
24	1,029	499	291	114	62	530
25	985	666	232	30	27	319
26	925	607	172	56	39	318
27	776	652	57	39	12	124
28	718	642	45	14	2	76
29	749	690	31	0	1	59
30	841	785	63	29	16	56
TOTAL	15,035	10,768	2,595	676	499	4,267

reported to have been reduced to tears on the street by the impossibility of her task.

In 1964 when our research began we were able to use the 1961 Census only as a guide and, in effect, it told us only what we broadly knew already: that most immigrants were in Sparkbrook 1. There had been an increase and change in composition of national immigration and immigration in the West Midlands since 1961, and we suspected that internal migration around Birmingham and Sparkbrook would have further changed the composition of the Sparkbrook population. Thus we attempted to make our own estimates of the 1964 population while carrying out a random sample survey with a questionnaire. We failed to do this adequately,[1] but we have made fresh population estimates which, allowing for all possible inaccuracies, considerably modify the Registrar General's 1961 picture. We have also been able to relate the population more sensibly to the three zones of Sparkbrook and have separated the Indians and Pakistanis.

We estimated the total population in 1964 to be constituted thus:

TABLE 4: POPULATION BY NATIONALITY (1964)

Nationality	No.	%	% in 1961 Census
English	11,941	67·0	71·23
Irish	2,299	12·9	17·25
West Indian	1,551	8·7	4·49
Pakistani	642	3·6	3·25
Indian	356	2·0	–
Others and not known	1,034	5·8	3·78*
TOTAL	17,823	100.00	100·00

* Others only

Whether because of errors in the Census or because of migration since 1961, the population of our survey area differs considerably in its ethnic composition from that which the Census suggests. Immigrants have increased from 29 per cent. to 33 per cent. of the population. Coloured immigrants have

---

[1] The population calculations were only incidental to our survey which was constructed for other purposes, but for a fuller discussion of this see the Appendix.

increased from 7·7 per cent. to 14 per cent. This increase shows even more markedly in our Sparkbrook 1.

Our sample was drawn on the basis of the 1963 rating and valuation lists for the area, since we felt that houses were the only things we could count with any accuracy in the first instance. An inspection of these lists suggested that lodging houses were more common among houses of Rateable Value £55 and above and we knew that a majority of the immigrants would be in these houses. To give us at least 50 per cent. immigrant respondents to our questionnaire, and incidentally to give us a fuller enumeration of those minority groups whose exact numbers were so open to dispute, we weighted our sample towards the higher Rateable Value houses.

We decided to interview every adult[1] in each dwelling. We felt that interviewing heads of households only might have deprived us of information, the value of which would outweigh the loss by duplication. This would be especially true where there were household structures with no formal or clear headship, where there was a mixed marriage, or where we wanted information about men and women separately.

A full account of how far we succeeded in this intention will be found in the Appendix. Most of the questionnaire data are used in Chapters III and IV; here we are concerned with gross population figures and the geographical distribution of the population. There were striking differences in the density of occupation and in the composition of the total population and of households in the three Sparkbrooks.

In our random sample we drew dwellings and households as follows:

TABLE 5: DWELLINGS AND
HOUSEHOLDS BY ZONE

	Dwellings	Households
Sparkbrook 1	76	232
Sparkbrook 2	69	80
Sparkbrook 3	44	46
Stratford Road	12	24
TOTAL	201	382

[1] I.e., person over sixteen years of age and not receiving full-time education.

We found twenty-one dwellings in Sparkbrook 1 with ten or more adults in them (nine with more than fifteen), one with more than ten in Sparkbrook 3 and none in Sparkbrook 2. There were thirty-five, three, and three houses in Sparkbrooks 1, 2, and 3 respectively, with eight or more people in them; i.e. 46 per cent. of the sample in Sparkbrook 1 and approximately 4 per cent. and 7 per cent. in Sparkbrooks 2 and 3.

The reason for this is obvious, since Sparkbrook 1 has far more large houses than any other part of Sparkbrook. Indeed, it was on characteristics such as were likely to give us the above figures that we originally delineated our three Sparkbrooks. When we look at the distribution of population by nationality of households and Rateable Value of dwellings our guess that immigrants are predominantly in the larger (multi-occupied) dwellings is confirmed.

TABLE 6: HOUSEHOLDS BY NATIONALITY AND
RATEABLE VALUE OF DWELLING: PERCENTAGES OF
EACH NATIONALITY IN HOUSES OF DIFFERENT
RATEABLE VALUE*

Nationality of H/H	English No.	%	Irish No.	%	W. Indian No.	%	Pakistani No.	%	Indian No.	%	Other No.	%	Mixed No.	%	Total No.
R.V. £55 and above	78	14·9*	61	56·2	68	58·9	34	65·6	6	50·3	14	32·0	21	100	282
R.V. £54 and below	75	85·1	8	43·8	8	41·1	3	34·4	1	49·7	5	68·0	–	–	100
TOTAL	153	100	69	100	76	100	37	100	7	100	19	100	21	100	328

* All percentages weighted to allow for sampling bias.

The percentage of Irish, West Indian, and Pakistani families in houses with Rateable Value of £55 or above is higher than 56 per cent. in each case. The percentage of all English families in these houses is just under 15 per cent.

It is also possible to look at this table in another way. Table 6 above shows the degree to which each ethnic group is concentrated in houses of a particular rateable value. It is also clear, as Table 7 shows, however, that the percentage of all those in the larger houses who are immigrants is very high, while the percentage of all those in the smaller houses who are immigrants is low.

TABLE 7: HOUSEHOLDS BY NATIONALITY AND
RATEABLE VALUE OF DWELLING: PERCENTAGE OF
POPULATION OF HOUSES OF EACH RATEABLE VALUE
BELONGING TO EACH NATIONALITY

Nationality of H/H	English No.	%	Irish No.	%	W. Indian No.	%	Pakistani No.	%	Indian No.	%	Other No.	%	Mixed No.	%	Total No.	%
R.V. £55 and above	78	27·7	61	21·6	68	24·0	34	12·1	6	2·1	14	5	21	7·5	282	100
R.V. £54 and below	75	75	8	8	8	8	3	3	1	1	5	5	—	0	100	100

This suggests a considerable degree of segregation within
Sparkbrook as a whole. We must now look at the extent to
which dwellings contain ethnically segregated or mixed populations. This is shown in the following table:

TABLE 8: HOUSEHOLDS BY NATIONALITY AND
PERCENTAGE IN MIXED DWELLINGS

	R.V. Greater than £55			R.V. Less than £55		
	Total household	No. in dwellings of mixed nationality	% in dwellings of mixed nationality	Total households	No. in dwellings of mixed nationality	% in dwellings of mixed nationality
English	78	23	29·5	75	4	5·1
Irish	61	38	62·3	8	1	(12·5)
West Indian	68	46	67·6	8	5	62·5
Pakistani	34	28	82·4	3	3	100
Indian	6	6	100	1	—	—
Other and Mixed	35	14	40·0	5	1	20·0
TOTAL	282	155	55·0	100	14	14·0

Thus although the immigrant and coloured populations are
concentrated in Sparkbrook 1 the houses there have markedly
unsegregated populations. In fact, multi-occupation amounts to
lodging-houses with mixed populations. We examined the
actual constitution of these mixed dwellings and found that
there was no particularly prevalent population mixture, but
the English tend not to live in the same houses as West Indians

or Pakistanis. The distribution of races appeared to be random. The single-race houses must have been set up as such, or made so by the landlord, rather than resulting from a taking-over process. At least, we can say that we found no evidence of such a process in operation—although this does not preclude its actually happening in certain houses.

Clearly some houses are crowded; but to see how crowded we need to examine household sizes and number of rooms per person.

TABLE 9: AVERAGE HOUSEHOLD SIZES BY NATIONALITY

	Under £55 Rateable Value			£55 Rateable Value and over		
	Average No. of persons per household (1)	Average No. of rooms (2)	Ratio rooms/ person (2)/(1)	Average No. of persons per household (1)	Average No. of rooms (2)	Ratio rooms/ person (2)/(1)
English	2·76	4·84	1·8	2·84	3·29	1·3
Irish	3·07	5·63	1·8	3·75	2·05	0·6
West Indian	2·31	3·33	1·4	2·75	1·30	0·5
Pakistani	2·41	*	*	2·33	1·39	0·6

* Insufficient data

Yet the number of single-person households is higher among the immigrants than among the English. This is due mainly to young West Indians and Irish coming to England as unmarried individuals and to Pakistanis leaving their wives behind in Pakistan with the intention either of returning or of bringing their families over here when they can afford to do so. The Irish also appear to have slightly larger households than other immigrants. ·Proportionally more of them are married and they have a tendency to produce larger families.

For actual living space we found that in houses of under £55 Rateable Value, half the English and Irish had exclusive use of four to six rooms (including whole houses), but in the higher-value, larger houses, 48 per cent. of the English, 82 per cent. of the Irish, 93 per cent. of the West Indian and 67 per cent. of the Pakistani households were in one or two rooms. In other words, most of the Irish and West Indian households live in one or two rooms in the larger houses. The Pakistanis seem to have more rooms at their disposal, though our sample included only six Pakistani households with more than three rooms. Even so, we would expect to find them having more rooms available to them as a result of their position as landlords in the area.

The rents paid for these rooms vary around the standard charge of £2 10s. od. a week per room. We found that 54 per cent. of the English, 74 per cent. of the Irish and 89 per cent. of the West Indians were paying between £2 and £4 a week for their rooms, though 65 per cent. of the West Indians were paying from £2 to £2 10s. od. These rents were roughly equivalent to the rents of whole houses in Sparkbrook 3.

TABLE 10: SAMPLE* BY AGE, SEX, AND NATIONALITY

Age Group	English	Irish	West Indian	Pakistani	Indian	Others†	Total immigrants
16–19	21	4	1	—	1	—	6
20–24	44	18	17	2	2	3	42
25–29	23	22	28	8	8	2	68
30–34	20	17	21	7	1	2	48
35–39	14	14	5	4	—	2	25
40–44	26	17	6	7	1	6	37
45–49	17	6	4	2	—	3	15
50–54	28	4	1	2	4	2	13
55–59	21	5	—	2	—	1	8
60–64	20	2	—	—	—	—	2
65–69	16	1	—	—	—	2	3
70–74	8	—	—	1	—	1	2
75–79	7	1	—	—	—	1	2
80+	5	—	—	—	—	—	—
TOTAL	270	111	83	35	17	25	271

* The sample in this case contains all those from whom we obtained details of age, sex, and nationality. See Appendix, Table 56.

† This column includes a few long-established European immigrants who, being older, tend to weight the final column towards the higher age brackets. Recent immigrants are younger than the last column might suggest.

The majority of immigrants arrived in the late 1950s and have had to find accommodation in the lodging-houses of Sparkbrook 1, but a notable point of similarity between the English and the immigrants is that two-thirds of English households set up in 1964 (either by migration or marriage) were set up in Sparkbrook 1. Housing needs cannot be met immediately by owner-occupation or by gaining the tenancy of a corporation or private house any more easily for the English than any other group. Another and related point of similarity is the comparative youth of the Sparkbrook 1 English population and of the immigrants.

The Sparkbrook 1 English population is significantly younger than Sparkbrook 2 and slightly younger than Sparkbrook 3. Though this latter difference is not statistically significant we suspect that it would be if our sample had been more adequate. The 1961 Census in fact shows the difference to be significant in that year.

TABLE 11: ENGLISH POPULATION OF SPARKBROOK
BY AGE AND SEX, BY ZONE (1964)

	Sparkbrook 1			Sparkbrook 2			Sparkbrook 3			Totals		
	Male	Female	Total	Male	Female	Total	Male	Female	Total	Male	Female	Total
Under 20	–	5	5	–	2	2	2	1	3	2	3	10
20–29	9	15	24	5	5	10	5	4	9	19	24	43
30–39	4	7	11	1	8	9	4	3	7	9	18	27
40–49	8	5	13	6	6	12	6	5	11	20	16	36
50–59	5	6	11	6	10	16	5	4	9	16	20	36
60–69	4	4	8	5	7	12	4	2	6	13	13	26
70–79	2	1	3	–	3	3	2	2	4	4	6	10
80+	1	1	2	1	–	1	–	1	1	2	2	4
TOTAL	33	44	77	24	41	65	28	22	50	85	107	192

If this chapter were to be summarized, we would say that our data modified but did not contradict the basic picture given by the 1961 Census. The central zone of Sparkbrook has a predominantly immigrant population of whom the Irish are the largest single group. The immigrants, alongside new or young English households, share rooms in the large Victorian houses of this zone. The whole of Sparkbrook has a 33 per cent. immigrant population, of whom 39 per cent. are Irish.

Perhaps, being familiar with Sparkbrook, we expect these figures to speak for themselves when only we ourselves (with others familiar with such areas) know what they mean in terms of the social relations and the 'feel' of Sparkbrook. This brief statistical analysis will be referred to in subsequent chapters dealing with the relationships and associations growing up

within the material framework they describe. Since nowhere
subsequently shall we give an impressionistic description to fill
in the details the figures present, we should like to take the
general reader for a walk down Claremont Road.[1] Claremont
Road is a cul-de-sac in the heart of Sparkbrook 1. At its farther
end the three-storey houses face one another across short gardens and a very narrow roadway, making the day seem darker
than it really is. About half the houses have drab, peeling paint-
work and the others are painted in various bright blues, purples
and reds. Two houses have every brick painted red and the
pointing and stonework white. The front doors stand open on
long, dark passageways. The narrow pavements are uneven and
cracked where the roots of the trees have pushed them up and
the narrow road is blocked at a number of points by cars in
various states of repair. One car is being washed by a cheerful
West Indian who jokes with his friends standing around the car,
as two Punjabi women laden with shopping walk past in
pajamas and shawls. Farther down the road a group of white
and coloured boys are throwing stones at an Indian boy and at
the end of the road six cats are stalking one another through the
front gardens. These gardens have overgrown hedges, a few
dead shrubs and hardened patches of grass and hard earth.
There is broken glass and torn paper on the pavement and
in the road. A few milk and beer bottles are lying in the
gutter.

From one window comes the sound of steel band music, from
another the latest Urdu pop song. Laughter and animated
conversation issue from a dozen windows, the sounds of a
family row from another. People are eating behind one window,
washing behind another, and just looking out of a third. As
evening draws in, lights come on in every window except those
which are occupied by shift workers who are thus immediately
identified. Even the skylights are illuminated and shadows
move across them. At this time of the day it is possible to stand
in the road and note what people are doing in every room, to
see what stage their daily routine has reached. By midnight
every window is covered by drawn curtains as people settle
down to sleep in the ground floor, first and second floor and
attic rooms. The only sounds are of occasional babies' crying,

[1] Plate 1 shows the top of Claremont Road.

III. The People of Sparkbrook

The English constitute approximately two-thirds of the population of Sparkbrook, but they are such a heterogeneous group that it is barely possible to speak of the 'typical Sparkbrookian'. They may be differentiated from one another by a variety of criteria: social class, status and status aspirations, mode of residence, actual and intended length of residence in Sparkbrook and their degree of identification with and activity in the life of the area. Given the variety of these possible dimensions of differentation among the Sparkbrook English, it seems to us sensible to use none of them directly but to make a very simple division of English society into the older, established residents on the one hand, and the young married couples on the other and to draw out the other differences within these groups as we progress.

Fourteen per cent. of the men and 16 per cent. of the women in our English sample were themselves immigrants from outside the West Midlands region and only about 50 per cent. of the sample could claim to be pure, second-generation 'Brummies' with both of their parents and themselves Birmingham-born. Birmingham has been experiencing immigration since the days of the One Mile Act, and especially since the industrial revolution, which raised the city to major industrial and commercial status. The definition of a Brummy is therefore as obscure as, if not more obscure than, the definition of 'an Englishman'.

In Sparkbrook itself we found that there was a significantly smaller number of Birmingham-born English living in Sparkbrook 1 than in Sparkbrooks 2 and 3. Thus, among the English, migrants to the area tend to concentrate in the same area as Commonwealth and foreign immigrants and for the same reasons; a fact first indicated by the age structure of the English population in Chapter II. The fact that the English have different life histories in the three zones of Sparkbrook suggests that there may be different social structures and different definitions of the total situation by the English in these three zones. This will become evident as we turn to an examination of English social types in terms of the very simple categorization given above.

The social status of Sparkbrook has fallen during the past two decades, so much so that we found a number of English who gave 'Sparkhill' as their address, even though they lived on the city side of Sparkbrook, saying that people looked at them pityingly and they in turn felt ashamed if they said they lived in Sparkbrook. In so far as the ideal Sparkbrook success story is that of working hard, making good and moving out to more desirable suburbs, the older people remaining (especially in Sparkbrook I) can be said to be failures. Few of them see it this way. The responses to the situation vary from withdrawal into the fantasy life of the old Sparkbrook, through individual efforts at self- and property-improvement, to militant activism and fierce loyalty to Sparkbrook in attempting to get things done, either on a locally organized basis or by putting pressure on local authority departments.

There is an element of fantasy for most of the older English who constantly refer to the 'good old days' when all the big houses were nicely kept, the area inhabited by respectable people and the streets safe at night. Typical of this response was Miss A.,[1] a retired nurse, caring for her aged and infirm father, owning the house she lives in and wishing she could move away —tied, however, not only by the two commitments to father and house, but also by an overpowering consciousness that there is nowhere else to go.

Among the rapid changes in the area that she listed for us she included the drying up of the supply of rented accommodation. She associated the rapid deterioration of the area with the arrival of coloured people and expressed the wish that they would go. At the same time she showed quite affectionate regard for her Kittician neighbour, with whom she was on friendly terms and whom she helped when a problem arose regarding

[1] Here we are to meet for the first time in this book the ordinary people of Sparkbrook. A friend of Miss A. told us that she knew much of the history of Sparkbrook. So we called on Miss A. and she became one of the many people with whom we had informal, and often long, talks in the course of our work. See Appendix, p. 292.

the transfer of the neighbour's child from one school to another. Miss A. has no relatives other than her father. She 'keeps herself to herself', devoting most of her life to her father, to keeping the large house in spotlessly good order and working for her parish church.

Another family living nearby has also decided to stay, the husband and wife are about to retire and the husband's niece, who lives with them, intends to work for some years more. This family, too, 'keep themselves to themselves', seeing the son, daughter-in-law, and two granddaughters who live in Sparkbrook more than once a week and other relatives in the West Midlands less frequently. They, too, bemoan the decline of Sparkbrook, especially in their own street, although they blame the Irish as much as coloured immigrants. They think it would have been worse but for the work of the Sparkbrook Association. They are digging themselves in for retirement, having many improvements carried out and the whole house redecorated. In affirming their intention to stay, they pointed out that their moving would only accelerate the decline of the street but that they might be able, whilst staying, to set a good example.

Mrs. T. represents the more active section of the English who intend to stay, believing that something must be done to prevent the 'social disease' spreading throughout and beyond Sparkbrook. It was, in her view, people like the old Sparkbrookians who made Birmingham a thriving city; she believes that if such people continue to move out, the disease will only creep out to newer areas and engulf those who have moved from the inner zones, when they are that much older and less able to handle the situation.

Mrs. T. has adopted a number of approaches to the problems of her part of Sparkbrook 1, as she sees them. She first attempted to befriend some of the Indian women, but met with little success. Later she tried to call a meeting of tinker women with a view to organizing them to improve their own living conditions and especially to help them care for the children more adequately. This met with even less success than her venture with the Indian women. Secondly, Mrs. T. has herself become a property-owner, owning a small number of the large houses in Sparkbrook 1, which she has had converted and set up as good examples of proper lodging-house provision. She selects her tenants carefully and occasionally helps deserving couples in poor accommodation by providing them with good flats. Thirdly, with a group of like-minded friends, she has organized campaigns to exclude the tinkers altogether from her street, to put pressure on local authority departments and the Press, to work through the Sparkbrook Association and, in co-operation with the Sparkbrook Association, to organize the 'face-lift' schemes for her street.

Mrs. T. may be untypical of the English residents, but she represents a more extreme type of activism, towards which a few of the English aspire and at times approach. These people constitute a significantly active minority of the English population. More typically, Mrs. T. and her husband held a series of stereotyped views about various groups. The Pakistanis do not work and are unscrupulous landlords (according to these stereotypes); they kill chickens cruelly and keep white girls locked in their houses. The 'Jamaicans' are friendly, easygoing, 'nice people' but with tendencies towards wild parties and drug-taking, while the Irish, the worst of all groups when they are drunk, are given to vicious fighting and vandalism. Mr. and Mrs. T. believed, in common with many of the English, that the police turn a blind eye to most of what goes on in Spark-brook,[1] and that by and large the authorities do not really care what happens there.

The T.s had attitudes, often vehemently expressed, that would make them potential recruits for a racist movement if no alternative modes of expressing and acting on their frustrations and resentments were available. But local, non-racist organizations, the Press, local authority departments, and the Sparkbrook Association provide them with sufficient channels for action and, in spite of their views, they obviously saw racism as an illegitimate response unlikely to solve their problems. The T.s took a continuing interest in our research and became two of our best friends in Sparkbrook. Perhaps partially as a result of this, their stereotypes underwent favourable modification. It seemed to us that many of the English displayed an underlying reasonableness which showed itself actively when they felt

---

[1] We observed two incidents; in one case the police arrived within 3 min. 50 sec. of being telephoned, and in the other (more serious), 10 min.

there were legitimate and effective channels of protest and action open to them.

Not all the established English respond by attempting to improve their own or the community's situation. Some never try, others go under after early failures and find themselves helpless, at the mercy of a situation they cannot handle. Typical of the latter are the J.s. They moved from one part of Sparkbrook 1 to another, taking a house in what they hoped would be a quieter part of Sparkbrook 1. They had retired and hoped to settle here, facing the Park, in a little house of their own into which they had sunk their life savings.

Soon after they moved, the house next door went into multi-occupation. They said that the combined noise of people living in every room, Pakistani music, shouting, door-slamming, the sight of refuse spread around the garden, and the view of Asian cooking in progress worried and annoyed them. The noise was especially bad in the room occupied by an Indian couple and their young children next to the J.s' bedroom. Talking, banging, and the sound of fire being raked out went on until 4 a.m. and started again at 6 a.m. The J.s slept with wadding in their ears and did everything possible to insulate their bedroom against noise. Representations to the next-door landlord, the Pakistani Liaison Officer, and the police brought only temporary respite and the J.s themselves were very worried lest through their complaints they would be thought a nuisance.

Over the months they became more and more depressed and demoralized in spite of a little abatement of the noise next door. Mr. J. had a mild fit during one noisy session and Mrs. J. was continually upset by the resulting state of his health as well as by the deterioration of the property next door, the health dangers it represented and the contribution it made to the overall deterioration of the whole area. The J.s would like to move and swear that they would never have come to this house if they had known that coloured people would be living next door. They suspect this was the reason for the previous owner's selling. Financial commitments in buying and improving the house prevent them from moving, however, and it is very doubtful if they could sell the house to anyone but a coloured person. Thus they have withdrawn into a private world of worry, complaint, and possibly deteriorating health, completely overwhelmed by their situation, with bitter but guilty racist comments increasingly tinging their views on it.

Mr. B. on the other side of the Park has also withdrawn: his children have grown up, gone away, and seldom come to see him; his conversation consists of almost continuous vituperation against coloured people, the Scots and Irish (who live on either side of him), the police, the Sparkbrook Association, the younger generation and the vicar. Although Mr. B. is not a churchgoer he feels that the vicar is *our* vicar (that is, white, English Sparkbrookians') but that he, in fact, 'favours the Niggers' and 'doesn't want to know you unless you have ten bob to put in his tin.' Mr. B.'s life seems to consist of sitting and brooding over the good old days in Sparkbrook, the evils of this generation and the shortcomings of people around him, punctuated by rows with his neighbours.

So far, we have been discussing the older people of Sparkbrook 1. While much of what we have described would be true for many of the older people throughout Sparkbrook there are a number of significant differences. The situation in Sparkbrook 2, for example, is slightly different, for three reasons. Firstly, the English here are, on the whole, of lower social and economic status than they are in Sparkbrook 1. Many of them are corporation tenants and not property-owners. Secondly, they are not immediately confronted by the problems arising from intense multi-occupation. They see little of it. It is mainly 'over the road' around the Farm. Thirdly, whereas the children of many of the residents in Sparkbrook 1 seem to have 'made good' and moved out of the area, most of the children in Sparkbrook 2 have had to find accommodation in the immediate locality, which has often meant sharing with parents or in-laws.

Mrs. L., a fifty-four-year old working-class housewife, provided the following account of change in Sparkbrook 2,[1] she herself having been born in the area:

People here used to rely on neighbours a lot, especially for child-minding and during confinements, but a lot of the old people moved out during and after the war. So now neighbouring is no longer a street-wide thing, but more a question of next-door neighbours. My next-door neighbour takes in parcels for me and I pay the rent and

---

[1] Reconstructed by us from a more colloquial account given at some length.

insurance for my neighbour on the other side. Before it was the whole street that would be doing this for one another. The housing manager has made this into a twilight area. Whenever a house becomes vacant rough families from slum clearance areas are moved in. This was a nice street, but the newcomers f'ing and b'ing a lot. They're a rough lot from Aston. For example, the woman opposite had ten children and then ran off with a coloured man. A few doors away a man brought a second woman into his house.

Houses are not available for local young married couples. As they become vacant outsiders get them. Our young people have to go into lodgings and pay £3 10s. 0d. for a room; they can share with parents but then clashes are inevitable. It's best to move out. Parents will always be there to help when they're needed, but it's best not to have them around all the time.

Mrs. L. had her son and his wife living with her for what she described as 'six nightmare weeks' before he found a house. Mrs. L. spoke for her son to the Corporation, but the only houses available were due for demolition. She has spoken to local Councillors about housing policy in Sparkbrook (she is herself active in Labour Party politics) but declared: 'I'm fed up with the local Councillors; I've talked to them until I'm blue in the face.'

Dissatisfaction with housing policy and uncertainty about the precise future of the area were constant themes in our conversations with people in Sparkbrook 2. Mr. S. lives with his wife and aged mother in a house scheduled for demolition, and in this lies his only hope for a new council house. But the Inner Ring road-widening scheme in Sparkbrook is so frequently changed that he is never quite sure which side of his street it is actually intended to demolish. The S.s displayed a vitriolic hatred of the Corporation and blamed them for everything from the lack of social amenities to declining standards of education and the influx of immigrants. In common with a number of people in this zone they believed Sparkbrook 2 to be a forgotten area, Sparkbrook 1 to have an unfair allocation of local authority resources and services, and the Sparkbrook Association to be an organization run entirely for the benefit of immigrants. 'You need a coloured face or an Irish accent to get anything there', was their comment on the Sparkbrook Association, a comment repeated by many other English people.

The prevailing mythology in Sparkbrook 2 seems to be that of a past in which strong working-class solidarity existed among a community living in peace alongside a respectable lower middle-class population, whose values strongly influenced the working-class outlook. Stories of the golden working-class past were recounted not only by the older generation but by people in their late twenties both from their first-hand experience as children and from the stories told and values upheld by their parents.

Did this close-knit working-class community exist? Certainly, to us as sociologists there were more than superficial signs that it did, and indeed we would have expected it in such an area. Many people who had migrated from Sparkbrook 2 returned on Saturday mornings to shop 'down the Lane' (Ladypool Road) and most of our informants in the area said how much they enjoyed meeting old personal or family friends and stopping for a chat to exchange all the latest news during the Saturday morning shopping. In part, the 1939–45 War was blamed for the breakdown of the old social patterns. Much more, however, the responsibility was attributed to the local authority which now constituted the main enemy of the people in the area.

Immigration has affected this zone; but because the houses are small the Irish, West Indians, and Pakistanis who live there tend to live more in single-family occupation. (Sparkbrook 2 may be on one of the routes out of Sparkbrook 1 for them, though we have no conclusive evidence for this.) Thus immigration does not loom so large in the consciousness of the English, except in so far as newcomers (including Brummies) reduce the supply of accommodation available which the local people feel should be their own, as of right.

As in all the zones of Sparkbrook we found old and isolated people. Mrs. K., a widow in her seventies, lives alone in a Sparkbrook 2 court. Except for a couple of old ladies like herself, the old-timers have left the Court and been replaced by newcomers, including an Irish and Pakistani family, none of whom are noisy or troublesome, according to Mrs. K. Mrs. K. does not go out much, as she is arthritic. Her daughters visit her from time to time and do her week-end shopping, though on the occasion of our visit neither of them had yet called, so we did her week-end shopping. The bill was 12s. 6d., of which 3s. was for Mrs. K.'s meat and 1s. 6d. for her cat's food. Mrs. K. was well known to the shopkeepers, as are most of the English in Sparkbrook 2, who are regular customers at a couple of the many local small shops.

Sparkbrook 3 presents yet another picture. The social status of the long-established residents is felt to be a 'cut above' the English residents of Sparkbrook 2. Some of the older people are the original tenants of the houses built by the Barber Trust in the late nineteenth century. Mr. B., for instance, a widower, immigrated to Birmingham from Leamington in search of work in 1892. He lived in Bordersley and Sparkbrook in lodgings for nine years. When he married in 1901 he went on the waiting list for a Barber Trust tenancy. He moved into his present house six months later. Others moved into the area in similar circumstances, but this generation is dying off. There are four widows and widowers on Mr. B.'s side of a short street. These people knew one another but were 'not too close'. There was some reserve over entering one another's houses and Mr. B. was a little worried in case anything happened to him and he has to call on his neighbours for help. 'I haven't ever been in their house.'

From accounts given and people we interviewed, and in view of the Barber Trust's own tenant selection criteria, it would seem that the residents of Barber Trust property had higher job status than the working class in Sparkbrook 2, being clerks, supervisory, and skilled workers, some of them working 'in the city'. Their sons and daughters similarly achieved higher status than their Sparkbrook 2 contemporaries, so that on marriage they were able to look for new accommodation outside the area rather than sharing with their parents. They moved away to Yardley, Shirley, Hall Green, and other 'desirable' suburbs, returning occasionally during the week, but more often at week-ends, to see their parents, as the shiny cars standing in the roads at week-ends testified.

Mr. B.'s own situation illustrates the point well. His schoolmaster son (aged sixty) comes to him for tea on Mondays and on Wednesdays has tea with his ninety-year-old mother-in-law (the son's wife is dead). On Saturday and Sunday Mr. B. goes to his son in Yardley and has his Sunday dinner there. Sometimes his son will pop in unexpectedly to ask, 'You O.K.

Dad?' Mr. B. has two married grandchildren with two or three of their own children. One lives in Devon and the other, whom he sees from time to time, lives in Birmingham. Similarly, the widower opposite Mr. B. is visited three times a week by his daughter and the son-in-law comes once a week on his motor-bicycle. There are others, though, who are not visited. We heard constant complaints from young and old about neglectful children who have got on in the world and no longer bother with their old parents. Some of the old, for this or for other reasons such as inability to cope with the loss of a spouse, retreat into isolation, or become 'semi-detached', as one respondent put it.

The older people in Sparkbrook 3 thus see changes in terms of the changing structure of their own family lives. Events in Sparkbrook 1 impinge upon them only through Press reports and rumour, and in so far as they resent Sparkbrook being called a 'twilight zone'. For them, Sparkbrook is a place where good, hard-working people lived out respectable lives, keeping themselves to themselves. This readily slips into an identification with the old gentry surrounding the Farm.

Their lives still centre around the family (or memories of it) and their community is in many ways an isolated village within Sparkbrook, with its own shops on the Walford Road, churches and social clubs (mainly clubs for older people run by the churches). If they are housebound, there is even less reason why the affairs of Sparkbrook 1 and 2 should feature meaningfully in their lives. This is certainly not true of the younger residents in Sparkbrook 3, as we see when we turn to consider the younger married couples in Sparkbrook.

In Sparkbrook 1, we found no young English couples in owner-occupation. A few were sharing parental homes, but most were in lodging-houses. Also in Sparkbrook 1, we found many mixed households where English girls were married to or occasionally living with immigrants (thirteen in our sample), and a number of single men and women. Given that all the English together constitute a little over a quarter of the Sparkbrook 1 population, it is hardly surprising that we had little success in building up a picture of the typical young English married couple. There are probably very few of them. From various passing encounters and a series of inferences we did, however, begin to see that such couples are most likely to be in transit, using Sparkbrook 1 rooms as temporary accommodation while seeking other alternatives either through the market or through corporation provision.

Fifty-five per cent. of all the English households in our sample in Sparkbrook 1 had been founded in 1960 or after, 54 per cent. of these in 1964, the year of our survey, whereas only 27 per cent. of all English households in the other two zones were formed in or after 1960. As will be seen from other empirical data later, the main ambition of these couples is to get out of the area to better accommodation. Although proportionately fewer of the English share with other nationalities than any other nationality, about 30 per cent. of them are so sharing and experiencing all the hardships and deprivations of lodging-house life.

In our sample in Sparkbrook 2 we found only five houses in multi-occupation, out of sixty-nine. Three of these were English people sharing with in-laws. Mr. and Mrs. C. lived with her mother in Marshall Street South for four years after they were married. They 'committed the greatest crime' of 'having children before we had a place of our own' and found great difficulty in obtaining accommodation. They now have two boys aged six and eight and obtained a rented house around the corner from Mrs. C.'s mother through foreknowledge of its coming on to the market. One of the owner's relatives wanted the house but decided it was in too poor a condition and so the C.s were able to move in and have obviously made very great improvements to the property.

Mrs. C., in her late twenties, is Sparkbrook 2-born and bred and can remember the old days when the children played, went to school and Sunday school together. People were poorer then, she said, and street outings and festivals were the only treats they had. Today affluence and the motor car have changed this and many of the 'old-stagers' have moved out and strangers moved in. In the old days you could go out leaving your front door open. Today you would not do this even for two minutes. Houses are often robbed and gas meters broken into (this was not just Mrs. C.'s personal opinion, as twelve gas meters had been robbed in the next street during one day in the previous week).

Crime and vandalism were the C.s' main complaints; the noise of motor bicycles and noisy parties inside the local café, and the wanton destruction of premises as soon as they were vacated. Again, the C.s' observations were confirmed by us throughout our twelve months in the area. The C.s thought that Brummies were as much to blame as anyone. Indeed, a Brummy had been arrested recently for breaking a nearby shop-window. Mr. C. saw the Irish as the main problem-group among newcomers. Riddled with North-South animosities, they 'got boozed up to the eyeballs', became fighting mad, and punched and kicked one another in the street.

The coloured people are occasionally dirty, but the C.s listed a number of West Indian families in the area who were well liked, respectable and gave no trouble. However, the C.s reckoned that race tension arose from the competition for housing and that most of the older generation were filled with prejudice because of this. The real hope lay with the next generation and the C.s hoped that their boys would grow up to have friends from all races and discriminate between people on grounds other than that of race. They also hoped that their children would settle in Sparkbrook, as they would not only learn the right lessons about race, but enjoy the improvements that were bound to come to the area in the future even though there are housing problems and rough elements present today.

Mrs. C., like all other respondents in this zone, remarked on the decline of street-wide 'neighbouring'. She herself looks in every day to see the man next door, his daughter comes in once a week to do the housework. We did notice, though (and social workers reported similarly, when visiting in Sparkbrook 2), that neighbours always came out to tell you exactly where someone was, whom he was with and how long he would be out, if you failed to knock him up. Neighbours would also 'protect' some of the older people from callers, a custom which was not very helpful to the social workers. Filial and parental ties still existed, but were attenuated by the housing shortage and by people moving out or dying. Although the motor car took people away on individual rather than street outings, it did enable sons and daughters from outside the area to visit their parents, to take them and other relatives or non-car-owning friends for days out. A number of respondents in Sparkbrook 2 said that this happened.

The community did, however, have its conflicts and we heard bitter comments, even from young people who could hardly have remembered the events, about those who left the area during the 1939–45 War, leaving the others to look after their houses and face the bombing. ('Everyone deserted during the War, all rushed to the country, and they'll do the same thing next time. Yes, they'll all clear out. Alf, look after me house will you?') Similarly, the fact that some husbands and sons avoided conscription whilst other families lost all their menfolk, was frequently remarked upon. These particular points of conflict are still very close to the surface and if they were not mentioned spontaneously, we could easily start our respondents off on quite heated descriptions of what 'went on' by asking a simple question about what it was like in the War.

The younger people in Sparkbrook 3 face a different set of problems; they are establishing themselves in a 'respectable' area either as owner-occupiers or corporation tenants, in houses that have many years' potential life. Thus those we met were invariably carrying out extensive improvements to their houses and were very conscious of Sparkbrook 1 constituting a threat to them. Firstly, this was because of the bad reputation of Sparkbrook 1 as a twilight zone which reflected unfavourably on their community, so that people automatically assumed that they lived in a run-down area. Secondly, they felt that the residents of Sparkbrook 1, and especially the coloured immigrants, would find the Barber Trust houses ideal for multi-occupation and would be able to buy up Sparkbrook 3 houses at the end of the five-year period, during which all houses sold had to be sold back to the Corporation.[1]

Thus events in the surrounding areas do impinge on them. They cannot live in the village of their predecessors. A couple of the younger men, therefore, formed the Barber Trust Residents' Association after a protest meeting held in the local school, when it was known that the Trust intended to auction

[1] When the corporation offered houses for sale to the sitting tenants (see pp. 45–46), it was stipulated that any sale within five years of purchase had to be made to the corporation at the original price. After five years houses could be sold on the open market.

the houses over the heads of the tenants. In fact, the Corporation became their landlord and the Residents' Association was able to achieve very little. Its functions then changed somewhat and it now concerns itself with amateur social welfare work, mainly among the older people, helping them improve their houses, taking parcels at Christmas and generally keeping an eye on them. The Association is not racist, but its officers say that maintaining standards and preventing the deterioration they have seen in Palmerston Road must be in large part synonymous with keeping coloured people out. They also object, however, to the Corporation's housing 'problem' families in the area. They said that there is a (small) maximum number of coloured or 'problem' newcomers who could be socialized into the standards and ways of life of the Barber Trust residents, and they spoke highly of a West Indian family that had settled in and adjusted to the area after initial difficulties. (We believe that this was the *only* West Indian family in the Barber Trust property.)

The political functions of the Association are now being carried out by the Chairman and Secretary of the Association, who rightly feel that they are making little progress. They said that the Labour Councillors were only interested in votes, and had plenty to say, but did little, and failed to recognize the Association as a legitimate organization. In fact, the Councillors can do little, as the Labour group in the city has decided its policy for Barber Trust houses already. We were told, however, that the Corporation is concentrating much of its repairs and maintenance effort in the Barber Trust areas, at the expense of new properties, to counter the residents' sense of being forgotten or neglected. The Trust tenants are all too conscious that these houses are ideal for large families and are situated in the inner ring area where we might expect the Corporation to rehouse coloured people.

So far, we have looked at the changing social patterns for the three zones as seen by a number of inhabitants, both young and old, the family lives they live, and the way in which they see the present situation. Two questions remain outstanding. Firstly, how far do the respondents we have quoted represent all Sparkbrookians or how far have our own biases selected only particular people? Secondly, what are the actual patterns of kinship, neighbouring and association in Sparkbrook? We shall attempt to answer both these questions by presenting statistical data from our questionnaire survey.

Desire to Move

We asked our respondents if and why they had any desire to move from their present house and whether they would continue living in Sparkbrook if they had a choice, hoping to elicit information both on housing conditions specifically and on the residents' views of the general environment. The answers given showed that they did not separate these factors; at least, not in answer to the questions we put to them. There was no doubt that the majority of English would prefer not to be in Sparkbrook; 65 out of 85 men and 87 out of 107 women said they would not choose to live in Sparkbrook. The reasons given were:

TABLE 12: REASONS FOR WISHING
TO MOVE FROM SPARKBROOK

	Men	Women
Do not like the people	9	19
Do not like the area	24	30
Don't know	24	–
Refused to say	8	41
TOTAL	65	87

There were many 'Don't knows' and refusals in answer to this question. We received similar but more pointed answers, and answers from a greater number of people, in response to the other specific question, 'Why do you want to move from this house?' Table 13 shows the answers to this question.

When asked where they wanted to move, only two men and six women expressed a desire for alternative accommodation in Sparkbrook. Just over a quarter of the men and women (25·4 per cent. and 27·6 per cent. respectively) preferred the Hall Green, Shirley, Acocks Green suburbs. A third (33·9 per cent. and 31·0 per cent.) preferred other parts of Birmingham and 29 per cent. (seventeen) of the men and 11 per cent. (ten) of

TABLE 13: REASONS FOR WISHING TO LEAVE PRESENT ACCOMMODATION

	Men	Women	Total	%
Want to own a house of their own	10	11	21	14·4
Because of bad living conditions in Sparkbrook	30	54	84	57·5
Other reasons	19	22	41	28·1
TOTAL	59*	87	146	100·0

* Only 59 men actually wanted to leave their house; 65 wanted to leave the area.

the women would have liked to move right out of the West Midlands.

Sixty-four per cent. (thirty-eight) of the men and 71 per cent. (sixty-two) of the women wanted to live either in a house or bungalow; only thirteen persons (six and seven) hoped for council houses, although fifty-two had their names down for them. It would seem from this and our more detailed interviews with particular residents that one needs to explain why English people live in Sparkbrook at all. They seem to be held there by ties of property and kinship, a few by loyalty to the area, but the majority by the sheer inability to move.

The ability to move out of Sparkbrook to more desirable areas is a mark of social and economic success which cannot be achieved without some effort. 75·3 per cent. (sixty-four) of our male respondents were manual employees of whom sixteen were skilled or semi-skilled, six and four were office workers and self-employed respectively, the remaining eleven consisted of unemployed, retired, and a student. The modal (and mean) gross wage for men was £15 per week.[1] The mean wage for women was £7 10s. od. per week; fifty-one of them were employed, twenty-nine in manufacturing, ten in catering and domestic work, twelve in offices, retail trade and self-employment (four in each). Household incomes averaged £15 with 30 per cent. receiving £10 or less a week and 33 per cent. £20 or more.

[1] It was not possible to allow for overtime in our small sample. Various amounts of overtime at varying rates were worked at each wage level. 43 men worked some overtime in the previous week, 22 of them working between 4 and 6 hours and 16 working more than 6.

Kinship and Primary Community

We gathered a considerable amount of data on kinship, finding out which relatives our respondents had in Sparkbrook, Birmingham, and elsewhere, and how often they saw them. This material is sufficient for, and perhaps proper only to, another study, but we use here those data which are relevant for comparisons between the English and immigrant communities and for testing what we were told or what we saw concerning English kinship patterns.

The English, as we would expect, have kin throughout England, many of whom they had not seen for a very long time and no doubt some they have forgotten or never known. Sparkbrook, as an established English community, could also be expected to contain many kinship links for any English person. We found that fifty-eight (30·2 per cent.) of our English respondents had relatives in Sparkbrook outside their own household, fifty-three of these had relatives beyond Sparkbrook and thirty-two had relatives beyond the Birmingham area. 169 (88 per cent.) respondents had relatives in Birmingham beyond Sparkbrook and 134 (69·8 per cent.) of these had relatives beyond the Birmingham area. Only four respondents had no relatives beyond their household.

This would indicate that the Sparkbrook English have a more Birmingham-wide kinship orientation than a local one, something that will be seen to be in sharp distinction to the immigrants when we examine their kinship patterns.

We would expect to find the relatives of the Sparkbrook English more dispersed than anyone else; since they are long-established, the effects of marriages, job changes, and rehousing will be noticeable. This does not indicate, though, whether a previous tight community has been broken up or dispersed in the normal course of events, as we are unable to compare these data either with other English communities or with the Sparkbrook of a decade ago.

The fact that the English have been dispersed around Birmingham rather than concentrated in Sparkbrook is shown by their patterns of visiting. Nineteen out of our eighty-five men saw a relative other than members of their own household every day, thirty-four out of 107 women saw such relatives every day. Of those seeing only one relative outside their household, three-quarters (eight) of the men saw male relatives and two-thirds (ten) of the women female relatives. 72 per cent. (sixty-one) of the men and 58 per cent. (sixty-two) of the women saw their spouses only every day, so that the women saw their relatives significantly more often than the men. Two men and five women saw no one. Two men and five women saw friends only.[1]

Turning to visiting patterns over periods of a week and a week to a month, we find that most visiting is done outside Sparkbrook, as might be expected, since nearly three times as many Sparkbrookians have kin outside Sparkbrook as in Sparkbrook itself.

TABLE 14: WEEKLY AND MONTHLY KIN-VISITING
BY ENGLISH

	Spark-brook	% M/F sample	Birming-ham	% M/F sample	Else-where	% M/F sample
Seeing relatives in last week:						
Men	15	17·6	40	47·1	8	9·4
Women	23	21·5	79	73·8	3	2·8
Seeing relatives in last week-month:						
Men	7	8·2	49	56·6	11	12·9
Women	10	9·3	62	57·9	14	13·1
% OF ALL CONTACTS	19·6		69·5		10·9	

From this we can see, firstly, that women visit in Sparkbrook and Birmingham more than men in a week, but over the longer period visiting is more equal, presumably because husbands and wives tend to make these visits together. Secondly, nearly 70 per cent. of all visiting is done in the Birmingham area but outside Sparkbrook.

We also asked respondents who would help them in an urgent situation, domestic crises such as accident or illness, in order to see whom outside the household they relied on immediately. The answers to this question are probably not very reliable since respondents may not have been able to think themselves into a situation that had never actually arisen. The answers given were as follows:

[1] One man and one woman gave no response.

TABLE 15: HELP SOUGHT IN TIME OF CRISIS BY ENGLISH

	Men	Women
Parent	9	16
Child	20	24
Other relative	19	22
Friend or neighbour	13	20
'No one' or 'Don't know'	21	25
No response	3	–
TOTAL	85	107

In view of the *prima facie* differences between the three Spark-brooks, we further broke down these data by zones, condensing and expressing the answers as percentages of the sample in the zone.

TABLE 16: PERCENTAGE SOURCES OF HELP IN CRISIS, BY ZONE

	Sparkbrook 1	Sparkbrook 2	Sparkbrook 3
Relative	48	68	58
Friend or neighbour	23	9	18
'No one' or 'Don't know'	26	23	22
No response	3	–	–
TOTAL	100	100	100

These figures give us some indication of the structure of primary communities and how far they depend upon kinship in the different areas. They indicate less reliance on relatives in Sparkbrook 1 and on neighbours in Sparkbrook 2. This is what we would expect since Sparkbrook 1 has a high percentage of migrant households, and since neighbouring is less important in Sparkbrook 2 than in either a very stable community (Sparkbrook 3) or a rapidly changing community lacking as many kinship ties (Sparkbrook 1).

Associational Activities
It seemed that associational life strengthened the primary community life of the English and at times was an alternative to

family life or primary community based on kinship. Also life in an association can, quite apart from the formal aims of the association, take on something of the nature of primary community life. Thirty-nine out of our eighty-five men and seventy-eight of our 107 women belonged to no formal social, political, or recreational organization; twenty-six men and nineteen women belonged to one organization only, twenty men and ten women to two or more. The largest group of organizations attended were social clubs of the Working Men's Club type, with twenty-two men and twelve women belonging to them. However, our respondents were not frequent *attenders* at any club or association, as the following table of attendances in the four weeks previous to interview shows:

TABLE 17: ASSOCIATIONAL ATTENDANCES

	Social Clubs	Sports Clubs	Trade Union Meeting	Mutual Aid Association	Spark-brook Association
Men	16	6	6	–	–
Women	9	–	1	1	1

Three men and three women claimed to be active members of political party organizations, but religion featured more often than politics in the lives of our respondents.

All but two men and three women claimed a church affiliation but only seven men and eleven women had been to a religious service in the last four weeks, between them accounting for sixty-four attendances. The life of the English churches consists mainly of activities among small quasi-family groups of people well known to one another, rather than pursuing the aims of some formal constitution through rational organization and action.

It is likely that the only significant associations for those who are not church members are informal; the small groups which gather in pubs being most important, both because of the numbers attending and because of the social welfare organizations represented there by the two or three collections made every Saturday night. In all the pubs which had maintained their English character we found groups of older men, many with few apparent ties beyond their friends in the pub. They include

TABLE 18: CHURCH AFFILIATION AND ATTENDANCES

Affiliation claimed	Men	Women	Total	Church attendances in past 4 weeks				
				None	1	2	3	4 or more
Church of England	68	72	140	127	7	1	2	3
Methodist	1	4	5	4	1	–	–	–
Baptist	3	2	5	3	1	–	1	–
Other	3	7	10	9	–	–	1	–
Roman Catholic	8	20	28	20	1	–	–	7
TOTAL	83	105	188	163	10	1	4	10

widowers, some living with children, but many clearly feeling themselves to be a nuisance around the house, and bachelors, most of whom were retired men whose conversation centred around the trenches of the First World War and the dole queue of the 1930s, and was often tinged with regret that they had not been able to join up in the Second World War.

Attitudes to Immigrants

Already we have seen, in quoting particular individuals, the ambiguity of the English towards immigrants and colour. Referring to social problems in the area may be a non-racist way of defining problems arising from the presence of immigrants. Conversely, immigrants may be seen as a problem only because there are social problems. This was borne out by evidence from our survey; only seventeen—seven men and ten women—cited immigrants as a problem as such or made racist remarks about them: 'They ought to be sent home . . . shot . . . put in concentration camps', etc.

We gave our 192 English respondents three open-ended questions, in none of which was race or immigration mentioned. They answered each one before having the next put to them.

The questions were:

1. What would you say were the most important changes in Sparkbrook in the last ten years?
2. What changes would you like to see in Sparkbrook?
3. Sparkbrook has been called a 'problem area'; do you agree with this—if so, what would you say are the main problems?

The answers fall into three main categories:

	Men	Women
1. There are social problems as such	24	25
2. There are social problems with which the respondent associates certain group(s)	25	32
3. There are groups which the respondent sees as responsible for particular social problems	22	29

And four smaller categories:

	Men	Women
4. There are social groups which constitute a problem in themselves	7	10
5. There are no problems	3	4
6. Ambiguous or confused comments about problems or groups	4	2
7. Don't know	–	2
	85	104

One woman thought that the area had improved during the period in question; two women refused to answer the questions.

From these we can see that 82·9 per cent. (157) of our sample gave an answer with an understandable rationale; only 8·9 per cent. (seventeen) expressed naked hostility to immigrants. Of course, those in Category 3 and some in Category 2 might be rationalizing prejudice, but it is important to notice that reflections about the immigrants were made in a specific social context and not always for their own sake. Moreover, there were twenty-four men and twenty-five women who mentioned social problems without mentioning immigrants.

These data can be further broken down as follows:

(1) Those who thought there were only social problems as such, said they were:

	Men	Women	Total
General decline in physical environment*	12	18	30
Decline in 'moral' environment†	2	3	5
Both	7	2	9
Other problems	3	2	5
All	24	25	49

Respondents = 25·9% of total sample.

* Crowding, deterioration of housing fabric, general physical decline of area.
† Crime, violence, decline in moral standards.

(2a) Those who thought there were social problems associated with specific groups, said the problems were:

	Men	Women	Total
General decline in physical environment	20	18	38
Decline in 'moral' environment	1	4	5
Both	4	8	12
Other problems	–	2	2
All	25	32	57

Respondents = 30·2% of total sample.

The main groups they cited* were:

(2b)

	Men	Women	Total
Immigrants	6	9	15
'Coloureds'	14	12	26
Pakistanis	1	1	2
Indians	–	1	1
Irish	2	5	7
Tinkers	2	4	6

* These tables based on first national group mentioned by the respondent; if other groups are also mentioned they appear under totals of unfavourable mentions in Table (5) below.

(3a) The respondents who thought there were social groups associated with particular problems said the groups were:

	Men	Women	Total
Immigrants	3	5	8
'Coloureds'	15	13	28
Pakistanis	1	2	3
Indians	–	–	–
Irish	2	2	4
Tinkers	1	6	7
	22	28	50

And the problems were:

(3b)

	Men	Women	Total
Decline in physical environment	17	8	25
Decline in moral environment	–	9*	9
Both	3	10	13
Other problems	2	2	4

* The women mention moral decline almost twice as often as the men—36 to 19.

(4) Those who thought certain groups were a problem in themselves said they were:

	Men	Women	Total
Immigrants	1	5	6
'Coloureds'	1	1	2
Pakistanis	–	–	–
Indians	–	–	–
Irish	–	1	1
'Jamaicans'	2	–	2
Refused to name them	3	2	5
All	7	10	17

(Respondents = 9·0% of total sample)

(5a) The total number of unfavourable mentions achieved by each group were:*

	Men	Women	Total
Immigrants	14	17	31
'Coloureds'	37	47	84
Pakistanis	7	6	13
Indians	1	3	4
'Jamaicans'	2	–	2
Irish	14	20	34
Tinkers	14	19	33

* Where more than two groups are mentioned by a respondent, only the first two are counted.

There is, of course, some ambiguity as to the meaning of 'immigrants', but if we take it to mean *coloured* immigrants, then the 'unfavourable mention' table looks like this:

(5b)

	Total	%
Coloured immigrants	134	66·7
Other immigrants	67	33·3
	201	100

(6) However, some groups were mentioned favourably even by those making adverse comments on others:

	Men	Women
'Coloureds'	5	9
West Indians/'Jamaicans'	7	4
Indians	1	—
'All immigrants'	2	5

(Note: No specific favourable mentions for Pakistanis or Irish)

From these data we may conclude that statements about race and colour arise not simply from wrong thinking or 'prejudice-in-the-head', but from an appraisal of an actual situation as seen by the locals. Pre-existing racial stereotypes may help people to identify people with particular problems, but the housing situation, which dominates the thinking of our respondents, and which we discuss in Chapter V, also helps to reinforce the stereotypes. We would not say that a large proportion of the English are prejudiced in a psychological sense. A large proportion merely make a connexion between the complex of social problems and the presence of immigrants. How they relate these causally *may* depend on their education, their social and political understanding, and their prejudices, but none of those factors is fixed, except perhaps education in the sense of schooling. Less than one-tenth of the English expressed opinions that might be simply called prejudiced. All the other views have at least a minimal rationale which is explicable by reference to the actual social situation in which the people find themselves.

IV. The People of Sparkbrook

(2) THE IMMIGRANTS

The English of Sparkbrook are, for the purposes of our study, people who were born in England. The likelihood, therefore, is that they have relatives in England and that their primary community life will be structured around these relatives. It is also likely that since they belong to England their friends and relatives will be found beyond Sparkbrook itself and that they will feel at home in other parts of Birmingham and England. For the immigrants, however, the situation is different. They are bound to be relatively lacking in kin, even though it is possible that those relatives who *are* here will mean more to them, as will non-kinsmen who are fellow-countrymen. In any case, the problem of finding a significant primary community is different for them and it will be our aim in this chapter to show from our survey data what kinds of primary community each of the main ethnic groups did form. We begin with the Irish, who are the largest immigrant group.

(i) The Irish

Of the major immigrant groups in Sparkbrook the Irish are the largest and longest established, although not as a fixed population. Sparkbrook is more an Irish reception area and a lodging-place for the single than an area of settlement. In the main the Irish disperse to settle. Of our eighty-nine Irish respondents, six came to England in the 1930s, thirteen in the 1940s, fifty in the 1950s, and twenty between 1960 and 1964. Even if they were not white, therefore, one would expect the structure of the Irish community to be different from that of the West Indians who came predominantly between 1956 and 1964 and the Pakistanis who mostly came after 1960.

Some of the earlier Irish immigrants have become completely anglicized. Such a man, for example, is Mr. F. He came from Dublin with his parents in 1934 and he and his father both served in the British Army in the Second World War. He married an English girl and now has a son at the Grammar school who, he hopes, will go to university. But for an accident at work, he would have moved out of Sparkbrook some time ago, and, indeed, as our research came to an end, he and his family moved from their lodgings in Sparkbrook to a council house in Acocks Green. Many other early immigrants have made similar moves, amongst them one of Sparkbrook's Labour Councillors. Obviously, by virtue of his position as a Labour Councillor, and as a prominent member of the Labour Club, he has found a place in the English working-class movement. He has also moved his home to Hall Green.

None the less, the majority of Irish in Sparkbrook seem to retain their Irishness. Perhaps losing their Irishness, succeeding, and moving out of Sparkbrook all come at the same point in a process of urbanization, anglicization, and assimilation. What we intend to do is to look more closely at those Irish who are either just beginning this process, have been forced out of it or who have opted out of it. In so doing we will be showing what is meant by being one of the Sparkbrook Irish.

We may divide the Irish community into three main sub-groups. These are: (1) the Dubliners; (2) the countrymen, known as 'Culchies' to the Dubliners; and (3) the tinkers, or 'travelling people' as they call themselves. The Irish freely admitted to there being a fourth, small sub-group within their population. We propose to say little about this group except that they live mainly by petty thieving (usually from shops) and/ or by finding various ways of living off a combination of casual earnings, Unemployment Benefit and National Assistance. One small group we found to be well organized, with a guarded hideout and a swift escape route to Ireland, but we did not find any 'organized crime' in the accepted sense of the term, only unorganized petty crime and sharp practices.

In terms of their place of origin, the Irish in our sample were divided as shown in the footnote on page 86, which shows that countrymen predominate and that Sparkbrook and Sparkhill are primarily 'Culchie' settlements. The nearest predominantly Dublin settlement was outside our area to the south-west. But there are, none the less, a good number of Dubliners in Sparkbrook and the division is a significant one within the area itself.[1] Thus we found that they were inclined to use different pubs and to attend different churches, St. Anne's to the north of Sparkbrook drawing the Dubliners, and the English Martyrs, to the south, the 'Culchies'. Dubliners regard 'Culchies' as slow and stupid; countrymen think of Dubliners as fast-talking 'smart alecs'. Little love is lost between them and when fights occur they may well become fights between Dubliners and 'Culchies'.

We found that kinship was important for the Irish, particularly in the early stages of the migration when contacts who could help with accommodation and employment were necessary. Some of the ways in which it operated may be seen in the following case histories:

(1) Mr. M. came from Dublin five years ago to lodgings arranged by his brother in Claremont Road in Sparkbrook 1. Now he lives with his wife, son aged four and daughter aged five in lodgings consisting of a bedroom, living room, and kitchen, on the ground floor of a house owned by a Pakistani who lives in West Bromwich. M.'s mother and father, her four brothers, three of them married, and her three sisters have all lived in this house while the M.'s have been there, especially when they have been changing lodgings. Similarly, Mrs. M.'s mother, father, and sister have all lived here, while her father died in this house and is buried in England. So for a considerable extended kin group the lodging-house in Claremont Road is an important point of reference.

Mrs. M. says that she will never return to Ireland. Her mother now has a patched house in Ladywood and one of her husband's brothers and a sister live in the same road. Mrs. M. claims to see all of her relatives every day. Her mother helps them out if there is trouble or illness. Mr. M. works with his brother and father and visits them and his sister during most week-ends.

ORIGINS OF IRISH IMMIGRANTS

	Republic of Ireland		Six Counties		
	Dublin	West Coast*	Belfast	Elsewhere	
Men	16	21	3	5	45
Women	15	24	2	3	44
All	31	45	5	8	89

* Mayo, Clare, Galway, Roscommon, Kerry

The M.s intend to settle in England, feeling that, while it offers little hope for them, things will be better for their children who will have a good education and not have 'religion forced down their throats' as in Ireland. They have been told that they have to wait five years before putting their names down for a council house, but even then, they pointed out, they would probably finish up with a 'patched house'. 'We'll have to wait fifteen years just to get something worse than this.' At present, paying £3 10s. od. for their accommodation and having young children, it is impossible for them to save for a house of their own. They felt that all immigrants were treated unfairly by the English and the local authority but they were 'quite resigned to [their] fate'. They were! Their rooms were untidy and shabby, the children dirty and constantly being shouted at by their parents, who bickered with one another throughout our interview, Mrs. M. nursing her eye.

(2) Farther down the road the D.s lived in one clean, well-kept room; a husband, wife, two children under five, and a baby. Mr. D. earned £12 a week as a dustman and they paid 30s. per week rent to their Irish landlord. Mrs. D. has three brothers in England, and Mr. D. a married brother with four children, and a sister. They both have parents, a brother and sisters in Ireland, and other relatives in the United States. Mr. D.'s relatives in England all live in Spark-brook and it was his sister who found them their present room and came to live with his wife when she had her baby six weeks earlier. The D.s want a house of their own ('Just a place with our own front door, that we can close and say it's our own'), but with young children they find it impossible to save and said that any further additions to their family would necessitate their obtaining larger and more expensive lodgings. Four months after our talk with the D.s, however, Mr. D. and the two eldest children contracted tuberculosis and the family was allocated a patched house in Aston on medical grounds.

(3) Mrs. H. (Mr. D.'s sister) had been married twenty-one months. She and her husband are both in their thirties and live in their own terrace house, for which they paid cash, at the north end of Spark-brook 1. Mr. H. has been here nine years during which he has visited Ireland on eighteen occasions. He has three sisters, one in London, one in Sparkhill, and a third living in his home. For seven and a half years, Mr. H. was in lodgings and, although he does not drink now, he went to the pub for company. He sees the Sparkbrook Irish as going through a stage he entered upon nine years ago.

The H.s are a little uncertain whether they will stay in England or not, but decided to buy a house in Sparkbrook as it was convenient for Mr. H.'s work. They felt that they ought not to put their names down for a council house as council houses were Englishmen's by right. They enjoy good relations with their neighbours. An English woman at the end of the street has a key to let in the gas man. The H.s' morale is high and they have settled, adapting to an English way of life, though only after nine years' struggle by Mr. H. and a late marriage.

(4) Typical of the larger family in a late stage of the family cycle are the C.s. Old Mrs. C. has four married daughters, four sons, three married and one unmarried, and seventeen grandchildren in England. The kitchen of the small cottage where she lives was so crowded during our visit that it was impossible to sort out exactly who lived where. One daughter lives in Bristol and is seen only occasionally; two others live close by in Birmingham and a fourth in West Bromwich, though her children appeared to live with Mrs. C. The unmarried son lives with his mother and a married son and his wife live next door, the tenancies of the two houses having been obtained together through information received from Mrs. C.'s clubman. Another son is in prison.

Mrs. C. is too old to work now and so lives on National Assistance, which she says is more generous than in Ireland. None the less, she says that she could not cope without her daughters to help her, and that if they were to become homeless, she would rather go out on the streets with them, than into a hostel without them. The daughter-in-law next door is a great help and the two of them are always popping in and out of one another's houses. The daughters and daughter-in-law do the shopping, come and see her and accompany her on her weekly outing to play Bingo.

Mrs. C. in turn helps the daughters when there is illness in one of the families and frequently minds the children, from which she gets great pleasure. One daughter became homeless and was put in a patched house. Another bought an old house in West Bromwich, but this is now to be demolished and Mrs. C. said that the daughter had been evicted without the offer of alternative accommodation. Most of the family in the kitchen joined in our first discussion with Mrs. C., though it was quite clear she was the family boss and had the right to the last word. The general consensus of opinion amongst the C.s was that, although the Irish should expect no special privileges in England, they were, in fact, heavily discriminated against, especially in housing. Things would, however, probably be better for the children, whom they saw as having a much brighter future here than in Ireland.

We met and heard of a large number of Irish families exhibiting a complex of personal, social, and housing problems, but those we met showed a remarkable resilience rooted in a sense of family solidarity. As long as they stick together the troubles of individuals can be shared and thus relieved by the whole family. Thus, although the large family may raise severe housing problems, it is itself a protection against the exigencies of the housing situation. The most severely disadvantaged family is the young couple with young children and no other kin.

Kin in Ireland may also be important for the Irish in Sparkbrook. Ireland is home for them all, including those who intend to settle here permanently. It is 'just across the water' and holiday visits are financially possible. The Irish immigrants thus enjoys a kind of support which is not available to the West Indian or Pakistani, though in some cases this can act as a barrier to assimilation.

Mrs. G. for the first eleven years of her life in Sparkbrook crossed regularly to see her mother and, as long as her mother was alive, it did not occur to her that she might settle in England. Thus she never registered for a council house. When her mother died Mrs. G. was living in a Pakistani-owned lodging-house. She put her name down for a council house and was told that if she had applied five years ago she would now be getting one.

Mr. L., forty and unmarried, visits his mother in Ireland every year. He has been in lodgings here for fourteen years, during which time he saved up enough to build a bungalow for his mother in Ireland—'but', he said, 'if anything happened to her (God forbid!) what should I do? Sell the bungalow and stick to my room or give up my room and live in the bungalow. There are lots of young people in the area [Clare]. I'd probably not get a job over there, yet I'm too young to get much sympathy if I didn't work.'

In these two cases, the ties of kinship in Ireland were pulling against settlement in England, and in the case of Mrs. G. had lengthened her stay in Sparkbrook.

Some of the younger Irish, however, are glad to be free of the ties of home. Many we talked to in the pubs and cafés had come to England with school friends who had gone back to Ireland with stories of a new life, good jobs, and high wages. They live either in rooms alone or with friends, or with relatives or family friends. Release from family control, earning more money than they had ever seen before, and having to find companionship in pubs and cafés, were reasons cited by older immigrants for the young becoming rowdy, irresponsible and, sometimes, sexually promiscuous. The young, themselves, said that they enjoyed the freedom from the stifling atmosphere of home life and the expectations of family and priest. Older immigrants also mentioned this greater freedom as a subsidiary advantage of their own migration.

These case histories and conclusions drawn from informal interviews help to give us a general picture of the quality of Irish immigrant life, and we regard this qualitative material as important. We must now see, however, what the picture is which emerges statistically from our survey data. We asked a series of questions to discover the meaning that immigration had for the migrants and the kinds of primary community which typically occurred.

Our first question concerned the reasons for migration and we received the following answers:

TABLE 19: IRISH IMMIGRANTS' REASONS FOR MIGRATING

	Men	Women
To earn money ⎱ To find work ⎰	17	15
To join relatives* or friends	6	16
To be away from the family	2	1
For a better way of life	6	1
To travel	4	4
No particular reason	3	6
Combination of reasons	6	2
	45	44

* Including migration to marry

The economic motive appears amongst the Irish about as often as it does amongst the West Indians, but not as frequently as amongst the Pakistanis. The main reason for leaving Ireland is population pressure on relatively unproductive land on the west coast, a cause of Irish migration for more than a century and a half. Forty out of the eighty-nine in the sample received some financial aid from friends or relatives in emigrating. This is rather less than amongst other migrants, as we should expect in view of the shorter distance and lower cost for the journey.

In all immigrant groups we see rural people moving into urban society. This is more true of the Irish than the presence of thirty-five out of eighty-nine immigrants from Dublin and Belfast in our sample might lead us to suppose. The following table shows the employment of Irish migrants in Ireland and at the present time.

TABLE 20: EMPLOYMENT OF IRISH IMMIGRANTS

| | In Ireland | | Present Employment | |
	Men	Women	Men	Women
Housewife	–	7	–	34
Agriculture	10	6	–	–
Handicrafts	1	1	–	–
Domestic and catering	3	9	1	1
Retail trade	4	3	–	1
Manufacturing	8	8	29	8
Other*	13	4	9	–
Under age/unemployed	6	6	3†	–
	45	44	42	44

* Transport, building, and miscellaneous unskilled
† 2 apprentices and 1 retired man

These tables not only show the shift from agricultural to urban manufacturing employment, but also indicate that 73 per cent. of the employed women have ceased paid employment in England. Marriage, however, did not necessarily take place immediately on arrival, as the table of first employment for female migrants shows:

TABLE 21: FIRST EMPLOYMENT OF
IRISH FEMALE IMMIGRANTS

Housewife	10
Domestic and catering	7
Retail trade	4
Manufacturing	13
Other	5
Under age/unemployed	5
	44

This suggests that a number of Irish women migrate to employment before marriage. We do not know whether Irish women marry earlier in England than they do in Ireland, although this was frequently suggested by social workers. But, in any case, it is clear that marriage or at least child-bearing takes women out of the labour market and reduces household incomes.

Nine per cent. of the men and 10 per cent. of the women in our sample came to England to take a specific job which was awaiting them here. Twenty-five found their first jobs through friends or kin. Another twenty-three 'just walked around' looking for employment. Only four men and two women waited longer than two weeks for their first job. The average wage for men was £16 and that for women £7 10s. od. Eleven of our respondents were sending money to dependants in Ireland.

Like the English, most of the Irish wished to move out of their present accommodation. Twenty-seven men and twenty-nine women said they wanted to leave, for the following reasons:

TABLE 22: REASONS FOR WANTING TO MOVE HOUSE
AMONGST IRISH IMMIGRANTS

	Want to own a house		Bad landlord		Poor living conditions in the area		Other reasons	
	No.	%	No.	%	No.	%	No.	%
Men	6	22	2	8	13	48	6	22
Women	12	41	–	–	12	41	5	17
All	18	32	2	3·5	25	44·5	11	20

Of the fifty-six in this table, two men and one woman said they would like to move within Sparkbrook. Eight men and thirteen women said they would like to move to Hall Green, Acocks Green, Sheldon, Shirley, Moseley; eight men and thirteen women to other parts of Birmingham, and ten men and seven women to other places. The most frequent reason for wanting to move was to enjoy better environment (ten men and eleven women). But seven women and twelve men said that they wanted to be near work, schools, or shops. Fifteen said they did not know why they wished to move to these places. Twelve men and fifteen women said they had put their names down for council houses.

Desire to change their accommodation did not exactly co-incide with desire to move out of or stay in the area, so we asked:

'If you could choose the area you could live in would you continue to live in Sparkbrook?' Sixteen men and seventeen women said 'Yes'; nineteen men and sixteen women said 'No'; five men and eight women said that they didn't know; and five men and three women gave no reply. We were somewhat surprised to find that only thirty-three out of eighty-nine definitely wished to leave Sparkbrook and therefore asked why people gave either of these answers. Unfortunately, their answers to this question were not always consistent with their answers to the previous one. They were distributed as follows:

TABLE 23: REASONS FOR WANTING TO STAY
IN OR MOVE FROM SPARKBROOK (IRISH)

	Men	Women	Total
Like the area	9	7	16
Relatives and friends here	2	1	3
Near to work/shops	3	4	7
Own a house	—	1	1
Neutral comments	3	6	9
Do not like the people	4	5	9
Do not like the area	13	7	20
Other reasons	2	3	5
Don't know why but want to move	7	7	14
Don't know whether want to move	2	3	5
TOTAL	45	44	89

Some obviously have ties in Sparkbrook. But although some may like the area, it is also possible that some who said they would not move were merely offering a rationalization in face of an apparent impossibility of getting out.

In the 1961 Census, the Irish had a sex ratio of 138 men to 100 women. This means that there was a surplus of Irish men over Irish women. The consequent problem could either have been solved by mixed marriages between Irish men and English women or by a proportion of Irishmen remaining bachelors. Thirteen out of forty-five of the men in our sample were, in fact, bachelors and only one woman out of forty-four was a spinster. This does not mean that there were no mixed marriages, since some of the married men in our sample might have been married to English women and some of the married women to English men. But it was the case that there were a considerable number of bachelors amongst the Irish in Sparkbrook.

Surprisingly, we found no less than thirty out of eighty-nine Irish respondents who claimed no kin in England outside their immediate household, and twenty of these reported that they had no friends whom they visited. Seventeen had kin in Sparkbrook itself, a much lower proportion than either the English or the West Indians, but fifty-one had relatives somewhere in Birmingham and fifty-seven had them somewhere in the United Kingdom. The relatively low figure of kin close at hand in Sparkbrook does not necessarily mean that the Irish are less settled than other groups. The length of their settlement and greater ability to find houses might have led to their dispersion, compared with the West Indians. But the English had more kin than the Irish in Sparkbrook, and both the English and West Indians had more in Birmingham. Thus the low proportion having kin in Sparkbrook would seem to mean either the presence of a considerable number of self-sufficient families or continued links with kin in Ireland. The latter is perhaps more likely and draws attention to the fact that this is the one migration which permits relatively frequent contacts with and visiting of the home country.

We also wanted to know how active kinship connexions were and therefore asked our respondents about the relatives outside their immediate household whom they saw or visited. Here we found that Irish visiting was less frequent than we had

TABLE 24: WEEKLY AND MONTHLY KIN-VISITING
BY IRISH

	Spark-brook	% M/F sample	Birming-ham	% M/F sample	Else-where	% M/F sample
Seeing relatives in last week:						
Men	4	9	13	29	–	–
Women	6	14	17	39	2	4·5
Seeing relatives in last week-month						
Men	–	–	8	18	4	9
Women	1	2·3	6	14	–	–
% of all contacts	18		72		10	

expected. Forty-one out of the forty-five men and thirty-three of the forty-four women saw no relatives other than members of their household daily. There were ten people without even immediate kin. Of these, six (three men and three women) saw friends every day. But four men saw nobody.

It was also true over the longer periods of a week or a month that the Irish saw less of their kin than the English. Table 25 below shows the numbers visiting kin weekly and monthly.

When we asked Irish respondents who would help them in a crisis we again found that the proportion depending on relatives rather than friends was not as high as we had expected:

TABLE 25: HELP SOUGHT IN TIME OF
CRISIS BY IRISH

	Men	Women
Parents	2 ⎱	2 ⎱
Child	5 ⎰ 15	8 ⎰ 21
Other relatives	8 ⎰	11 ⎰
Friend or neighbour	13	8
No one or don't know	15	15
No response	2	–
TOTAL	45	44

These data do seem to show that, although there is a strong sense of family solidarity amongst the Irish, kinship is not of immediate day-to-day importance to the extent we had imagined. We still believe, none the less, that in certain matters such as finding accommodation and help during confinements, kinship links are important. And they may be especially important at the beginning of the immigration.

Only ten (5·4 per cent.) of our English respondents claimed to have visited or been visited by friends in the month prior to interview. All these visits were outside Sparkbrook or made by people living outside Sparkbrook. Thirteen Irish (14·6 per cent.) had visited friends in Sparkbrook over the same period and six (6·7 per cent.) friends in Birmingham outside Spark-brook. Clearly, friends are important to the Irish, especially perhaps friends from their home-town and school.

We had intended in this study to draw a fairly sharp distinction between primary communities and groups on the one hand

and associations on the other. This distinction we found difficult to maintain, and although we do reserve our major comments on the immigrant associations till a later chapter, it is
important to notice here the extent to which associational
membership and participation helps to strengthen primary
community life.

Twenty-two men and thirty-seven women amongst the Irish
belonged to no formal social, political, or recreational organization. Nineteen men and seven women belonged to one, four
men to two or more. Attendances by men in the previous week
included one to a social club, three to a sports club, five to a
trade union meeting, one to the Labour Club, and one to the
Sparkbrook Association. One woman had attended a social club
and seven a trade union meeting. One woman was an active
member of a political party, and two men and one woman had
attended a Bingo session in the previous week.

Seventy-nine out of eighty-nine Irish respondents, comprising
thirty-nine men and forty women, were Roman Catholics. Five
men and seven women also belonged to church organizations.
Attendance at Mass during the month prior to interview was
as follows:

TABLE 26: FREQUENCY OF ATTENDANCE AT
MASS AMONGST IRISH

No. of times attended	0	1	2	3	4	5 or more	No reply	Total
Men	10	1	—	1	24	1	2	39
Women	11	—	1	3	21	1	3	40
TOTAL	21	1	1	4	45	2	5	79

Thus 57 per cent. of our respondents attended mass weekly
compared with 5·3 per cent. of our English sample who attended Church weekly. Among English Catholics only 25 per
cent attend Mass weekly (see Table 18). This striking difference
is probably due to two factors. Firstly, the greater urbanization
and secularization of the English and, secondly, the fact that the
local Catholic churches are essentially Irish institutions, thus
forcing the English Catholic to travel farther to church and
thereby increasing opportunities and excuses for a falling off

in practice. The only two Irish Protestants had both been to church four times in the previous month. Fifteen of our respondents said their children went to Catholic schools, but there were less than fifteen groups of children here since our sample did include some married couples.

The Church appears to be one of the most significant social organizations for the Irish and the main one of the women. We shall discuss its role in relation to the structure of the Irish community in Chapter VI. We shall also discuss there the role of the County Associations, pubs and clubs which, though they have no formal membership, may be of great importance as the focus of primary group life amongst the Irish men.

Finally, we sought to find out how far the Irish intended to settle permanently. Nine men and nine women in our sample intended to return permanently to Ireland. Thirty-four men and thirty-five women intended to settle in England permanently, although nineteen men and nineteen women among these intended to return for visits. Two men were uncertain as to their future. Asked when they intended to visit or permanently return to Ireland they replied as follows:

TABLE 27: INTENTION TO VISIT IRELAND

	Men	Women
Next month	2	1
Within a year	9	8
Within 2 years	2	1
Within 5 years	2	—
Every year	4	3
When trained	1	—
Not sure	8	10
'When I have the money'	1	2
Not at all	14	16
No reply	2	3
	45	44

We shall return later to the question of the degree of permanence of the Irishman's migration and to the relation between his life in an Irish colony in Sparkbrook and his life in English society. Here we may say, however, that most Irishmen suffering the hardships of life in Sparkbrook hope for a better future for their children in England. Before they or their children finally become anglicized they must succeed financially and re-house themselves. In the meanwhile, their aspirations remain confused, as they live balanced between an Irish society in an English urban setting and a totally English society.

Before we leave the Irish it is necessary to say something about the 'tinkers', if only because their reputation affects all Irish-men adversely. We did not have a tinker in our sample, but we were able to observe them frequently and occasionally to speak to them in the streets. We did also visit and interview one tinker household informally.

In Ireland the tinkers are travelling odd-job men, though they included an elite of horse-dealers. There they have desig-nated camping sites and are kept on the move by a law which allows them no more than twenty-four hours in one place. Some have migrated to England and to Europe. The family we inter-viewed had come over gradually since the early 1950s.

In England the tinkers deal in scrap metal and feathers, col-lecting scrap, furniture and old mattresses and pillows from Birmingham and from surrounding areas as far distant as South Wales. They unpick the mattresses to obtain feathers for sale and burn the covers. They are much disliked for having turned houses in Sparkbrook into feather factories. Originally they had come to Sparkbrook in their caravans, but the Public Health Department, public pressure, and highly unfavourable camp-ing positions drove them, women first, out of their caravans and into houses. From what we saw ourselves and from questioning landlords, residents, and social workers, it is obvious that the tinkers have been extremely destructive in these houses, smash-ing furniture for firewood or selling it, stealing from and assault-ing other tenants and squatting in empty houses or rooms.

One or two of the older generation are glad to be off the road and have settled down, keeping spotlessly clean rooms, albeit decorated like the inside of caravans. But the younger ones are a constant source of trouble, especially when the tinker population swells from seventy to about two hundred. This often happens at week-ends when friends and relations come in from the country in fleets of vans looking for lodgings and entertainment. As a result the tinkers unite coloured and white, landlords and tenants, against themselves.

The tinker girls contribute their own quota of mischief. Unmistakable in their bright frilly dresses, with their high piled-up dyed hair, they are high-spirited girls, who sometimes amuse themselves by ragging passers-by or even throwing water over them from upstairs windows. But all the tinkers seemed to regard rooms as prisons, and walls as things which you travel between or sleep inside in bad weather rather than as making a home. They found it more natural to be in a street than in a house and we were able to watch them sitting on broken-down garden walls for hours on end or sleeping unselfconsciously in their vans among piles of old mattresses.

From all reports the tinkers are devout Catholics, and we saw some of the most regular trouble-makers at Mass. Their personal and family standards of morality are high, but, as a marginal group pursuing what appear to most people as objectionable trades in an alien environment, they behave publicly in a manner that brings them into immediate conflict with those around them. The whole Sparkbrook tinker community consists of three intermarried, large, extended kinship groups with no normal contact with outsiders.

The future of this group in Sparkbrook is likely to be a troubled one. They form no part of Sparkbrook society and have not sought to come to terms with it. Their activities produce continuous incidents in Sparkbrook, a number of which we observed at first hand. Their presence is an explosive element in the total situation and many of Sparkbrook's resentments are focused on them. In fact, it may be that their obviously aggressive behaviour channels against them a sense of grievance which might otherwise be directed against the coloured population.

(ii) The West Indians

More than any other group in Sparkbrook the West Indians display a heterogeneity that defies simple categorization. Usually lumped together as 'Jamaicans' by the other inhabitants, the West Indians come from a number of islands. Our sample included eight Jamaicans, fifteen Barbadians, fourteen Kitticians and eleven others from Trinidad, Monserrat, and Dominica. Among West Indians were found families reminding us of Victorian middle-class families, men and women living in a series of temporary liaisons, stable 'Common Law' marriages, and single people. Some live in single-family occupation in well-kept houses in Sparkbrook 2, others in the worst, most crowded, lodging-houses in Sparkbrook 1.

Unlike the Irish, the West Indians are recent arrivals; 83·3 per cent. (forty) of our sample had come to England between 1956 and 1964, of whom eighteen (35·7 per cent. of the total) came in 1961 or after. They came to England for the following reasons:

TABLE 28: REASONS FOR WEST INDIAN
MIGRATION

	Men	Women	Total
To earn money, find work	8	3	11
To join relatives or friends	2	9	11
For a better way of life	4	5	9
To travel	5	1	6
Combination of reasons	2	2	4
No particular reason	6	1	7
	27	21	48

Sixty per cent. (twenty-nine)[1] of them received some aid in coming over from friends and relatives either here or in the West Indies. Twenty men (76·9 per cent.) and fifteen women (71·4 per cent.) first came to live with relatives or friends in England.

Just as the Irish are divided into Dubliners and countrymen, so the West Indians divide themselves into Jamaicans and the rest. People from other islands speak of Jamaicans as noisy, fast-talking, idle trouble-makers: 'All brawn, no brain, big mouths', as one Kittician woman put it. The Jamaicans whom we spoke to regarded the others as unsophisticated people from little islands, overcompensating for a sense of inferiority. Jamaicans and non-Jamaicans tend not to live together and to avoid one another. If they do live together, relations may not be very close. We found a Barbadian who never spoke to the Jamaican with whom he shared a room.

A second general point about West Indians is that we confirmed the popular notion that West Indians come to England as to their mother country. Imbued with a deep sense of Eng-

---

[1] Including one brought over by his employer.

land's traditions of fair play, they expect equal treatment and no colour discrimination. These beliefs and hopes are almost universally destroyed after a few weeks in England.

The variety of family structure and modes of living will be seen from the following brief accounts of various West Indian households in Sparkbrook.

(1) **Mr. M.** comes from St. Kitts. He has two brothers and three sisters at home; a sister in Trinidad, two sisters in Manchester, brothers in Nevis, Leeds, and King's Heath (Birmingham). On our second visit the two sisters, both nurses, were staying with M. in the two rooms which he, his wife and five children use. The house in which they live is quite crowded. The Pakistani landlord lives with some friends on the top floor, another Pakistani lives on the back landing, two Pakistanis have the front rooms downstairs and a Scottish woman and her daughter the back room. The M.s live on the first floor. They took these rooms because there was nowhere else available and they had had long experience of difficulties in finding accommodation in various parts of Birmingham. There being no bath, the M.s take the children to a friend's house for a bath twice a week. There is a shared gas cooker on the landing. They pay £5 a week rent. Most of Mrs. M.'s time is taken up with caring for the children, although the eight-year-old eldest girl is expected to help her with them whenever she is at home. If the M.s wish to go out to a social in the evening Mrs. M.'s aunt comes over to look after the children.

The M.s think it would be 'lovely' to live on a council estate, but have been told by local Councillors that they have a long time to wait. They tried to register in 1960 but were told to come back in 1965; in 1965, soon after we first met the M.s they had been to register for a council house and were told that they would now have to wait one year to get on the waiting list. M. was very angry about this. Before this experience he suspected that there was discrimination against West Indians for jobs and housing. Now he is convinced.

M. organized a local football team and social club. He went to hear the speeches by the party leaders in Birmingham Rag Market during the General Election campaign. He helps the Sparkbrook Association and takes a general and intelligent interest in current affairs, which he discusses with great insight and cogency. Our last encounter with M. was late one night when we met him on the street searching for rooms. His landlord had (quite illegally) served notice to quit but M. saw no real point in contesting it.

(2) We paid a visit to J. (whose surname we never discovered), a Kittician woman in her mid-fifties. Her house is so crowded that we were unable to work out how many people actually lived there. All the residents seemed to be West Indians. The rooms are all in bad condition. J.'s room could only be called a cubicle. She has divided it into two with a partition. On the 'living room' side she has managed to fit three wooden chairs, a chest of drawers and a paraffin stove. However, J. is a very cheerful person and she talked about her activities in the local Methodist Church, of which she is an active member, and discussed moral questions, especially the problem of young West Indians going astray in England.

(3) Sid lives with his mother, his sister and her baby in Sparkbrook. They came from Barbados and appear to be a very tight-knit family group, although neither Sid's mother or sister are married. They pay £6 a week to a Kittician landlord who lives next door and whom they accuse of snooping on them. (It is a common complaint that West Indians make bad landlords for West Indians.) They live in two rooms, although they rent the whole of a small terraced house, Sid sleeps in one room and his mother and sister in the other, which also serves as a sitting-room. They do not use the other rooms except for storing furniture and luggage, as they intend to move as soon as possible. The landlord forbids the use of electric fires so they normally use a paraffin stove; but sometimes they lock the doors, draw the curtains and bring out an electric fire from under the bed. Sid's main problem is to find a woman, but he is not very articulate and a little unused to social gatherings, coming as he does from a very poor, low-status peasant community in Barbados. So he has little success socially. He watches a lot of television, his friends call once or twice a week and sometimes they go out for a drive in a car. Sid recently became the only coloured member of a local Judo Club, an enterprise which brings him in for a lot of good-natured teasing from his friends.

This family's main concern is to stay together and find good living accommodation, though they live in a far better physical conditions than many of their fellow-countrymen. They take little interest in affairs outside their home but are vaguely resentful of the way West Indians are treated in England.

(4) Mrs. I. is in her forties, has been here five years and lives in a two-roomed attic. One room is a bedroom and the other is partitioned to form a sitting-room cum kitchen. The rooms are expensively and well furnished and kept in good order. There is no bathroom. Mrs. I. works at a factory, as do her son (nineteen) and

daughter (twenty-one). She also has a son and daughter of twelve and sixteen respectively. Mrs. I. is not married and left the children's father in St. Kitts. She has two or three regular West Indian visitors and herself regularly visits a fellow member of the West Indian Fellowship (Methodist Church) but at work she prefers to mix with the English women as the West Indian women (mainly Jamaicans, according to Mrs. I.) fight and swear at work. This was confirmed by another West Indian worker at the same firm.

(5) Mr. and Mrs. G. also live at the top of a house, in one room partitioned to form a bedroom and sitting-room. The sitting-room has a radiogram, a television set, and a glass cabinet with all the best crockery laid out in it. They share a kitchen with two other familes; at least fourteen people live in the house, owned by a Pakistani who does not live on the premises. Mr. and Mrs. G.'s marriage is a Common Law union and she has two children in Jamaica, where she also owns a piece of land which she had refused to sell in spite of good offers for it. Mr. G. works at a car factory and comes home at five p.m. every day. Mrs. G. is an auxiliary nurse at a hospital. She works twelve hours a day, never knows when she will have a Sunday off, and often works a seven-day week. She is very tired at the end of the day, but Mr. G., who arrives home much earlier than her, refuses to put the dinner on to cook, as 'that's a woman's work'. He never takes her out in his car either, so that Mrs. G. has genuine grounds for a series of complaints about her husband. Mr. G., how-ever, is a placid man who mainly ignores his wife's complaints, so they live together quite peacefully, intending to stay in England indefinitely and hoping to buy a house as soon as they can afford one. Mrs. G. went for a holiday to see her mother in Jamaica last year.

(6) Mr. and Mrs. N. were born in Barbados and St. Kitts res-pectively, though they came to England from Curaçao, Mr. N. two years ahead of his wife and family. They have three daughters and Mrs. N. has a married son and daughter by a previous husband in the West Indies. The family, having lived in Curaçao for some time, all speak a little Dutch, and one of the daughters speaks it fluently. They live on a whole floor of a house divided into two flats, theirs being very well kept and brightly furnished, with new furniture. Mr. N. took charge whenever we called. His daughters (and, by implica-tion, his wife) were told to sit down properly and keep quiet. Mr. N. does all the talking and he knows all the answers. He works at a car factory and as a spare-time insurance agent. He believes that West Indians who try do well in England, but they must work hard

and behave themselves. He said that he has no trouble with jobs or accommodation and is quite happy here. The family are stalwart members of the parish church which provides their only associational activity. They intend to settle permanently in England. Mrs. N. minds babies for working West Indian mothers. There is a great demand for baby-minders among West Indian women and this is usually done by the older woman, either unable to work or with large families of their own. The children of working mothers in the West Indies would be cared for by the grandmother, aunts or sisters, but these are seldom readily available in England.

(7) Daniel C. we first met when we tried to stop him coming to blows with his Pakistani landlord, who was trying to throw him out.[1] He came from St. Kitts two years ago. He was a blacksmith at home, but is content to have a labouring job in a factory near his lodgings in Sparkbrook. He lives in one room and spends a lot of time in pubs and cafés, where we often saw him in the evenings. He likes England and does not want to go back to St. Kitts, though he says he misses the cheap fruit. He had a woman and some children in St. Kitts. The children are still there but his woman is now married in England, 'without telling me'. Daniel would like an English girl. West Indian women are crafty and put on airs in England, but really they are no good, he says. So far, he has had no luck with English girls. Two white 'business girls' asked for his room one night, so he shut them in there and went to stay with a friend, but he would not take any money from the girls; 'Prostitutes' money doesn't do you any good'. So Daniel, in his late thirties or early forties, and only a couple of inches over five feet tall, lives on his own, cheerfully hoping that one day the right girl will turn up. Meanwhile, he has more or less 'adopted' a family of seven little Irish girls. 'They are my friends now.' He first met them in previous lodgings and was glad to find them again in his present street; they, too, seem to have adopted him.

(8) F. and J. came from the same street in Kingston, Jamaica, and now they are married, living in a Birmingham suburb, but having passed through the lodging-houses of Sparkbrook and elsewhere. Their present house is the second they have started to buy on mortgage. Their first mortgage was obtained for a fee of £45 and at 8 per cent. interest for a house in Yardley Wood. Along with many other West Indians they lost their money when the mortgage company went bankrupt with the Jasper Group companies. The agent went to jail for fraudulent conversion. At least this company offered some

[1] See page 143.

hope. Others had made many excuses in refusing J. a mortgage, including the assertion that English birth is a necessary qualification for a mortgage. Now they have a mortgage from one of the large national companies, which raised no difficulties. F. and J. have thus been able to move out of Sparkbrook; but F. works below his skill in order to earn higher wages and J. works nights as an auxiliary nurse. They see little of one another and have almost no social life except in so far as J. is able to call on a sister in Sparkbrook after church on Sunday.

F. and J. were two of the most intelligent West Indians we met, well read, socially and politically conscious. These qualifications helped them to understand and explain their misfortunes and plan the comeback necessary for eventual success. We are sure that most people without their mental resources and persistence would have been beaten at an early stage of the struggle.

Taking an overall view of West Indian life in Sparkbrook, we note that there is often instability between partners in the West Indian family, leading to separations and new relationships being formed. This has been noted in other studies of West Indian migrants and of West Indian society itself. Marriage has only been legal in the West Indies for a little over a century; the Common Law marriage, conjugal instability and formal marriage late in life as a mark of middle-class status are all still very common. The care of children falls almost entirely to female kin and many children are brought up by their grandmothers or aunts, although their (biological) fathers may help support them financially. Many of the West Indian families we knew in Sparkbrook had children from more than one union, both here and in the West Indies. We found single people without a mate. Some, like Mrs. I., settle quite happily with their children and friends around them, but others, especially the men, like Daniel C., are unsettled and looking for a partner to settle with. The young men's conversation in the pubs almost invariably centred around the problems entailed in getting a woman, though they were not always looking for a life's partner. These men have no immediate kin here and therefore find their primary relationships among other men in the pubs or as members of small clubs.

Although a number of our West Indian informants and local

ministers told us that West Indians were now experiencing a pressure towards formalized marriage, so as to attain full English respectability, we did not notice this as an at all significant factor. While we found many stable, happy couples, we also found many unstable relationships; we witnessed one pair parting with blows in Farm Park. The man was complaining bitterly that his wife had given him three fried eggs for breakfast when he had only asked for two. The wife retorted that this was no reason for punching her in the face. A white acquaintance standing near by (the future use of his spare room depending on the outcome of the row) told us that this couple, who have two or three children, part regularly every year, usually in the course of just this sort of issue flaring up. It was not uncommon, either, to see a West Indian man throwing gravel at a window and pleading to be let in by the woman he loved, or men and their baggage being ejected from the erstwhile connubial lodging-house. Such partings, and the underlying instabilities which they represent, seem to be accepted, the only complaints arising when actual physical injury is done in the course of parting or where a woman who cannot support herself is left unsupported. Older women would not hesitate to tell their daughters to leave their man if he was 'no good'.

The isolated men like Daniel C. may have to fend for themselves but the women are more likely to have people with whom they can form a viable set of primary relationships, usually children or relatives here in England. Other women may only be able to send children home to a mother or sister in the West Indies so that they can be free to work here. The break-up of a small familial West Indian group in England has a special significance for the woman in so far as mothers, sisters, and aunts are not so readily available to look after the children if the woman wants to work. Thus for these women and working women in general the system of paid baby-minding has grown up in Sparkbrook. The woman who fails to adapt or succeed in English society can return to her family in the West Indies and expect support from them. For the man this is not so, nor would they find the loss of face, in returning as a failure, tolerable. The men therefore look to their friends for support and transient liaisons for comfort.

Forty-three (86 per cent.) of our West Indian respondents

said they had friends and relatives in Birmingham; 72 per cent. (thirty-six) had them in Sparkbrook itself; only 12 per cent. (six) said they had no friends or relatives in England at all. When we look at the proximity of kin we see that 70·8 per cent. (thirty-four) have relatives in Birmingham, 41·7 per cent. (twenty) actually in Sparkbrook. A higher percentage of kin are contacted in Sparkbrook than for either the English or Irish, but outside Sparkbrook the contacts are considerably less.

TABLE 29: WEEKLY AND MONTHLY KIN-VISITING
BY WEST INDIANS

	Spark-brook	% M/F sample	Birming-ham	% M/F sample	Else-where	% M/F sample
Seeing relatives in last week:						
Men	8	30	7	25	–	–
Women	6	29	5	24	–	–
Seeing relatives in last week-month:						
Men	5	19	3	11	2	7
Women	–	–	1	5	–	–
% of all contacts	51·4		43·2		5·4	

This would point to a generally higher concentration of West Indian immigrants in particular areas; thus, if a Sparkbrook West Indian has kinsfolk the chances that they are in Sparkbrook also are higher than they would be for an Englishman or Irishman. Indeed, the West Indian is likely to have come to Sparkbrook because he has kin there. He may even live with them on arrival or in accommodation found by them. Interestingly enough the importance of kin was stressed by many of the Irish in our discussion with them, but was not shown statistically to be more significant than for the English in our two samples; whereas the West Indians did not mention kinsfolk very often, but the data from our sample show that in Sparkbrook they are more important than for the Irish, in the sense that they are seen and 'used' more often, and in so far as they actually provide an obvious basis for a local community in which one can live, or at least feel one lives.

Nineteen (39·6 per cent.) of our West Indian respondents could rely on kinsmen to help them in time of need. To our question, 'Who would help in the house . . .?', the West Indians answered as follows:

TABLE 30: HELP SOUGHT IN TIME OF
CRISIS BY WEST INDIANS

	Men	Women
Parent	–	1
Child	3	2
Other relatives	10	3
Friend or neighbour	6	8
No one or 'Don't know'	8	7
All	27	21

Over a period of a whole month, eleven men and nine women (40·7 per cent. and 42·9 per cent. respectively) had visited or been visited by various numbers of friends in Sparkbrook; four men and four women (15·4 per cent. and 19·0 per cent.) had visited or been visited in Birmingham, and a woman had visited friends outside Birmingham.

The change in employment in coming to England, representing also a change to a more urban, industrial way of life, is as important for the West Indians as for the Irish. Kinsmen are important here too, in that fifteen of our respondents (31·9 per cent.) found their first job through relatives, ten (21·3 per cent.) found them through the Labour Exchange and fifteen by 'just walking around'. Their employment in the West Indies and England is shown in Table 31.

It is interesting to notice that far fewer West Indians than Irish came from agricultural employment; however, they do come mostly from small, mainly rural islands.

All the women entered paid employment on arrival in England; twenty-eight (58 per cent.) of our respondents obtained a job within two weeks of arrival, nine (19 per cent.) in the next two weeks, eight waited longer (one woman for over a year). The average wage for men was £15 and £7 10s. od. for women. Twenty-two men and fifteen women send money home to kinsfolk in the West Indies.

TABLE 31: EMPLOYMENT OF WEST INDIAN IMMIGRANTS

| | Employment in West Indies | | Present Employment | |
	Men	Women	Men	Women
Housewife	–	4	–	7
Agriculture	2	–	–	–
Handicrafts	5	4	1	–
Domestic and catering	–	7	3	2
Retail trade	1	2	–	–
Manufacturing	7	–	10	8
Other	7	–	13	3
Under age/unemployed	5	4	–	1
	27	21	27	21

The West Indians are evenly divided in their desire to stay in or move from Sparkbrook. Asked whether they would choose to continue to live in Sparkbrook, they gave the following answers:

TABLE 32: WEST INDIAN DESIRE TO LEAVE SPARKBROOK

	Yes	No	Don't know	% Yes
Men	14	12	1	54
Women	10	8	3	50
All	24	20	4	52

Their reasons were as follows:

TABLE 33: REASONS FOR WANTING TO STAY IN OR MOVE FROM SPARKBROOK (WEST INDIANS)

	Like the area	Relatives and friends here	Near work, shops, etc.	Neutral comments	Do not like the area	Do not like the people	Don't know
Men	6	3	1	3	6	2	3
Women	5	3	2	2	7	1	4
All	11	6	3	5	13	3	7

However, eighteen men and thirteen women definitely wanted to move from their present accommodation, for the following reasons:

TABLE 34: REASONS FOR WANTING TO MOVE
HOUSE AMONGST WEST INDIAN IMMIGRANTS

	Want to own a house	Bad area	Bad living conditions	Other reasons	Total
Men	3	–	14	1	18
Women	1	1	10	1	13
All	4	1	24	2	31

Again we see respondents citing the poor living conditions in
their houses as the main reason for moving; that it is this alone
and not only a desire to improve their social standing by moving to 'better' areas, was also shown. When the West Indians
were asked where they would like to move, a preference was
shown for places outside Sparkbrook, though not such a marked
preference for the suburbs seen to be desirable by the English
and Irish:

TABLE 35: PROPOSED DESTINATIONS OF MOVES
BY WEST INDIANS

	Hall Green, etc.	Elsewhere in Birmingham	Anywhere else	Sparkbrook	Total
Men	1	5	7	5	18
Women	1	5	5	2	13
All	2	10	12	7	31

Table 36 shows the reasons for choosing these places.
Our sample responses showed, therefore, that although
Sparkbrook did not offer them the most desirable environment
or good living conditions they experienced some ambivalence
about moving. This may be due to any one, or any combination,
of three factors: low expectations of becoming an owner-
occupier or getting a good council house (only three men and
two women had their names down for council houses); uncertainty about staying in England or a definite decision to
return home (see below); or the presence of kin, friends, or

TABLE 36: WEST INDIAN REASONS FOR SEEKING HOMES IN PARTICULAR AREAS

	Near shops/ work, etc.	A better environment	Other advantages	Don't know or no specific reason	No response	Total
Men	5	3	–	4	6	18
Women	3	3	–	–	7	13
All	8	6	–	4	13	31

fellow-countrymen forming a viable community that they are unwilling or uneasy to abandon in pursuit of better living conditions.

In answer to the question, 'Do you intend to return home?', our respondents replied:

TABLE 37: WEST INDIAN INTENTION TO RETURN TO WEST INDIES

	Yes		Not at all	Don't know
	Permanently	For a visit		
Men	15	7	2	3
Women	12	7	1	1
All	27	14	3	4

This is in striking contrast to the Irish responses. Only 20·2 per cent. of the Irish intend to return for good, but 56·3 per cent. of the West Indians intend to do so, although the intention may never be translated into action for either group. The West Indian reasons are shown in Table 38 below.

The West Indians do not appear to be very heavily engaged in formal associational life. One man and two women had been to a social club in the previous four weeks, one man to a sports club and seven to a trade-union meeting. None said he was an active member of a political party and this was confirmed by our own observations that no West Indians at all took part in the routine social and political activities of the political party organizations. Of those entitled only 40·7 per cent. (six) and 30 per cent. (six) of the men and women respectively were registered as voters.

TABLE 38: WEST INDIAN REASONS FOR
WANTING TO RETURN HOME (PERMANENTLY)

	Do not like England/ the English	Inability to settle, homesick, etc.	Other reasons	Combin- ation of reasons	Don't know	Total
Men	3	6	3	–	3	15
Women	3	7	1	1	–	12
All	6	13	4	1	3	27

We found sport to be a significant activity among small groups of West Indian men in Sparkbrook. The St. Christopher's Football Club was started in 1959 by a West Indian who thought that the playing of football would be a good way to raise the morale of his fellow countrymen. Initially he undertook the financial responsibility for the club, but now it supports itself from membership fees, weekly subscriptions, a 'tote', and occasional 'socials'. It has about twenty members, all of whom have been friends for some years, some since before the foundation of the club. On the way home from matches they stop at one of their favourite pubs to talk about the game and to discuss their personal activities during the previous week. The team has been quite successful in nearly winning the Birmingham Coronation League and in winning Birmingham Parks cricket competition. The team plays in one of the most exposed playing fields in Birmingham and we observed it turning out in some of Birmingham's worst winter weather. It seems, however, that not only does this relative success and dedication to the game bind the team together, but the fact that it is a small, essentially face-to-face group of Kitticians, for whom this is the major associational group to which they belong. It may be the nearest thing to a family that some of them have in England. In 1965 they planned to go on a tour of Ireland. The very closeness of the group led to a split in it about a year ago.

Mr. M., whom we have already mentioned, had a personal disagreement with the organizer-manager of the St. Christopher's team, he left the club, and formed the Basseterre Celtic Football Team. This team plays in a league much less well organized than the Coronation League, so it does not have a game every week. It tends, therefore, to concentrate on social events, organizing dances and socials every two weeks, which has aroused some of the keener footballers to conflict with M., though he says that the worst complainers are the men who do not pay their subscriptions. The dances and socials are important events for both teams, as not only do they raise funds this way but are also able to get together with their friends and meet girls—an important factor hardly catered for in any other way for the young West Indians. Men from other islands are almost always excluded from these social occasions.

Both clubs are run by a committee, but in fact each revolves around its respective founder-manager. We noticed that many West Indians are willing to join in recreational activities organized for them but few are willing to help with the organization. However, this complaint was made not only by the officers of West Indian associations, but by the organizers of every activity in Sparkbrook.

Whereas the Irish have provision made for their social life on a relatively well organized basis, the Harp Club and the County Association are essentially secondary associations within which smaller kin or village groups could exist. The West Indian Football Clubs we suggest fall between being familial groups and more formally organized secondary associations. Here we are interested in the function of such associations in enabling the individual to overcome isolation.

Party-giving is an activity which from time to time brings the West Indians into conflict with local residents, although there were very few such incidents during our stay in Sparkbrook. The parties that we visited in the area (with the exception of a birthday party) were run on a commercial basis by individuals in their rooms or houses. The majority of those present were men, the few West Indian and English girls being in great demand for dances. Some West Indians avoid these parties as the sale of liquor in this manner is illegal and they are not willing to risk being caught in a police raid.

West Indian religion will be discussed in Chapters VI and VII but we have already seen how a group like the West Indian Fellowship at the Methodist Church is the base for friendships and visiting among certain West Indians. J. would have been isolated without it, and Mrs. I. would have been left with no contacts outside her family or work. Religious adherences among West Indians were claimed as follows:

TABLE 39: WEST INDIAN RELIGIOUS ADHERENCE

	No religion	Church of England	Church of Scotland	Methodist	Baptist	Others	Roman Catholic
Men	2	10	—	7	1	5	2
Women	—	10	1	2	1	4	3
All	2	20	1	9	2	9	5

The Roman Catholics had all been to Mass at least once in the previous month, but only one man had attended four times. Nine men and six women in the non-Roman Catholic churches had been to a service at least once in the previous month; one man attended on four or more occasions.

How, then, do we see the West Indian community in Sparkbrook? It consists of people drawn from a number of islands, living in Sparkbrook largely because ties of kinship and friendship draw them here in search of living accommodation. Although West Indians may have more local kinship links than the English or Irish, they lack the extensive, dense kinship network of their home. Crucially for the women, this deprives them of aid in caring for children. Men particularly are thrown back on small secondary associations for company and aid and to make common provision through dances and socials for meeting girls who, numerically, are not so available as at home. The lack of coherence of the West Indian social life, and the lack of kin also, make the break-up of couples a slightly more serious event in terms of its economic consequences and the need for alternative accommodation to be found for one party. But we can say that the West Indians have sufficient of their kin and/or fellow countrymen around them to make life possible and tolerable in Sparkbrook but not to make it desirable. This, combined with obviously poor living conditions, prevents the West Indians settling satisfactorily in the area and leaves them undecided as to whether to seek better accommodation elsewhere, though mainly they are determined to return to the West Indies. This return and its acceptability must in turn depend on economic factors and the immigrant's ability to earn and save enough to return with enough money to set himself up comfortably in the West Indies, or his willingness to return without. It is perhaps an understatement to say that the West Indian's situation in Sparkbrook is ambiguous.

(iii) The Pakistanis

The Pakistanis are the smallest of the three major immigrant groups in Sparkbrook but they have a presence and exert a special influence out of proportion to their numbers. The apparent tightness of their community organization, the fact that they speak a different set of languages, and their particular role as housing entrepreneurs make them a largely unknown and widely disliked group. Typical of English ambivalence is that whereas West Indians are criticized for being noisy, Pakistanis are accused of being too silent, 'coming and going like shadows'.

The origins of the Pakistani immigrants show how the events of world history impinge on a small section of English society today. Our sample consisted of eighteen Azad Kashmiris[1] from the Mirpur district, eighteen from the Campbellpore district of the North West Frontier Province, and four from the remainder of Pakistan. There is in Sparkbrook a small group of Bengalis from the Sylhet district; but the one Sylheti household drawn in our sample refused to be interviewed. The Pakistani community in Sparkbrook is roughly half Mirpuri and half Campbellpori; emigration from these districts is a result of British imperial activities. Mirpur and Sylhet were districts from which British steamship companies recruited their cheap labour; some of these seamen jumped their ships, especially between 1943 and 1949 when there was an acute labour shortage in England. Further potential emigrants were displaced in the Mirpur district during the early days of the Kashmir dispute and now more are being displaced by the flooding of villages in a hydro-electric scheme. Campbellpore district was the area in which the British North West Frontier Army recruited its bearers, cooks, batmen, and caterers. Thus early links were formed between England and these areas. Immigration from

---

[1] Strictly speaking not Pakistanis, but in their own opinion they are, and we would identify them as such by virtue of their culture and religion.

them has been a slow but accumulative process which accelerated in the late 1950s.

Pakistani immigration follows a pattern different from that
of any of the other groups; six (15 per cent.) of our sample came
to England before 1955 (two before 1950), another six (15 per
cent.) between 1956 and 1959 and twenty-eight (70 per cent.)
came in the remaining five years between 1960 and 1964.
However, not all of these earlier immigrants have spent all the
time between first arrival and the present in England. We
found a common pattern of returning home and re-immigration, the immigrant staying in England for between three and
five years and returning home for anything between six months
and two years before again returning to England. There are
also cases of brothers emigrating in rotation, one coming to
England as another returns to Pakistan. These patterns are
possible only if the individual or family has a *pied-à-terre* in
England. This is so for most Pakistanis. Fifteen out of twenty-
two respondents who were willing to say whether they owned
the house in which they were living were either owners or part-
owners. Non-owners can, however, always expect to be housed
by a relative or friend from their home districts.

The most obvious fact about the Pakistani population is the
predominance of men. In 1961 men outnumbered women by
twelve to one (and we obtained only two women in our sample
of forty-one). Pakistani households in Sparkbrook are therefore
typically male households. This may be liable to fairly rapid
change as during the increase in public discussion of immigration control it seemed that more of the men decided to bring
their wives and families over, in many cases before they had
originally intended to do so. The lack of the female presence
becomes very evident after visiting a few Pakistanis' houses.
The male households have something of the quality of a railway
waiting room; the households with wives present are comfort-
able, homely, and private. The men without women have to
cook for themselves, something which they rapidly learn as a
matter of survival, but if the husband has a wife in purdah he
still has to do the shopping unless there is a son old enough to
do it for his mother.

We are aware that the Pakistani community in Sparkbrook
and throughout England has a very complex structure, the

surface of which we were only just able to scratch. There are three major sets of relationship existing in the Pakistani community in Sparkbrook. Firstly, the kinship relationships which merge with village and district loyalties. This means that co-villagers are freely referred to as cousins and we experienced difficulty in sorting out blood relationships from village ties.[1] Kinship terms were not in themselves used consistently by Pakistanis, who also recognize and name kin beyond English recognition and terminology.[2] Thus we were told how a man lived with his mother's cousin-brother or father's sister-cousin, the exact meanings of which were seldom revealed by probing. Among kin we found distinct patterns of deference. Thus a Pakistani would consult his brother before answering a question, not because he did not know the answer or have an opinion but because he felt he could not answer without deferring to his brother. Deference received seemed to be in direct proportion to the recipient's command of the English language, in most instances when Pakistanis were speaking to us, though this may have been enhanced by a desire to be sure that the conversation was being understood. Age seemed important also and elder brothers and kin were clearly held in respect, even when they spoke little English and were less literate in their own language than the younger kinsman.

Secondly, there are patterns of factionalism under village, political or religious factional leaders. These are seen most clearly when any community-wide decisions need to be taken, such as at meetings or welfare organizations and the mosque committee. Factional arguments and factional leaders appear to carry a weight proportional to their factional membership and thus effective action at the community level can be, and mostly is, blocked. However, our study of the infra-structure of Pakistani associational and political life was not sufficient for us to say much more about it.

Thirdly, there is a whole series of patron-client relationships. Kinsmen will receive loans or practical aid without charge; a landlord will charge his kinsman only a nominal rent; the obligations of kinship are fulfilled with expectations of recip-

---

[1] We are sure that Pakistani kinship terminology would have been clearer to us had we been studying it in the actual Pakistani village situation.

[2] One of the authors became 'elder brother' to a Pakistani and an Indian.

rocity but without the intrusion of market relationships. A
client, however, seldom receives (or expects to receive) a service without some payment in cash or kind. For writing letters
this is a small fee, but a signature for an official document can
cost £25, and standing surety for a hire purchase agreement
much more. Some Pakistanis have set up as moneylenders
mainly providing house-purchase loans; others act as middlemen in obtaining bank loans. Much of this is done 'on trust' (as
a private loan between kin) but the cost of trust can be very
high. The boundary between patronage and entrepreneurial
activity is hazy. Some others give loans for fares back to
Pakistan, to bring relatives over or obtain labour vouchers.
These services involve buying a ticket or voucher on hire
purchase, with a house as security. We have *prima facie* evidence that some Pakistanis are combining the business of estate
and travel agents and are thus able to keep some of their
countrymen permanently and heavily indebted to them. A
man's debt network may be as extensive, complicated and
permanent as his kinship network and may exert as many
obligations on him.

How these three types of relationship—kinship, political, and
economic—overlap is of crucial importance. The roles of
patron and factional leader are often performed by men of
property, shopkeepers, *restaurateurs*, and so on, but we wait
for further studies to amplify this while concerning ourselves
mainly with the primary associations of the immigrant. It is
perhaps of interest to note that we were under various pressures
from a number of Pakistanis in Sparkbrook to act as sponsors,
middlemen and mediators and that we did at times perform
such services where they were of a transparently ethically
neutral nature.

More than for any of the other immigrant groups, it is
possible to speak of the typical Pakistani. Similar life histories
and the same modes of life in England were recounted to us by
informant after informant. Our most articulate informants
divided the community into two groups. Themselves, astute
men who would get on in English society, and the 'innocent'
people, poor simple peasants who would never be out of debt
and never cope with life in England. This we find to be a gross
oversimplification. There certainly are Pakistanis with a com-

paratively good education, skill, or business acumen who quickly succeed economically and socially in their own community in England, and there are shy country boys who find England somewhat bewildering. But these, too, become lodging-house owners and some of them are successful in business. Some of the most successful Sparkbrook Pakistani shopkeepers are illiterate.

To refer to an immigrant as an 'innocent', rather than as a 'Culchy' or with the comment, 'all brawn, no brains', is a kind way of pointing out that many of the Pakistanis are countrymen, shy and ill at ease in the industrial city. Only three of our sample were employed in manufacturing (unskilled) in Pakistan, whereas thirty-seven (four skilled) are so employed in England.

TABLE 40: EMPLOYMENT OF PAKISTANI
IMMIGRANTS*

	Employment in Pakistan	Present employment in England
Agriculture	9	—
Handicrafts	2	—
Domestic and catering	4	—
Retail trade	3	—
Manufacturing	3	37
Other	13	1
Under age and unemployed student	5	1
	39	39

* Our two female respondents are not included in any of these tables

Not only do the Pakistanis come from the country, but they speak different languages[1] and come from an Islamic culture which, *inter alia*, gives them no framework within which to handle relationships with women beyond their own kin. Thus, a number of English women who know Pakistanis in Spark-brook say how a lot of them are extraordinarily shy and unsure of themselves when they meet.

The Pakistanis have come here mainly to earn money[2] and this they mainly gave as their reason in response to our question:

[1] Campbellporis: Urdu, Pushtu and Punjabi; Mirpuris: Dialect, mixture of Urdu and Punjabi; Sylhetis: Bengali.

[2] Average annual per capita income in Mirpur is £19.

TABLE 41: PAKISTANI IMMIGRANTS' REASONS
FOR MIGRATING

To earn money	12
To find work	13
To join relatives	2
To travel	4
Combination of reasons	3
Better way of life and education	4
No reply	1
	39

This does not mean money for themselves alone. Emigration is a joint, family venture. Twenty-three (59 per cent.) received help from relatives at home or in England in coming over and informants constantly stressed how one man's migration is his whole family's enterprise. On arrival in England only five of our respondents lived among strangers; eighteen stayed with relatives and sixteen with friends. Kin or friends found the first jobs for eighteen of our respondents, nine found their own and three went to the Labour Exchange. But our Pakistani sample had to wait significantly longer than any other immigrants for their first job, twelve (38·7 per cent.) having to wait three months or more.

The average weekly wage for Pakistanis is £13, and contrary to our expectations they work less overtime than any other group, though night-shift work and working on unpleasant jobs may in part account for this. Eleven (29 per cent.) of our respondents were in receipt of rents. Thirty-seven (90 per cent.) of our respondents sent money home, either to their fathers for the whole extended family or to their wives. Sums sent varied widely from 'as much as possible . . . as often as possible' (usually a sum of £5 or £10) to regular large sums of £50 to £100; some sent larger sums more irregularly. Three-quarters of our sample had sent over £20 on the last occasion prior to interview.

The Pakistani immigrant comes to England, launched by his family, sheltered and sustained by relatives or co-villagers in England who help him to find a job so that he may be independent and able to send money back to his family.

(1) A.K. comes from Campbellpore, where he worked on the family farm, six years ago. He has worked for short periods in Bradford, Sheffield, Cardiff, and Smethwick but left all these jobs as he objected to paying bribes to avoid the dirtiest and heaviest jobs. He now lives with his brother in Sparkbrook and works at a motor-car factory where he says there is no bribery. He does not much like English workers but thinks that his present Managing Director is a 'good man'. A.K. speaks very poor English and seldom goes out. He spends a lot of time reading his Qoran and is deeply religious (which his brother takes as a sign of his mental simplicity). When we first met A.K., he was sitting in his room playing a small harmonium-like instrument and singing to himself. He is quite happy in England now, but yearns for his wife. He will not bring her to England as he believes it would be impossible to maintain Purdah here. It would not be good for his wife to see English ways (kissing in public). England is a morally corrupt country with thousands of divorces to prove it. A.K. was deeply shocked to learn that one of us was nearly thirty years old and unmarried. He firmly believes in early, arranged marriages, preferably at about the age of sixteen. He thinks he will return to Pakistan 'some day', but he is not sure when. Meanwhile, he lives in a room with the kitchen attached, acting as manager for his brother who owns the house and lets it to West Indian and Irish lodgers. A.K. does his own cooking and cooks for his brother (who also has a flat and a café in Aston) when the brother is in.

(2) E.K. is a Mirpuri, owning and living in a house in the centre of Sparkbrook 1. He has a Pakistani lodger in the back room over the kitchen, his brother-in-law in the upstairs back room and two other Pakistanis in the front, an Irishman and his twenty-one-year-old wife live in the front room downstairs.[1] E.K. has been in England for over four years, the last two of which have been spent in this house. He has a mother, father, wife, and four children in Mirpur, all living on the family farm. He sends money to his father, wife, and children separately. E.K. intends to return home in eighteen months' time, when he will hand over the Sparkbrook house to his brother. But he is really very confused by the prospect of returning home. His confusion arises because he needs money to return but at present only has debts. He earns £12 10s. od. for a sixty-hour week in a small foundry and collects £5 a week in rents. Recently he has

---

[1] When we talked to the Irish girl and her girl friend (also twenty-one) we found that neither of them was able to read or write, thus showing that illiteracy is not confined to non-European peasants.

been off work, ill, and has only had National Insurance sickness benefit and his rents. While staying in his house he has carried out £15 worth of repairs in one week and spent £500 on repairs overall (which are not yet paid for). He still has not paid off the loan for buying the house.

E.K. regards himself as a good Muslim although usually his working hours preclude attendance at Friday prayers and daily prayer, but he goes to the mosque for the main Muslim festivals. He drinks whisky on doctor's orders (he has a pain in the chest) and has a few drinks in the pub with his friends in the evening. This he feels in no way runs counter to Islamic teaching.

During our first meeting with E.K. a group of friends called to see him. This is a normal Sunday routine among many Pakistanis; groups of friends dressed in their best suits go calling on other friends at about lunch time, usually staying, drinking tea and gossiping until they all go off to the pictures together. This particular group (with whom we had an animated conversation on colour prejudice in the trade unions) had walked across the railway bridge from Small Heath.

This purely local visiting is supplemented by longer cross-country expeditions to see friends, kinsmen, or patrons. Not only are Birmingham Pakistanis to be seen crowding into the Friday evening Leeds and Bradford trains, but Bradford Pakistanis can be seen walking around Sparkbrook. We spoke to a number of such visitors, some of whom had only a piece of paper with a bus number and a misspelt address to help them find the right house in Sparkbrook.

(3) G.H. is a Rawalpindi Pathan. He has relatives in the Pakistani Government and judicature. A graduate in Islamic Studies, he was himself an official for Pakistani International Airlines before he came to England. He arrived in 1956 and lived with his brother, who supported him during the three months it took him to find a job. By choice they later separated. Now G.H. lives in one room in a friend's house. In this room he has a bed, a chest of drawers, wardrobe, paraffin stove, and all his belongings. G.H.'s first (and so far only) job is as a driver for the Fire Brigade and Ambulance Department in Birmingham, a job requiring no little skill. He sees this job as an agreeable form of public service while he finds a very much better job, more suited to his talents, at leisure. By mid-1965 G.H. was appointed as a purser in British European Airways. He was also

about to bring his schoolteacher wife over.[1] He had been sending. money to her and the children regularly as well as saving up here. Now he has a house in Acocks Green and will move into it as soon as his brother returns from Pakistan with both their wives.

G.H. is very class-conscious and sees most of the Pakistani immigrants as low, rather dirty, unintelligent peasants and 'domestic servant class'. In spite of this he is very much in demand among the immigrants around him for advice on passport matters and reading letters, which services he appeared to perform free of charge ('they are only simple-minded people'). G.H. is a devout Muslim and a student of world religions. He was approached by some Pakistanis and asked to form a Campbellpore Association, but he declined. Clearly, he is soon to leave the Sparkbrook Pakistani community with his eyes set on integrating into British society, which he will probably achieve in large measure.

(4) Abram K. we first met in an Irish pub. He explained to us that Islam always adapts to the culture in which it finds itself. Soon it would give way on drinking. Thus he saw himself in the 'Black Horse' as in the vanguard of theological reform. His wife he kept in strict Purdah and she has not been out of the house for two and a half years. She was, however, the only Pakistani woman we were able to interview at length. Mrs. K. has four children, a boy of fifteen (by Abram's first wife), two girls of three and two, and a baby. She keeps the family room spotlessly clean and the children well dressed. She enjoys friendly relations with the tenants.[2] However, she does not go out of the house in the normal course of events. During her recent pregnancy she was taken to and from hospital in a taxi dressed in her *bhurkha*. Having no female kin to help with the housework and children she found her pregnancy very difficult and she always misses her own family. She has no visitors, no women to chat with. Mrs. K. would prefer to be back in Pakistan and would prefer her husband not to drink. She wants her daughters to be brought up as strict Muslims.

Abram has been back to Pakistan many times (once to collect his wife and children). He works in a factory and owns his house. His earnings are used mainly to finance a farm in Campbellpore. This he has equipped with modern irrigation and cultivation equipment. Abram was a merchant-seaman who jumped his ship at the end of

[1] Restrictions on the emigration of qualified personnel from Pakistan delayed her departure.
[2] Her husband interprets purdah as being secluded and kept from meeting *Muslim* men; the Polish tenants and ourselves were free to talk to her (though she covered her head while we were there).

the war and sought work first in London then in Birmingham. He has a number of kinsmen, brothers, and brothers-in-law here in Sparkbrook and has no intention of returning to Pakistan permanently. This is in spite of strong pressure from his wife. He will not take her on his next visit as he fears she will not return with him. (Mrs. K. hopes to enlist the support of her brother, soon to arrive, to pursuade Abram to let her return.) The only reason Abram gives for not returning to Pakistan permanently is: 'no pubs'.

Abram took us to a gathering of his kinsmen in Sparkbrook. This was a farewell party for his brother who was returning to Pakistan after seven years. The party was very subdued, with five men and three boys sadly drinking tea. The conversation was mainly on religious topics, presumably because the brother was returning home via Medina and Mecca (where he was to do *haj*[1]). Through another brother we asked if he had been happy in England. '*Acha*' ('O.K.') was the reply. Abram's brother was returning to his wife and leaving four sons in Sparkbrook. As each relative departed he shook hands and embraced the older brother, wishing him '*Salaam Alegum*' ('God's peace').

We have not so far more than mentioned the Pakistani entrepreneurs in Sparkbrook. They form a distinct class and perform functions beyond that of selling oriental food and spices. Their shops are meeting-places and gossip exchanges for immigrants. They advertise the films at the local Asiatic film clubs and distribute the Urdu newspapers. The shopkeepers themselves maintain continual contact with large sections of the English Pakistani community, through delivering, travelling, and knowing dealers all over the country. No feature seems to distinguish the successful entrepreneurs except their success. The businesses always seem to be joint (often family) concerns, started on loans. It is possible that their ability to set up in business derives from having among earlier immigrants relatives who are now in import-export and wholesale business, but we have no conclusive evidence for saying this. Even the most illiterate can succeed, it appears, once the initial loan has been raised. The interesting question remains; how do Pakistani peasants have the entrepreneurial spirit and business acumen

---

[1] *Haj*: attendance at sacred Muslim rituals performed annually at Mecca.

when West Indian and Irish peasants lack them? We feel that these differences may be worthy of further study.

Besides having relatives or co-villagers in their own house, eleven of our Pakistani sample had relatives[1] in Sparkbrook and beyond, eleven had relatives in other parts of Birmingham outside Sparkbrook and nineteen had relatives in other parts of England. Our table of contacts with relatives may not be either reliable or relevant in so far as Pakistanis have kinsmen and villagers around them in such a way that 'visiting', as such, is rather meaningless.

TABLE 42: WEEKLY AND MONTHLY KIN-VISITING BY PAKISTANIS

	Spark-brook	% Pakistani sample	Birming-ham	% Pakistani sample	Else-where in England	% Pakistani sample
Men seeing relatives in last week	6	15·4	3	7·7	1	2·6
Week-month	1	2·6	5	12·8	3	7·7
% of all visits	36·8		42·1		21·1	

This table does show that just over one-fifth of all visiting is done outside the Birmingham area, pointing to a possible confirmation of our notion that Pakistanis do visit kinsmen over a wider geographical area than any other group in Sparkbrook.

In a crisis situation the Pakistanis would be heavily reliant on kin:

TABLE 43: HELP SOUGHT IN TIME OF CRISIS BY PAKISTANIS

Parent	1
Sibling	12
Other relatives	13
Friend or neighbour	6
No one or 'Don't know'	5
No reply	2
	39

[1] By 'relatives' we mean here persons classified as relatives by respondents.

We may see that the Pakistanis are less without immediate aid than any other group in Sparkbrook.

TABLE 44: PERCENTAGE 'NO ONE' OR 'DON'T KNOW'
FOR HELP SOUGHT IN TIME OF CRISIS,
BY NATIONALITY

English	Irish	W.I.	Pak.
24	33·7	31·9	13·5

Thus we can see that the Pakistanis have a large number of kin both more concentrated than either the Irish or West Indians in Sparkbrook and more numerous in other parts of the country, and that they have strong and meaningful ties of friendship based on common nationality, religion, and village which provide them with an adequate community within which to live.

However, they also have close kin in Pakistan. Thirty-two had wives (thirty-one with children) at home and two others have children only there, leaving five only with no immediate family in Pakistan. We asked our respondents if they intended to bring their families over to England and received the following answers:

TABLE 45: PAKISTANI INTENTION TO
SEND FOR FAMILIES

No	19
Yes, next year	2
Yes, other time specified	4
Yes, don't know when	9
'Don't know'	5
TOTAL	38

(1 respondent already has his wife and children here)

The existence of immediate family in Pakistan clearly affects the respondent's future. This, and the pattern of the 'return and re-emigrate' cycle, were shown in answer to our question, 'Do you intend to return home?'

TABLE 46: PAKISTANI INTENTION TO
RETURN HOME

A.	YES	
	Permanently	8
	For a visit	12
	For a visit and possibly for good	1
	To bring back relatives	8
B.	DON'T KNOW	9
C.	NO. Not at all	1

It will be noted that only one of our respondents said positively that he would not return to his home country. Of the eight intending to return for good, five gave family reasons and one specified homesickness and inability to settle in England.

In the light of all the foregoing, it is not surprising that the Pakistanis' attitude to living in Sparkbrook and their aspirations deviate markedly from those of the other immigrant groups and the English. Twenty-one (53·8 per cent.) of our Pakistani respondents expressed no desire to move from Sparkbrook and fourteen said they did not like Sparkbrook (one 'Don't know'). The main reason given for staying was the presence of friends and relatives (47·8 per cent. of all those not wishing to move).

TABLE 47: REASONS FOR WANTING
TO STAY IN OR MOVE FROM
SPARKBROOK (PAKISTANI)

Own a house	3
Like the area/people	4
Friends and relatives here	11
Near work, shops, etc.	5
Neutral comments	1
Do not like the people	–
Do not like the area	7
Don't know	4

Those who wanted to move from their particular house (eleven) showed no particular preference for where they wanted to move, as Table 48 indicates.

Only one Pakistani had his name down for a council house, but single men do not qualify for council houses in any circumstances.

TABLE 48: PROPOSED DESTINATIONS OF MOVES
BY PAKISTANIS

Hall Green, etc.	2
Elsewhere in Birmingham	2
Anywhere else	5
Elsewhere in Sparkbrook	1
Don't know	1

And they were fairly evenly divided in their reasons for wanting to move:

TABLE 49: PAKISTANI REASONS FOR SEEKING
HOMES IN PARTICULAR AREAS

Near work, shops, etc.	3
Better environment	2
Other reasons	4
Don't know	2

We can see, though, that men without wives and families
in an alien land are unlikely to want to move from an area
which offers them the bare necessities by way of accommodation and the company of fellow countrymen.

The associational activities of the Pakistanis in the four weeks
prior to interview consisted of two men attending trade-union
meetings, one a mutual welfare club and one attending a Bingo
session. Although there are a number of welfare associations for
Pakistanis in general and the Commonwealth Property Owners'
Association for landlords in particular, these do not arrange
social events. Attendances are made by individuals as clients
seeking help or advice from a committee member. No Pakistanis are active in any of the English political parties, but
50 per cent. of those entitled, in our sample, were registered
voters.

Every pub seems to have one or two Pakistani regulars; the
smaller the number of Pakistanis the more they seem to associate
with the West Indian and white clientele. It was in the pubs
that we observed the friendliest relationships between Pakistanis
and other inhabitants, although in one or two of the larger
pubs where they constitute a significant group, the Pakistanis
tend to keep themselves to themselves. We never saw a
Pakistani drunk and found no prosecutions for drunkenness
among them. No policeman in Sparkbrook could remember
any cases.

All our sample said that they were Muslims, and ten of them had been to the mosque in the previous four weeks. The Friday prayers are held at lunch time, when only the self-employed men or night-shift workers can attend, but the major *Eid* prayers, held in a larger hall, were attended by six to seven thousand Pakistani and Indian Muslims from all over Birmingham. Muslims are also required to pray five times a day, but many are unable to fulfil this obligation because of their hours of work. Others do not wish to, believing strict religious observance to be something from which they have escaped in this country. Thirteen of our respondents said prayers daily; ten said them four or more times, though the prayers are often saved up for the end of the day.

The cinema is another major Pakistani and Indian social institution. Every Sunday the two Asian cinemas near Sparkbrook are filled for the three showings of the week's film. A number of fans take tape-recorders and use the songs thus recorded for their home entertainment. The films and the actors and songs are the subjects of constant discussion during the week. Some of the film stars are also wrestlers and they occasionally visit Sparkbrook and perform at the Embassy Sportsdrome on the Walford Road. Although there are occasional traditional Pakistani wrestling bouts, the fighting is mainly Western-style. The Pakistanis and Indians turn out in force to see their stars and to bet heavily on them. At one match, now passed into Sparkbrook folk-legend, a Pakistani wrestler beat a notoriously tough Irish fighter. The Pakistanis present threw over £200 in coin into the ring and garlanded their hero with £5 notes. The whole community was jubilant for weeks afterwards.

The future for the Pakistanis in Sparkbrook seems unlikely to be very different from the present. Groups of men from limited areas of Pakistan and Kashmir will live without women in their bleak rooms in a sort of male transit camp, sending home money and missing their wives, serving their English stint in an immigration, return, re-immigration cycle. For some, however, this will not be the future. Those who stay will either (like G.H.) settle in single-family occupation outside Sparkbrook with their wives and children, or (like Abram K.'s young nephews, busily studying English) will find a new way of life that is neither Pakistani nor English.

The chances of these patterns being fulfilled by substantial numbers of Pakistanis depends in the former case on their ability to house themselves in the market for private housing, and in the latter case on the degree to which Pakistanis become acceptable in English society and can themselves master language and skills. If the housing market closes against Pakistanis or if they are increasingly treated as a pariah group, then these alternatives will not be open to them and the few who have so far succeeded will have been the early, lucky few.

(iv) Minority Groups

There are three minority groups in Sparkbrook. The first we might more adequately describe as precipitants rather than immigrants. These are people who have drifted into Spark-brook from various places in Birmingham and England; they are the social misfits and deviants, socially and/or mentally inadequate people, two score or more of types one might find very infrequently in suburban areas. Also some methylated-spirits drinkers, an indefinite but small number of discharged prisoners, a few unmarried English girls with babies and a number of prostitutes. These people are in Sparkbrook either because they have found a society making only minimal de-mands of them, or because Sparkbrook offers a high measure of anonymity.

Secondly, there are the remnants of various waves of European immigrants who passed through Sparkbrook soon after the war—Poles, Italians, and Greek Cypriots being the main groups. They all live as families (including, for example, an old Polish couple with four bachelor friends in their forties), they have their main contacts with the larger society through work and, for Poles and Italians, the Roman Catholic Church. A few belong to city-wide National Associations.

Finally, there are the Indians, the largest minority group, constituting some 300 people, of whom fifty-six are Gujaratis[1] from East Africa and Gujarat and the remainder Punjabis from East Africa and the Jullundur district of the Punjab. Like

---

[1] For a fuller study of the Gujaratis in Birmingham, see R. S. Desai, *Indian Immigrants in Britain*, London, O.U.P. for I.R.R., 1963.

the Pakistanis they came partly as a result of a long history of migration, an aspect of the story of British imperialism.

The Indians live predominantly in families, even the single men living as boarders in the family homes of relatives. The tightness of the Gujarati community was demonstrated when we sat down with one family and were told the names, addresses, places of origin and family structures of all the Gujaratis in Sparkbrook. There are six men and a woman from East Africa; eight men, ten women and thirty-one children from Gujarat. New arrivals are known to all the community, as were the general activities of the permanent residents. Most of the Gujaratis (certainly those from East Africa) seem to have come with small sums of capital and have set their families up in small houses; one man who brought his wife over to a lodging-house was very severely criticized by the other Gujaratis. Friendly acts abound among them. For example, one family we visited frequently we once found at home with a newly arrived family, helping them make curtains for their newly obtained house. This same family have relatives in the Black Country who frequently visited them. The Gujaratis seem intent on settling; those who thought they might return wanted their children to be educated in England first. The prospects may be good for them providing they can always cope with housing themselves, they are settled families with strong face-to-face community ties, most of them speak very good English and some have never seen India.

The Punjabis, who are mainly Sikhs, have their main settlement in Smethwick. There are some 250 in Sparkbrook; our actual sample of Indians[1] was not large enough for us to say much about them with certainty, but we met a number of them and formed some impressions. The men in this group had more skilled jobs than the Pakistanis; most had skilled or semi-skilled jobs in light engineering or construction work.[2] The Punjabi women, who come and go freely, unlike their Pakistani counterparts who are in purdah, would on the whole prefer to be at home in India, but seem content here, though they expressed concern that their daughters should marry

[1] Totalling seven, of whom five were Muslims and therefore culturally more like Pakistanis than Indians.
[2] Some of these may have had previous industrial experience in the East African dockyards and railways.

within their own community and not be corrupted by English life. We found a number of families who had taken, or intended to take, their daughters away from the local schools at puberty and send them to private girls' schools where they would not be able to mix freely with boys. A higher proportion of Punjabis than in any other community seem to be shopkeepers in Sparkbrook. The son of one such shopkeeper was the only child who passed the 'Eleven Plus' in the local Primary school. We could not be certain, however, that these characteristics applied with equal force to the whole of these communities.

These, then, are the people of Sparkbrook; English, Irish, West Indian, and Pakistani, and a small group of English and Irish social misfits. Alongside these exist a series of very small groups; the residue of a number of waves of European immigrants and a few recently arrived Indian and Arabian immigrants. We are mainly concerned with the former section of the population. We turn now to an institution known to them all and experienced by many, but peculiar to the twilight zone: the lodging-house.

V. The Lodging-House

We have already seen, in Chapter I, how the new arrival in Birmingham suffers especially severely from the general housing shortage in the city. We also know that of all newcomers the coloured immigrant suffers worst of all because he has limited access to the market in private housing. Perhaps the earliest coloured working-class immigrants to Birmingham attempted to obtain digs with white landladies and were turned away; or they stayed with kinsmen, as a very small, inconspicuous number of coloured immigrants must have been in Birmingham for a long time.

The large houses such as we find in Sparkbrook 1 were already in multi-occupation when the main waves of coloured immigrants arrived and it was to these areas that the immigrants were drawn as tenants and later as potential landlords. These large houses offer great advantages to immigrants. First of all, an immigrant (especially a Pakistani) comes to England to earn money; the cheaper he can house himself the more money he will be able to save and the sooner he will be able to return home. If he can own a house and let rooms he can pay for the house's maintenance and purchase and himself live free, or even gain extra income. Secondly, with a large house he will always have room available for any kinsman or friend arriving in Birmingham, thus solving the immediate housing problem for the next newcomer. In the tight Pakistani community the obligations of hospitality, sheltering and supporting kin who are not able to fend for themselves are mandatory. Thirdly, a house is a *pied-à-terre* in England, ready for the owner's return to England if he goes home for a visit, or available for the use of kinsmen while he is away. At the least, a house is a source of realizable capital which can probably be sold at a price higher than the purchase price.

In fact, none of it works out quite like this. In order to buy a house the intending purchaser needs money. A mortgage may

be available only with a very large deposit (over 50 per cent.
in some cases) and at a high rate of interest (8 per cent. is
not uncommon). To raise the deposit or enough cash to avoid
taking a mortgage at all the purchaser will first need to obtain
a loan. This he will do among his friends in the first instance
and then from either a moneylender or a bank. He will need
an introduction to the bank, which will involve a fee to his
sponsor, and will then have to pay the loan back to the bank
quickly, since banks, like mortgage companies, see an old house
with a short lease remaining as a poor security. Thus by the
time the purchaser has a house he also has many debts. It
becomes, therefore, a matter of economic necessity for him to
let off as many rooms as possible at the maximum rents
obtainable.

If our purchaser now wishes to accommodate kinsmen or
fellow-countrymen he has either to cut down his rent-producing
capacity, or charge his other tenants higher rents. A third
possibility, which in the late 1950s and early 1960s was the
most often taken, is to let more space by converting a bathroom
or landing into a bedroom, or by multi-letting single rooms on
a *per capita* rent. A kinsman will not pay his way; we found
that most Pakistani landlords accommodate their kin free of
charge or for a contribution to the housekeeping; fellow-
countrymen are generally charged a nominal rent of £1 a week.

Lastly, the house will not realize much capital if and when it
is sold. This is for two reasons. The first is that the house is
unlikely to have a long lease left to run. Many of the houses
in Sparkbrook 1 were built in the 1880s and 1890s and their
ninety-nine-year leases expire in the 1970s and 1980s. The
ground is owned by a well-known public school which has not
made its intentions known yet. They could either renew the
leases or redevelop the land for more profitable uses. Even if a
house has a substantial lease remaining it is not likely to fetch
a high price. The second reason for loss of value is that of the
practice of multi-occupation itself. The houses are already in a
state of neglect. The various tenants have no stake in maintaining the value of the property; passageways, stairs, bathrooms will be neglected, and sheer over-use of the fabric
accelerate its decline. The landlord may also be catering for a
specialized class of tenants. The Pakistani landlord will be the

last resort of many white tenants and he will thus have more than his fair share of deviant and destructive tenants, especially large families and tinkers. He will, in fact, be accommodating people who have been unable to find accommodation elsewhere or who have been evicted from other lodging-houses. Our landlord, striving to pay off debts and faced with difficult tenants, is unlikely to have sufficient money available to maintain his property. He may have to calculate his profits and losses on the basis of a total loss of productive plant.

It is not surprising, therefore, that rents are high, £2. 10s. 0d. per room being a standard charge. We asked an Indian landlord whether he thought £3. 10s. 0d. was an exorbitant rent for an Irish family of five to pay for one of his rooms. He replied that it was not, saying that they were poor people who would have to pay £7 for two rooms, so he was doing them a service. In the context of an acute housing shortage he argued with irresistible logic.

However, the activities of the landlords do not go unnoticed. The attentions of the Public Health Department in areas such as Sparkbrook 1 create a rather different situation for the landlord. The two main concerns of the Health Department are crowding and the provision of amenities in houses. In pursuit of their objectives they use mainly Sections 13, 15, and 19 of the 1961 Housing Act (see Chapter II) and Orders to carry out repairs or abate nuisances under various other Housing and Public Health Acts. These can be backed by the more powerful but less-used sanctions described in Chapter II.[1]

Once the enforcement of Sections 13, 15, and 19 is under way in an area, the would-be house-purchaser is likely to get himself into difficulties. He may buy a house unaware that an order under Section 19, limiting the number of tenants, is in force. This is especially likely if the sale is not conducted through a solicitor who will search for such restrictions on a house's use on behalf of his client. If the landlord then starts taking in tenants, he may receive a summons for contravening Section 19. An established owner faces similar difficulties, although he knows about them, and may find that the Section 19

---

[1] We should like to record our admiration for the Public Health Inspectors, especially those in Sparkbrook, who carry out a difficult job with tact and firmness, always explaining and attempting to persuade before using official sanctions.

limitation puts him in a position where he can run the house only at a loss. He will then be tempted to contravene the order. A double order to thin out tenants and carry out repairs can be crippling. Genuine misunderstandings do arise, especially among landlords whose command of the English language is poor. They think that because the inspector has seen the house and has not taken action with a number of tenants in residence, they can maintain this number, thus taking on new tenants as others leave and not complying with the order which intends them to run down their numbers by not replacing tenants. Others fail to appreciate that children are counted among the total tenants, as is the landlord himself if he lives on the premises. The boundary between genuine misunderstanding and 'playing dumb' is a fine one, and the delay between serving an order and prosecution may mislead some landlords into thinking that nothing will happen, or that they can get away with contraventions. Others just see fines as a normal running cost.

Clearly, the landlords soon begin to see the Health Department as the enemy and we heard many stories of 'persecution' of landlords by them. Usually this was a simple clash of values, an immigrant not seeing why he should not be able to maximize profits from the use of what is his own personal property. Sometimes we were told that landlords carried out £100 worth of repairs or alterations so that the Inspector would approve the house for a promised ten tenants; then on subsequent re-inspection the Inspector would only clear the house for eight tenants, thus destroying the economic advantage of the land-lord's outlay. We suspect that such cases arise from mis-understandings such as those mentioned above.

The Public Health Department *is* the enemy of the lodging-house landlord, if he is the landlord we have described as letting rooms without proper conversion or provision of amenities. This is shown by the Birmingham Inspections and Prosecutions for 1963.

It is very striking how Indians and Pakistanis feature among bad landlords, although they may not predominate among lodging-house landlords, and how many of their prosecutions are for multiple offences. We shall see in Chapter VI how associations arise to defend the interests of the landlords and

TABLE 50: BIRMINGHAM CORPORATION INSPECTIONS OF
HOUSES AND PROSECUTIONS ARISING:
8 JUNE 1962 – 8 FEBRUARY 1964

Owners	Houses inspected No.	%	Ill-managed houses	Houses lacking facilities	Over-occupation	Summonses issued No.	%
Pakistanis	658	42	61%	75%	83%	530	70
Indians	292	19	56%	71%	83%	210	27
Others	611	39	5%	8%	9%	16	3
TOTAL	1,561	100				756	100

mediate in the conflict between the Public Health Department
and landlords. At the end of this chapter we give an account
of two lodging-houses and their owners which typify the situation we have described above.

It seems to us that the Public Health Department is
making an impact on the situation. Many informants in Sparkbrook, especially social workers, reported a considerable reduction in crowding over the past four years and we have confirmed
this from such records as are available and through the Health
Department. A sign of the effectiveness of Public Health action
is the number of large houses now standing empty and for sale
in Sparkbrook 1; six that we passed almost daily were up for
sale for at least four months and were still unsold when we left
the area. This success, however, does nothing to ease the
housing situation for the immigrant.

The exact pattern of house-ownership could not be established with certainty. Three relevant data were established
however. Firstly, twenty-two out of forty-seven multi-occupied
dwellings in our sample had Pakistanis in them; thirteen with
single Pakistani households, seven with two, and three with
three. Secondly, eighteen of these dwellings were owned by
Pakistanis in single or joint ownership. Thirdly, we separately
identified sixteen Pakistani landlords in the sample; fourteen of
their houses were in multi-occupation. Taken together, these
facts tend to confirm, though they do not prove, our suggestion
that Pakistanis own the houses they live in and let rooms to
other nationalities. It is highly likely that the eighteen multi-
occupied houses above were owned by one of the Pakistanis

resident in them. If Pakistanis also own houses that have no Pakistani households in them, as we know they do, then they are clearly over-represented as landlords in the area. This points to the specialized landlord role of Pakistanis.

A lodging-house is in itself a sociological phenomenon of some interest. We saw in Chapter II that a lodging-house tends to be a multiracial unit. The primary communities of the inhabitants of Sparkbrook are essentially within the ethnic groups if not actually within village or family groups.

Secondly, the lodging-house is both a home (or a set of homes) and the scene of intense market competition. In all normal circumstances the one place a man can be sure of being free of market relationships is in his home, but the lodging-house situation is different.

Given, then, that the relationships cross-cut normal associations and bring a new factor into home life, we would expect to find special institutions or modes of behaviour to emerge to cope with the new, or special situation. The total situation is essentially one of conflict; any fear, distrust or dislike of another ethnic group is sharpened by market competition. We found that under normal day-to-day conditions tenants and landlords deliberately avoided one another. Tenants behaved similarly among themselves. Thus tenants at home stay in their rooms, sometimes with the doors locked, and in some cases cooking on the fire or a paraffin stove to avoid sharing facilities. But facilities do have to be shared; passageways, stairs, and toilets especially, and it is over the use and cleaning of these that conflict most frequently breaks surface. In a few cases this was partially resolved by the landlord appointing a relative or tenant as manager-cleaner, in the case of a tenant usually for some *quid pro quo*. Where tenants shared cookers they either had one on each landing or one among themselves, in either case separate from the landlord. Again, conflicts break out over shared cookers; even with a rota for their use there are bound to be arguments over who cleans it or who put the last shilling in the meter. There can be no complete conflict management without a common will to achieve it, formulated in some routine, equable and acceptable manner of execution. It is difficult to see how this can ever be achieved when large numbers of people, in proportion to the available facilities, all want to use the facilities at the same time. In one Pakistani-Irish house with one cooker we found the senior Irish woman cleaning the stove (for her own benefit) before she used it. Eventually the Pakistanis gave her a box of chocolates for what they saw as a service performed for them all, but this worked only because one woman was willing to work alone.

The general tendency to withdrawal in multiracial lodging-houses is quite noticeable in contrast with single-race houses. On entering the latter and knocking on the first door or calling out for anyone at home, most of the doors will open and the visitor will find himself in a cross-fire of chatter. In a mixed house a similar entry will encounter closed doors and silence; even the door knocked on will need two or three knocks and perhaps a little calling through before it yields.

Landlord-tenant relationships are usually what the American sociologist, Talcott Parsons, would call affectively neutral, particularistic, self-oriented and specific; in other words, confined to paying the rent. We noted, for example, that West Indians in particular behaved very formally towards their landlords, often addressing them as 'landlord' and only coming to them to pay the rent or inquire about repairs or amenities. A few Irish women seemed to conceal the potential conflicts with a form of joking relationship, addressing the landlord over-affectionately, like a small child, to the great amusement of the Pakistani landlord. Another (with a landlord called Malik) often addressed him 'O Great King' and made a mock curtsey. By and large we would say the highly formalized relationship is more common, but both seem adequate ways of coping with day-to-day or routine relationships.

The ultimate stage in formalization of rules of conduct (relating to both the domestic and market situation) would be reached where one party imposed an articulated or written code of conduct. We heard stories of West Indian landlords who frequently 'laid down the law' verbally, giving times for tenants to be in, times for radios and gramophones to be off. West Indian tenants found this very irksome and they felt that the landlord was not treating 'his own kind' in the right way.

However, we encountered one Indian landlord who wrote the rules down and required his tenants to comply with them and signify their compliance by signing the rules over a 2d. stamp. Such a charter could emerge from either side, but the landlord's superior market position and the fact that he is not likely to be divided against himself make it more likely that his will emerge first and be imposed. Here are the rules set out by the landlord, preceded by a list of details required of his tenants.

(1) Name (full)...
(2) Last address ....
(3) Nationality........Married ....Children...,......
(4) Wife or husband's name and address..................
(5) Employer's address ....
(6) Kind of work.......................................
(7) Friend's name and address ....
(8) Rent one week in advance ....
(9) Deposit for the articles ....
(10) Furnitures.............. How Many? ....

Table	Pillow-cases
Chair	Sheets
Double or single bed	Bedspread
Sofa	Quilt
Cupboard	Carpet
Heater	Curtains

Conditions
1. The landlord has a right to make any change.
2. Regular payment of rent on Friday evening or Saturday morning, to landlord/landlady.
3. Notice of termination of a tenancy on either side.
4. No disturbances at any costs—wireless, radio, television, gramophones, etc. very low within the room.
5. No visitors allowed after 8.30 p.m., without the permission of the landlord or landlady.
6. Very quiet after 10 p.m.
7. Always co-operation as the landlord–tenant.
   I have received the Rent Book.
   Date........ Stamp and signature of the tenant.

The more difficult situation arises mainly from the second peculiarity of the lodging-house, when the more naked market forces show themselves. The market is most clearly impinging on the tenant when the landlord wants to obtain possession of his room. In theory, the tenant is protected by the law; the need for four weeks' notice and a County Court Order, at least until December 1964 when the Rent (Protection from Eviction) Act gave the tenants more substantial rights. However, such a law barely operates in Sparkbrook; indeed it does not protect the illegally evicted tenant at all. In Sparkbrook a landlord asks or tells a tenant to vacate a room, the tenant looks for another room and moves. As long as the pause exists both parties see the request as essentially reasonable. The tenant's reasoning runs: 'The landlord has a right to say who will live in his house, and anyhow the tensions created by living as an unwanted tenant in the same house as the landlord would be intolerable.' Thus there is a high turnover of tenancies in Sparkbrook, people constantly leaving one room for another, either as a result of a landlord's request or from choice. Short notice is also of advantage to tenants. If a tenant finds a better room he wants to be able to occupy it quickly; a lengthy period of notice for his existing room would lose him the better accommodation. Tenants are themselves in competition for more adequate accommodation The enforcement of the law relating to landlord and tenant would ruin their competitive position, which depends on rapid mobility. We are saying, then, that a system of norms, a code of conduct relating to landlord-tenant relationships develops outside and apart from the formal law of the larger society.

A different situation arises when the landlord wants to throw his tenant out on to the street or where a tenant is determined not to move. Here the parties are not obeying the norms of their market community and so sanctions have to be used to constrain one side or the other. For the landlord these will be violence or the threat of violence, physical ejection of the tenant or his property, locking the tenant out of his house or room. The tenant is now faced with either conceding to the landlord and taking his chance on the streets or mustering such sanctions as are available to him. At this point reference may be made to the formal law and the tenant draws attention to his plight either through the police (who can act only to prevent an actual 'breach of the peace'[1]) or a social welfare organization such as the Sparkbrook Association.

In such a situation possession is nine-tenths of the law and the tenant may find his goods in the street on his return from the Sparkbrook Association or before he can get to a rent tribunal (before December 1964) or the County Court. In this case he will most likely drop his proceedings and tackle the more immediate problem of finding a new room. Regaining possession of a room after three months on the streets is a pyrrhic victory that it is pointless to pursue.

Open conflict is most likely at this stage, where the tenant, perhaps assisted by a social worker, attempts to persuade the landlord (possibly with threats of legal action) in order to gain time. The immediate crisis passed, the tenant will then seek new accommodation at leisure; or, if he wants to keep his room (possibly as a matter of principle, and backed by some external agency) he will go into the necessary routines for a County Court action. In using a rent tribunal or court the tenant needs assistance. The rent tribunal will be sympathetic to him, but the landlord may have a solicitor, or himself tell a long and untrue story about his undesirable tenant, or claim to provide more services than are actually given. The tenant may find these tactics hard to cope with. Court proceedings are as likely to intimidate the tenant as the landlord and he may experience difficulty in getting legal aid for cases under the Protection from Eviction Act. Indeed, the magistrates may not give judgement with reference to this legislation unless the tenant specifically claims its protection. Thus a landlord-tenant conflict at this point passes out of the sphere of local norms and sanctions and is taken up by outside agencies acting in a legal, rational manner with reference to formally codified rules.

It was reckoned that 80 per cent. of the cases arising from multi-occupied dwellings coming to the rent tribunal involved Indian and Pakistani landlords; of these cases, 50 per cent. were concerned with security of tenure and the remainder with

---

[1] General opinion is that the police are on the landlord's side. We heard of two cases (one very well authenticated) of policemen assisting a landlord with an illegal eviction. This presumably is one way of preventing a 'breach of the peace'. On the other hand one landlord complained that the police refused to assist him, inviting him to call again for aid 'when they hit you'.

high rents. Over half the security of tenure cases arose after receipt of notice, but the tenant often stood a good chance of winning in these cases as landlords seldom served valid notices unless they referred the case to a solicitor first. Tenants evicted as a result of valid notice followed by a court order would not gain a council house but only hostel accommodation, as described in Chapter I. Rent tribunal officials noted the high proportion of West Indian tenants bringing cases against Indian and Pakistani landlords, the basic market antipathy frequently being backed by complaints about dirty houses, provision of poor furniture and intolerable cooking smells. Here we see all the conflicts arising from the multiracial situation in the lodging-house coming to the surface once conflict has been brought into the open, through competition for living space.

At present there is probably a slight advantage with the landlord. Landlords are now aware that there is a formal, legal procedure for removing tenants; thus they take advice from solicitors. A notice to quit on solicitor's headed notepaper usually (and quite unnecessarily) results in the tenant taking to the streets immediately.

For the formal legal rules of conduct to apply in rented accommodation it is necessary firstly that the contestants know the rules and secondly that life should still be tolerable when the rules are applied. Thus the rules are either not applied or referred to only as a threat of sanctions when the normal, informal rules, which are accepted and tolerable, are broken. In other words, open warfare with legal sanctions is not normally tolerable or possible, whereas conforming to the informal rules is acceptable and normal. Actual compliance with the formal, legal rules can account for behaviour in only a few cases of the many sets and types of landlord-tenant relationship in the lodging-house area.

The sociologist sometimes has to step outside his role of disinterested observer. This happened to one of our authors who thus found himself in a position to study the history of two lodging-houses from 'inside'. One night he was called to mediate in a violent altercation between Daniel C. and his Pakistani landlord who was trying to evict him. The land-lord's case was that Daniel C. was a bad tenant who gave noisy parties for his friends and had women in his rooms late at night; also, he failed to pay his rent. He had been asked to leave. C. had that day packed his belongings and moved them out, so the landlord assumed that he was going. The landlord had re-let the room to a married couple who had given their landlord notice and were moving in the same night.

C. replied that he had offered to pay the rent to his land-lord, A., but A. had refused it and said 'out'. C. would have liked to have moved but had nowhere to go at the time. He was still looking for another room and had meanwhile removed his property to a friend's room to protect it from A.

We pointed out that, whatever the merits of the case, A. would break the law by putting C. on the street. (We were hoping, incidentally, that the new tenants' old room was not to be occupied by new tenants the same night.) The police arrived soon after and listened to these stories; they then asked for C.'s rent book. A. immediately said that C. had no rent book. Rent books were issued to good tenants after a probationary period. Such a procedure would, in fact, prevent a landlord proving that a tenant was a bad rent-payer, so was hardly a good tactic on A.'s part. The police advised A. to leave C. alone and suggested that C. found more congenial lodgings as soon as possible. A. said that C. could stay the night but must pay the rent that was owing. C. said the landlord should have taken it when it was offered, as the money was now spent. C. and A. then departed to their separate rooms and locked themselves in. C. moved two days later, cutting off the electric light flex at the ceiling as he left.

A. lived in this house with brother E., also a landlord. He took over the house from a Pakistani friend and had the mortgage transferred to his name. Soon after taking over the house he was served an Order under Section 19 of the 1961 Housing Act instructing him to reduce the number of occupants to six persons. The Public Health Department informed the mortgage company of this Order. The company, which had a 'no-letting' clause in its mortgage agreement, threatened to institute proceedings for possession of the house if A. did not remove all his tenants. This latter action A. regarded with contempt saying that no one could take his house from him and that in a court of law the transparent honesty of his case would defeat the evil men. A.'s solicitor thought otherwise and wanted to negotiate a new mortgage for A. to save him from eventually either losing the house or falling into the hands of moneylenders. We arranged an appointment for A. to see his solicitor, but he failed to keep it, saying that he could not spare the time from work and that Justice and Allah were on his side, so he could not lose.

Eventually A. was summonsed for breach of the Section 19 Order. This puzzled him. We counted up the numbers in his house and there were eight occupants. 'But that is including my brother and I,' said A., 'We only have six lodgers.' We later established that one of the tenant families had small children, so A. had exceeded his limit of six occupants by four persons. A. appeared astounded that children too should have to be counted.

We discussed this case, and the difficulties that A. (and other Pakistani landlords) had in understanding the legal language of the Order, with the Public Health Inspector. The Inspector replied by telling us how he had carefully explained the meaning of the Order to A., who had said that he understood, and had later warned him about not complying with it. A. did not attend the court hearing and he was fined £30.

E. was served Orders under Sections 15 and 19 in respect of his house. He thinned out his tenants gradually and provided some of the additional facilities required under Section 15; in doing this he ran up bills that his rents would not cover. Knowing the risk involved he took in some tinkers so that he could raise the money to cover the bills. Three days later the Health Inspector called. E. immediately evicted his tinkers but was nevertheless summonsed for failing to comply with the Order under Section 19.

E. duly appeared in court. He sat at one end of the courtroom with a little group of Pakistanis, who one by one went up to the other end of the room to face the magistrate, Clerk of the Court, and a group of Health Inspectors. The Health Inspectors reeled off the details of their cases with the bewildered landlord looking on; a few mumbled and inaudible replies from the landlord, and then the fine swiftly imposed. E. became particularly confused when the Clerk of the Court asked a series of questions in rapid succession about the numbers in his house on various dates. E. had two previous offences against him. He was fined £10 for failing fully to comply with Section 15 Order and £75 for contravention of Section 19. A policeman leaned across to inform us that E. could well afford to pay these fines as he collected £20 in excess rents every week.

It seemed to us that justice was done. E. was guilty beyond all reasonable doubt, but justice was not seen to be done by the Pakistani landlords. Seeing them in the court and talking to E. and others, it was obvious that neither housing law nor the proceedings in the magistrates court had any legitimacy for them. Trips to court and fines were just part of the inscrutable and unalterable order of things, somehow connected with the unfair and eccentric British custom of letting officials persecute house-owners.

Far from being able to pay his fine easily, E. did not know where to raise the money for it. He asked us if he would be put in prison for non-payment and if he could avoid payment by hiding in another town. E. decided to sell his house to pay the fine. He had great difficulty in selling the house, as it was in a very dilapidated condition, and at one stage E. said he would take any reasonable offer for the house. Eventually, one of the West Indian tenants bought it.

These cases have been abbreviated and no short written account can bring out the confusion in the thought and actions of the two landlords, who found themselves in the wrong with various agencies, whatever action they took and with whatever intentions. It was also extremely difficult for us to sort out whether various actions and attitudes arose from real or assumed peasant stubbornness and ignorance, genuine mis-understanding, or sheer (ineffective) cunning. The truth must be that a mixture of all these attitudes and motivations are at work in a situation fraught with many pitfalls and unexpected difficulties for the uninitiated country folk from overseas, who constitute a high proportion of that section of the Sparkbrook 1 population which especially needs to seek the solution to their housing problems through lodging-house ownership.

VI. The Immigrants and
their Associations

In Chapters III and IV we considered some of the basic facts about the various ethnic groups in Sparkbrook and saw the mosaic of tiny primary communities which they formed. To some extent, however, each of the major ethnic groups, Irish, West Indian, and Pakistani, is organized as a whole and it is the aim of this chapter to show the ways in which this occurs. We shall also be concerned with the functions which ethnic group organizations have in relation to the different interests of the several groups and in relation to Birmingham society as a whole. Each of the groups has its own distinctive features, with regard both to the scale of its organizations and to the coherence of its culture. It is convenient, however, to begin with the Irish, both because the Irish immigration is the largest and because the position of the Irish community is not complicated by questions of colour.

The Irish, as we have seen, constituted 12·9 per cent. of the population of our area, and this clearly is the kind of proportion which will make a difference to the area. It is not surprising, therefore, that Irish culture is much in evidence in the daily life of Sparkbrook. So far as contacts in the street and pub or café are concerned, there are sufficient signs of Irishness for the Irish immigrant to feel culturally and socially at home.

The Stratford Road is Sparkbrook's market place, not merely in the sense of a place where buying and selling is done, but in the sense of a place where people make superficial and yet significant contacts with others outside their own intimate primary communities. They are not the precisely defined contacts which take place around a village pump. But neither are they the purely impersonal kinds of contact which occur in New Street, two miles away. There is some sense in which men feel at home in the Stratford Road.

Certainly, at least the Irish do. There are many places in which they may meet their own kind and many familiar cultural signals which indicate to a man that co-operative activity is possible. Hence, perhaps the first thing that may be said about the Irish is that they have a kind of community life in the streets and the shops, the pubs and the cafés. For many this may be as important as their membership of the Roman Catholic Church, for although, as we shall see, membership of the Church is large, it is still the case that the Church does not touch everyone and that there are some whom it touches only lightly and sacramentally, so that other forms of group partici- pation are more important for them.

Reference has already been made to the importance of the shop in Sparkbrook as a larder and of the cafés as dining-rooms. This is particularly true amongst the Irish workingmen. Even though the Irish are not great shopkeepers and there are few shops or cafés which bear Irish names, it is none the less the case that in the Central Café, the Mocambo and in Jones' Café, the clientele is overwhelmingly Irish. Here at teatime the Irishmen may be seen eating a mixed grill or, in the Mocambo at least, a huge steak and a pint of milk. And despite the uniform formica and juke-box appearance of the Mocambo, the posters from the Irish Tourist Board, as well as the accents of the waitresses, are sufficient to make the young Irishman feel at home.

Nearly all the pubs include Irishmen amongst their clientele, but in some, such as the Black Horse, the Irishness is over- whelming. One may buy draught Guinness or Sweet Afton cigarettes. A notice tells of a cheap week-end trip to Dublin arranged by the pub's own social club and it is not uncommon for someone to come round selling Irish political newspapers or tracts. Here, too, one night we met an Irish ballad-monger selling the 'recitations' which he had written to celebrate Kennedy, Chessman, and others, who in accordance with Irish experience had been shamefully and wrongly done to death. An admirer of the Behans who had worked and gone on strike on the Shell-Mex site in London, he was now working his passage as the father of a 'homeless' family, after being evicted by his 'Indian' landlord, and though he complained about the amount of food his children ate he accepted as inevitable and

right the fact that he should have a large family. Out of such
life-stories and the social relations which they imply the life of
the Black Horse is woven, and it is a warm life even though the
room is drab and the furnishings bleak.

As one walks south down the Stratford Road there are many
other signs of Irishness. There are advertisements for the Harp
and the Shamrock club dances and social evenings, printed in
green, and occasionally notices of Old Irish concerts in the
Town Hall itself. At the big Embassy Sportsdrome round the
corner, where the Brummy boxer Johnny Prescott fought his
way to fame, the programme often includes Irish contestants
and here and there one sees notices advertising Irish football.

An Irishman in the streets, therefore, can, if he wishes, live
fairly completely 'in the colony', but in this free-and-easy
atmosphere there is also the possibility of gradually making
more English contacts by talking to the marginal Englishmen
in the Irish pubs or moving his pub to another 'more respectable' one which does not simply reproduce the atmosphere of
Dublin. He is also aware, however, that not all the shops and
cafés are his. There are corner shops which refuse to stock Irish
cigarettes or newspapers on the one hand and whose proprietors
aggressively assert their old Englishness, and many of the cafés
and groceries in the Stratford Road are owned and used by the
Pakistanis. Here, perhaps, there is some applicability for the
concepts of ecology. The Stratford Road is marked out in
culture areas within which different groups may lead segregated
lives and as the stores and the cafés change hands one sees the
invasion by members of one group of another's area. Yet, by
and large, this situation is one of segregated and peaceful
coexistence.

This world of the pubs and the streets and the cafés can be
a source of demoralization. To have no home, to eat in cafés,
to spend one's night in pubs and occasionally to pick up a
prostitute for the night, does not provide an adequate substitute
for family life. But while some may go under in this world,
many others find their feet there and from that first experience
of urban society go on to make other and more lasting adjust-
ments. It is a world not without its own moral significance in
the sense that men without roots anywhere else find roots there.

It is not, however, a world of ancient ritual and there is

for an Irishman the possibility of making contact with this other world in the form of the Roman Catholic Church. We must now turn to this other aspect of Irish life, for as we often remarked to each other during the research, the Roman Catholic Church is the biggest Irish immigrant organization of all.

The ordinary Roman Catholic parish church in a British city, of course, already offers a spiritual home to the Irish immigrant, both because it is a universal church and because in its British branch it is very largely staffed by Irish priests. Yet by tradition Sparkbrook itself did not provide such a home, since there was no Roman Catholic church there at all and the atmosphere of the area was predominantly Protestant.

Pastoral responsibility for Irishmen in the area therefore came to rest with St. Anne's Church to the north and with the Church of the English Martyrs in Sparkhill to the south. It was, however, supplemented as a consequence of an agreement between the English and Irish hierarchies for the sending of missioners from Ireland to work among Irish migrants. One of these missioners sent by the Bishop of Kilaloo has taken up residence in the Catholic Presbytery attached to the Sparkhill church and assumes responsibility for the Irish of Spark-brook. In carrying out this responsibility he has established a Mass Centre in the Harp ballroom, opposite the Embassy Sportsdrome on the southern edge of our research area.

The attendance of Roman Catholics, and especially Irish Roman Catholics, at the two neighbouring churches and the Mass Centre is regular and large in numbers. About 7,000 had attended Mass at the three centres at the last yearly count. There is no other organization which unites so many people in Sparkbrook. Yet before we draw conclusions from this too readily, it must be asked what such church attendance figures mean.

To try to answer this question involves treading on difficult theological ground, and it may be that since neither of us is a Catholic, it has been impossible for us to appreciate the true meaning of these attendances. We have, however, said that Irish Catholics participate 'lightly and sacramentally' in the life of their church, and we mean by this that attendance at Mass may have little significance in giving a special moral and cultural shape to men's lives. Not merely did it seem to be true to us that Catholicism did not imply any great withdrawal from the world of the flesh and the market place, but also it seemed that it was compatible with a variety of different types of group participation. We felt that attendance at Mass, like the daily prayers of a Muslim, might not be the sociologically most significant aspect of membership of a religious group. What matters far more are those activities of the Church which seek to involve people in new social roles or moral attitudes.

We had expected to find two aspects combined in the pastoral work of the Roman Catholic Church, namely, concern for spiritual welfare and concern with social problems. To some extent this was the case and at first the Legion of Mary and the charitable societies like the Society of St. Vincent de Paul seemed to us to reflect this division exactly, one being concerned with 'talking to people about religious subjects', reclaiming the lapsed and saving others from lapsing, the other being concerned with giving material help. But we gradually became aware that there was another aspect to the work of the Church in the zone of transition which was of prior importance.

This other aspect is best described perhaps as Catholic puritanism. We were surprised to find that the missioner-priest, intellectually able though he was, and capable of under-standing sociological as well as theological issues, had a quite simple vision of the evils of drink and sexual irregularity as the main evils which he had to fight.

We say this, however, not in any spirit of criticism, but to draw attention to the social function of the Church in this situation. What the priest saw was a vast mass of Irishmen, many of whom would be lost to the Church through drink and sex. Against this he saw his role as helping individuals to find the moral strength to fight the temptations to which they were subject and to achieve a stable marriage, sound family life, and good housing conditions. The pubs and unsupervised mixed-sex lodging-houses stood in the way of this ideal. One prevented saving and the other encouraged extra-marital sex.

The virtues of self-help were actively encouraged by the Church and one facet of this was the work of the Catholic Housing Aid Society. This Society invited its members to join a compulsory savings scheme and helped those who joined to find the deposit on a house. But the priest at the Irish Centre in Birmingham who administered this scheme was clear that it touched only a minority and felt that little could be done for some of the Sparkbrook Irish who wasted all their money on drink.

On the negative side the consequence of these attitudes was that there were large numbers of Irish Catholics who simply attended Mass, but lived morally in the world of the pubs and cafés. On the positive side there was the clear enunciation of a puritanical ideal, which for those who accepted it provided a means of survival and success in the city. Thus even though the Church had its roots in a peasant society and embodied values derived from that society, it also had its urban puritanical side which helped men to fight against demoralization and attempted to equip them for living in difficult conditions in the city. And this two-sidedness of the Church is of some importance for understanding immigrant organizations in general. For the maintenance of a special community with its own signs and rituals is not incompatible with an active attempt to launch men and women into a cosmopolitan urban society. It may be, in fact, that the existence of a separate colony is an essential part of the social machinery necessary to the process of assimilation. The colony maintains the overall morale which is a precondition of learning new values. And no other community had a better organizational machinery for doing this than the Irish had in their Catholic Church, with all its complexity of attitudes.

Another aspect of the Church's role in promoting assimilation derives from its connexion with a larger organization. If we have emphasized the role of the Irish priest, it is also important to note that there are also English priests in the Sparkhill Presbytery and it could be that the committed Catholic gradually passes from an Irish to an English style of Catholicism, so that it is possible for him when he moves to the suburbs, to make the transition without moving outside the Church. He becomes, and his children become, unnoticed assimilated English Catholics.

Yet, when this has been said, there are some qualifications which should be made to this picture of the Catholic Church as an assimilating agency. One point is that it does not typically and normally play a large part in the management of the larger community. The missioner to whom we have referred did do so and offered help to outside bodies like the Sparkbrook Association quite freely. But he seems to us to be only the exception who proved the rule. Generally, the clergy were concerned to get on with their own work amongst their own people and had little to do with members of other communities. If the Church was promoting assimilation it was doing so by more subtle methods than by an overt concern for promoting an integrated community.

Two other aspects of Catholic practice possibly hindered assimilation. These were the Catholic attitude to education and the Church's teaching on birth control. The education of Catholic children in Catholic schools was a strongly held ideal and, although this was not by any means entirely realized, its partial realization had the effect both of segregating the Irish children and of concentrating the coloured children, few of whom were Catholics, in the state schools. And while rationalist social reformers were urging family planning as a partial answer to Sparkbrook's problem and as a means of adjustment to urban life, the Catholic Church made no concessions and in effect encouraged large families, who could not house themselves easily and tended to stay in the immigrant ghetto.

For these reasons and because urbanization involves secularization, a large number of Irish Catholics in Sparkbrook had lapsed or remained nominal church members. For them urbanization and assimilation would occur through other agencies, partly through formally structured organizations, but partly through informal group life.

One type of organization appears to be of some importance in providing a secular colony structure. This is the County Association. There are a number of these for different counties but the most successful one in Sparkbrook was the County Clare Association. This was started by four County Clare men who were dissatisfied with the social facilities available in Birmingham. It now has about two hundred members out of two or three thousand immigrants from County Clare in Birmingham.

The Association performs a number of functions for its members. It arranges sick visiting, it helps with travel arrangements and it provides informal contacts through which County Clare men can get jobs. It also organizes regular weekly dances and 'socials' which are attended by Dubliners and people from other counties besides Clare.

This kind of organization, however, probably does not affect the lives of more than a minority of the Irish in Sparkbrook. More than anything it is an organization of respectable immigrants looking for something more by way of social life than is commercially provided. These members come from all over Birmingham, though Sparkbrook is an important centre for them because socials and dances are held there. On the other hand it should be noted that, being a County Association, it institutionalizes the distinction between 'culchies' or country-men, and Dubliners. Generally, Dubliners look down on 'culchies' and a respectable County Association does something to redress the balance.

The 'Harp Club', like the 'Shamrock' in another part of Birmingham, is a commercial undertaking run by an Irish-man who was originally an immigrant from Kerry. He has succeeded commercially and operates two Irish Centres of some importance in Birmingham. Being commercial under-takings they do not provide the sort of structured organization which the Clare Association does, but they provide facilities for the Associations' socials and, through being always open, make a stronger impression on the community than the Associations can.

Two other aspects of Irish community life are sport and politics. A Gaelic football league exists in Birmingham and is supported by the more energetic and respectable young immigrants. But the numbers involved here are far smaller, of course, than the numbers who support Birmingham City or Aston Villa. Similarly, there are a few members of organiza-tions such as the Connolly Association who preach socialism and anti-partition, but those Irish who are interested in politics are more likely to join the Labour Party which, as has been pointed out, is sufficiently Irish for them to feel entirely at home.

It should be remembered in all that has been said that there are many different kinds of Irish of varying degrees of respect-ability and status. The 'respectable' ones tend to assimilate easily into the English working class and eventually to migrate to the suburbs, where their children become absorbed into English society. But there remains a pool of less settled people with slender family ties or perhaps with large familes and these loom large in the problems of Sparkbrook's lodging-house area. None the less, there is no Irish-interest organization which fights for the interests of Irishmen as such. There appears to be no need for one because the opportunities of assimilation are there. What does exist is a colony structure in which people may live before they finally become assimilated.

An exception to all of this must be made in the case of the tinkers. Most people in Sparkbrook regard them as a nuisance and there is continued agitation carried right up into the City Council Chamber for their removal. They live on the margins of the law, but have succeeded in making other groups afraid of them. There were incidents like those referred to in Chapter IV and we heard frequent complaints about their rowdyism in pubs and about their use of violence against their landlords. Here, in fact, we have a group which has no wish to become assimilated and which lives not in a state of integration or accommodation but in a state of highly uneasy truce with its unwilling hosts.

We found that many people blamed the tinkers for the deterioration of Sparkbrook and, indeed, they may have a positive function for the other immigrant groups in that they channel prejudices towards themselves. We believe, however, that far from the tinkers' being the cause of Sparkbrook's problems, they are a symptom, for when one has an area which is rapidly deteriorating and which has become permissive to the extent that Sparkbrook has, it will attract, among others, nomads who have no wish to be assimilated to respectable society. Some Sparkbrook residents talk of providing sites and camps for the tinkers. But what they ignore is that Sparkbrook is a camp where life is possible with the minimum adjustment to social norms for those who find norms oppressive.

The West Indians are the next largest immigrant group, but they do not make anything like the same organized impact upon the community as do the Irish or the Pakistanis. This seems to be due to two causes. One is the absence of institutions of their own which are significantly different from those of their hosts and the other is their affiliation to norms and organizations of the host society.

Because of the fact that they were the first coloured immigrants of the post-war period the West Indians are often thought of as the typical immigrants. Yet their image is compounded from those of all other immigrants and they tend to get the worst of all possible worlds, lacking the organization to make a colony of their own, yet not easily accepted into the host society.

Again and again as we read our research notes we find our West Indian respondents protesting that they are no different from anyone else. They want homes for their families. They want acceptance into local organization and have little time for exotic cultural exercises. As one of our interviewers put it: 'Everything a Pakistani says is wildly sociological. I find the West Indians dull by comparison.' It is worth emphasizing this point by some quotations from our interview notes.

G.M. 'Thinks it would be lovely to live on a council estate. Could travel to work, and perhaps visit friends only once a week or once a month. Does not have many English friends—but then one has to work away at this—he will have many friends in his new job after a time.'

C.T. 'C.T. is trying very hard to make a reasonable statement of the West Indian case. He is quite unfanatical though and conscious that he can't really secure the unity and co-operation of all West Indians. He expresses doubt about the importance of Pentecostal sects and says, "I'm not a fanatical person myself." How much more sophisticated he is than his white neighbours!'

F.R. 'Is a joiner by trade but now has a better job in a factory making aircraft parts. His wife is a nursing assistant working nights. They came from the same street in Kingston. F.R. came over in 1952 and J.R. in 1955. They married in England in the Methodist Church of which they are both members although F.R. doesn't go much himself, because he prefers religious discussion. Thinks he should be able to argue with the parson. Sermons are outdated and usually very boring.'

G.B. 'He lives with his mother and also has a brother who joined the army and is now in Cyprus. Another brother also lives with them and has passed several examinations since he has been in this country. The mother is about forty-five and like G.B. is very pleasant. The relationship between mother and son is very close and G. spends a lot of time at home with his mother. He spends a lot of time watching TV and is quite discriminating in his choice of pro-grammes.'

All these comments suggest ordinary working people with similar ranges of interests to British people. The young men meet and talk about sex and about motor cars. The older people discuss housing and their children. All talk about a wide range of social and political topics. Very few deliberately spend their time trying to sustain or build up a West Indian way of life.

But one thing which distinguishes the West Indians is that they are all forced to discuss discrimination. Contrary to a common view we found no evidence that West Indians arrived in this country with a chip on the shoulder. Rather, they came expecting acceptance and were shocked and grieved to find that they did not have the same rights as other citizens. We recorded this for instance in an interview with a West Indian couple:

A central theme in their conversation was the brainwashing of West Indians at home about Britain. They had been told about the Queen and Parliament, but no one had told them there was a colour bar. They had thought that they could get a flat where they chose and that Frank could get a job like any other carpenter. They were appalled by the effect which the bitterness of returning migrants would have on West Indian society. He said he wasn't bitter, but his wife said that she was. She was bitter because those who discriminated seemed to her to be not quite human.

Many of our interviewees said that they simply tried to avoid contacts in which discrimination was likely to occur. But all were pained by it and the events in Smethwick during the 1964 General Election were a common topic of conversation. The secretary of one West Indian organization concerned with discrimination said that 1964 had been a very painful year for him and there was a deep sense of disbelief and shock when Ku-Klux-Klan crosses were burnt in Birmingham in 1965.

The West Indian community had little in the way of organ-izations to deal with these problems, because it had few organizations of its own, its members belonging either to no organizations at all or to those of the host society. The problem was further complicated by the tendency of many West

Indians to respond to these problems by avoidance. Thus very little was done and those who were most politically conscious complained bitterly that their community had failed to produce leaders capable of speaking on their behalf. When they made these criticisms they directed them towards the various welfare societies which had been started, towards the High Commissioner's representative and towards the Birmingham Liaison Officer for Coloured People. It is necessary to look at the criticisms in order to understand something of the problems facing West Indians in Birmingham.

In Sparkbrook the main organization was the Commonwealth Welfare Association. This organization is Birmingham-wide in its scope but its members are in fact mainly from Barbados and St. Kitts and mostly resident in and around Sparkbrook. The organization is much weaker, however, than the Irish County Associations, and, although its officers help individuals with their housing and other problems, its main activity is a Friday night meeting, sometimes a purely social occasion, but commonly devoting itself to hearing a speaker on some topic of interest.

These meetings fall somewhere between being occasions on which immigrants protest about discrimination and occasions where they can learn facts about the host society. They might be devoted to a talk by a representative of the Housing Department or about insurance or any topic of general interest. The feeling about the evils of discrimination is there, but there is also an unwillingness to look at this problem and tendency to think of the situation instead as one in which mutual and self-education will provide the answers. On one occasion the committee even invited the principal instigator of the Immigration Control Association to speak, thus typically turning the other cheek and pretending that there was an important view here which it was significant that West Indians should understand. One of the audience asked the speaker if he would accept blood from a Negro donor and was told that he would in order to survive and fight to send the immigrants home! If the audience were shocked by this reply they suppressed their shock and treated their guest with courtesy.

In fact, this organization was uneasily balanced between being a protest organization and an organization to promote interracial goodwill. Moral Rearmament which, to say the least of it, is not a militant protest movement, had seen the potentialities of the Commonwealth Welfare Association and offered to send a speaker. Typically, the officers of the Association were uneasy about this offer but took it very seriously.

The achievement of the Commonwealth Welfare Association in checking discrimination must be negligible, and it would be surprising if it is not displaced in time by some more militant organization. We did not find, however, that there was any response to Michael de Freitas' Racial Adjustment Association, even though the newspaper *The Magnet* in which de Freitas stated his views was widely read. And it is easy to understand the tactics of the C.W.A. There are possibilities here and there of gaining acceptance for West Indians by polite promotion of goodwill, and it is felt that this must go on even though other activities of a more militant nature are promoted elsewhere.

There were in fact about eight or nine organizations of a type similar to the C.W.A. in Birmingham, some of them primarily social, some of them more educational and political. One of these was the West Indian Federation in Winson Green to the north. We called on the Public Relations Secretary and former Secretary of this organization, because we detected some animosity in the attitudes expressed by members of the C.W.A. towards him. We discovered that the Federation was, if anything, more moderate than the C.W.A.

The Federation is housed in rather mean premises opposite the gates of Birmingham's most famous gaol. It had originally been started, before it obtained these premises, by a West Indian doctor who had been in England for some years before the big migration. The Public Relations Secretary who lived on the premises was a defects inspector in the Corporation Transport Garage. He was particularly interested in youth work and had previously run a Boys' Brigade amongst what he called 'bad boys' in Bermondsey. He had taught them cricket and 'the bugling and the drum'. Currently he was putting in some of his Youth Club members for the Duke of Edinburgh's Award. He spoke very highly of Birmingham's Liaison Officer for Coloured People and as we shall show below this sentiment was reciprocated. His organization claimed about a hundred paid-up members.

The Secretary of the C.W.A. had been concerned to promote
unity amongst West Indians in Birmingham and had in fact
organized a Standing Conference of West Indian Organizations,
of which he became Chairman. He tried to use this organization as a platform to oppose discrimination and when we met
him he had spent the morning giving a Press conference
expressing the Standing Conference's views on various problems
in Birmingham. He received about eight column inches in one
local paper, much of which space was devoted to the tactful
qualifications he had made to his protest.

Clearly, voluntary organizations amongst West Indians had
not got very far in making an effective West Indian protest
against discrimination. It must be asked, therefore, whether the
West Indians received much help from the more official
agencies such as the office of the High Commission or the
Liaison Office for Coloured People. Here we found that neither
had done very much about discrimination, though both had
performed useful services in helping with travel arrangements
and directing people to social welfare agencies and solicitors
who could help them.

The Liaison Officer for Coloured People, however, occupies
a very complex position and it is necessary to understand his
role and how he and his employees see it, in order to understand the situation of the West Indians and other immigrants
in Birmingham. Obviously, his is a very delicate job which
could require great skill as a social worker as well as a politician
mediating between races.

The man chosen for the post had entered the police force in
York and has served as a police officer in Palestine and East
Africa before returning to police work in Bridlington. When
we asked members of the Council about this we were told that
he was chosen primarily because of his 'overseas experience'.
Little thought had apparently been given to the complex
questions of social policy and social work which the appointment involved; and none at all to the possibility that coloured
people might resent, as they told us they did, their being
entrusted to the care of an ex-police officer.

Difficulties had arisen precisely over this question. The
secretary of the Commonwealth Welfare Association was reported to have questioned the Liaison Officer's fitness for his

job in a speech in Cambridge and, although he had denied the remarks, this had led to a complete rupture of relations between the two men. The secretary of the C.W.A. had tried repeatedly to contact the Liaison Officer in connexion with the Jamaican Independence celebrations, but was told that he was too busy or that he was away.

When we asked the Liaison Officer what his policy was regarding co-operation with immigrant organizations he told us that he could not co-operate with anyone who was 'political'. At first we thought that he was referring to men with extreme left-wing views, but he explained that one of the men who he wished to avoid was in fact a 'big Tory'. In fact, he was un-willing to have contact with anyone who made 'political statements' about discrimination. One could easily understand a local government official taking a non-political stand. This, indeed, is what should be expected of a good bureaucrat. But in this case it meant the loss of many valuable contacts with the immigrant community and, in fact, the only immigrant leader whom the Liaison Officer expressed his willingness to work with was the Public Relations Secretary of the West Indian Federa-tion mentioned above.

This loss of contact with the organized immigrants meant that the Liaison Officer had to deal directly with individuals. He was well satisfied with this and claimed to have interviewed or arranged interviews for all the English-speaking and about half of the non-English-speaking immigrants, a claim in no way substantiated by our own respondents, very few of whom had had dealings with the Liaison Office.

The Liaison Officer defined his task as the integration of the immigrants, by which he explained that he meant seeing that they got their rights and that they conformed. He had helped many immigrants to get lodgings, but had found that they preferred to be with their own people. He had also helped to increase opportunities for employment. Again we must record that very few of our respondents had received these services and those who had done so complained about their inadequacy. But in any case, these services were no longer in operation. Emphasis now was on the second stage of getting the immigrants to conform. Housing standards and eating habits were among the most important issues, in the Liaison Officer's opinion.

The Office had, in fact, lost several of its small staff in the latter part of 1964 and they had not been replaced. We were surprised to find leading Councillors arguing that this was because the job had been at least partly completed. With race a major subject on the political platforms of the 1964 General Election this view seems surprising. But it should be borne in mind throughout that Birmingham's Councillors regard themselves as having done a good job on the racial question in contrast to the neighbouring authority of Smethwick. If there are immigrant grievances they do not register in the City Hall either through the Councillors or through the Liaison Office. Even the Liaison Officer's collations of statistics gleaned from Local Authority Departments and reported to the Council through its General Purposes Committee have had the effect of strengthening the demand for immigration control rather than of drawing attention to the disadvantages of immigrants.

One small outlet exists for immigrant feeling in the form of the other-wordly Pentecostal sects which are discussed in another chapter, and the number that there are would appear to signify some social discontent. But they touch only a few believers and their message of a great social reversal at the latter day encourages quietism. There was no specifically West Indian political organization and few West Indians had contact with the major political parties except as clients in their surgeries.

There were few West Indian landlords and only a handful of shopkeepers in back streets, who had an insignificant share even of West Indian trade. In this respect the contrast between Pakistanis and West Indians is remarkable. The West Indian community lacked any kind of commercial middle class and its leadership was entirely in the hands of skilled workmen.

There remain to be mentioned only the purely social activities of the West Indians, which helped to provide some sort of colony life for them. The most important organizations here were the football clubs. In Sparkbrook, as we saw in Chapter IV, there were two teams called St. Christopher's and Basseterre Celtic. Both of these drew their players and supporters largely from Kitticians and both were social as well as football clubs. Although they played against white teams and inevitably took part in negotiations about matches, this did not imply any social meeting off the field. A league of football teams may institutionalize a state of accommodation. It does not promote integration or assimilation.

Private individuals, the social and sports organizations which we have mentioned, and commercial entrepreneurs all provide parties and these parties form an important part of the life of West Indians. Most of those which we attended were marked by the petit-bourgeois respectability which pervades so much of West Indian life. They were symbolized by the shiny radiogram found in so many West Indian homes. But there were others at which there was more noise and drink and at which an occasional white prostitute might be present. Generally, however, we found that young men who wished to avoid a steady relationship with a woman went to few dances and parties.

To sum up, the West Indian residents of Sparkbrook have a largely English culture pattern and organization beyond the limits of the family does not occur spontaneously. Their organizations, where they do exist, are formal and weakly supported. None the less, precisely because the West Indian has English aspirations, he experiences discrimination and it falls to his organizations to try to remedy his grievances. The leaders of these organizations find themselves in a dilemma. Are they to fight and possibly rupture the ties with the white community which do exist, or are they to use educational and goodwill activities to help assimilation? They have generally chosen the latter alternative, but they have failed and know that they have failed because discrimination still exists. A largely working-class community, they have made no inroads in commerce or business and the ordinary day-to-day community activities are concerned with sport or with pure sociability. But for all this we found a great sense of grievance amongst the West Indians, coupled with a sense of impotence to do anything about their condition. This situation is still a relatively new one, for in the 1950s there was still hope that they might overcome discrimination and be assimilated. It seems likely that there will be a growth both in the religious sects and in more overt forms of political organization.

The Pakistanis are fewer in numbers than the West Indians in Sparkbrook, but their impact on the area is far greater because of the role which they play as landlords and shop-keepers. Moreover, whereas the West Indians so largely share English culture and affiliate themselves to its institutions, the Pakistanis have a culture and institutions of their own, so that their presence is doubly visible. They are seen not only as coloured but as culturally foreign.

We have already referred to the Irishness of the Stratford Road. We now have to notice that there are, mixed up amongst the English shops catering for Irish or English needs, some dozen Pakistani-owned stores and several Pakistani-owned cafés. The clientele of these shops and cafés is predominantly Pakistani, but includes also a strong minority of West Indians and a few English and Irish. In a very striking way these shops and cafés declare the Pakistani presence, for they not only have their shop signs in Urdu or Bengali, and sell Oriental spices; they also serve as social centres. In the New World Stores, for instance, a Pakistani may bath and eat, meet his friends and pick up news of Pakistani community activities. Thus the Pakistani, like the Irishman, has a supporting social world in the High Street and one which is if anything stronger, because it is based upon property-ownership.

This world of the High Street, however, has to be understood in terms of the structure of the Pakistani migration which is different from and more complex than that of the Irish or the West Indian. It is a foreign migration in a way that the Irish and West Indian migrations are not. It is based upon relatively short-term migrants and its strength and capacity to sustain and support itself depends upon property-ownership.

As we have shown in another chapter, the typical Pakistani migrant is a peasant-turned-worker, who has left his wife, if he has one, at home. He will suffer the trials and tribulations of the city for a period of five or more years but intends to return home at least for a time. He seeks a temporary home to establish himself as a worker, but in the great majority of cases does not aim at assimilation. None the less, as we shall show, his immigration is organized and supported to a far greater degree than the West Indians and in most respects than the Irish.

The original Pakistani immigrants to Birmingham were absconding seamen. They came almost entirely from two areas,

Sylhet in East Pakistan and the Campbellpore district of West Pakistan where shipping companies recruited seamen. The later migrants of the big migration which began in about 1958 also came very largely from these districts and were able to establish an initial contact with the seamen's colonies.

These immigrants were faced with formidable difficulties in finding accommodation, yet turned these difficulties into an advantage. They could not find accommodation because all immigrants found difficulty in finding accommodation. But they had the necessary commercial skills and confidence and became in effect the main entrepreneurs of immigrant housing. In a technical sense they were a pariah group, that is, a group which remains morally and socially outside the society, yet performs services for it and has a caste-like relationship to it. Like the Jewish usurers in mediaeval Europe they were performing a vital function for the society, and like them they took the blame for the more unpleasant aspects of the role they had to play, in their case that of landlords.

There is a complex and unresolved sociological problem as to why Islam encourages commercial motives. We do not pretend to have resolved this. But we do know that the spirit of Islamic culture is a world apart from the plantation culture of the West Indians or the Roman Catholic culture of the Irish as regards the norms it prescribes for economic behaviour. Whereas the Irishman or West Indian lacks the self-confidence or assurance to risk his future commercially, the Pakistani, even though he may be a peasant with no experience of the city, takes quite naturally to commercial ventures.

And if the individual worker can handle the business of his domestic economy so easily it is not surprising that those who have some experience of the city or those who are just more able than their compatriots can tackle larger ventures. Some become shopkeepers or café proprietors. But a number go even beyond this and provide secondary services. Thus we found that the Pakistani shops were well served in Sparkbrook by their own wholesalers and there were two Pakistani banks with which they could deal. Further to this, the organization of house-purchase and travel provided other commercial opportunities which were eagerly taken up. And finally, the community in Birmingham was serviced by at least three weekly newspapers, one of which was produced a mile or so from Sparkbrook.

In a curious way, however, this spirit of commercial enterprise was not linked with an individualist ethic. The successful entrepreneur was seen as having obligations to his kinsman. If he had a house, his fellow-villagers and kinsmen could reside there for a nominal rent. And if he had a successful business he felt that he had an obligation to do charitable works which was felt more immediately and carried out more conscientiously than might be the case with a pious Christian businessman.

This is essential to the understanding of the various associations which were to be found amongst the Pakistani immigrants. These were marked, it is true, by class features. Their leadership tended to fall to the economically successful. There was a margin of shady economic activity which made some of them evasive respondents to our questions. And there was a fairly open struggle for power and influence amongst their leaders. None the less, we could not see these organizations solely and simply as the organizations of a successful middle class. They were in an important sense organizations serving a whole community which was strongly commercially oriented.

The most obvious organization in Sparkbrook was the Pakistani Welfare Association, because it had premises in a green-painted, boarded-up shop in the Stratford Road in the centre of Sparkbrook. This Association had been set up by East Pakistanis in 1945 and was originally simply a Bengali Film Society. Its current President was not at all clear on what precisely its present functions were, but said that 'it helped Pakistanis with their personal problems and provided premises for functions'. Among the personal problems which he was willing to discuss were problems relating to obtaining Muslim food in schools and hospitals and helping landlords in their dealings with the Public Health Department. But clearly these premises were a place where much immigrant business was transacted, relating to work, housing, travel, and personal domestic problems. It also appeared that the organization had complained to the Chief Constable about the inadequate protection from assaults by hooligans against Pakistanis, and had achieved some success.

We heard complaints about the Pakistani Welfare Association being an East Pakistani organization, and if it was so, this was of some importance, for most of the Pakistani residents of Sparkbrook were from West Pakistan or Azad Kashmir. But the only man we met who claimed to have organized West Pakistanis was a man closely associated with the domestic mosque in the neighbouring suburb of Balsall Heath. His organization, the Pakistani Sports and Welfare Association, had few members and seemed to be primarily an extension of his own personal contacts. The President of the Pakistani Welfare Association denied that his was an East Pakistani organization and asserted that it was truly representative of the Pakistanis of Birmingham.

We could not really hope to discover the truth of this. Few Pakistanis claimed membership of these or any other associations, but this of itself is not sufficient evidence since many might none the less have been formal or informal clients who simply did not see themselves as members. What did seem to be the case was that amongst the more economically successful there were many who saw it as part of their duty to offer services to their fellow-countrymen for reasons of charity or profit or a mixture of both. The result was a complex of associations, interlocking, conflicting, and overlapping and providing a basis from which some claim to community leadership could be made.

The organizations which we have mentioned thus far were diffuse in their functions. But in all of them one problem was very much to the fore. This was the conflict between Pakistani landlords and the Public Health Department over the enforcement of provisions of the 1961 Housing Act relating to multi-occupation. There was a straight clash of interests here, since it was in the interest of the landlord to put as many tenants in his house as possible and to do the minimum of repairs, and it was the goal of the Public Health Department to reduce overcrowding and preserve property. The activities of the officers of the Pakistani Welfare Association on this issue were considerably more 'militant' than those of the officers of any other immigrant community association. They were willing to accept some limitation on numbers, but most of them agreed with the Indian landlord who accused the Public Health Department of trying to 'undercrowd' the houses.

One organization which came into being specifically to deal with this issue was the Commonwealth Property-Owners' Association. This was organized primarily by a Pakistani wholesaler and the Indian proprietor of a linen shop. It came into being when it became apparent that the vast majority of landlords being prosecuted were Pakistanis and Indians. They told us that that they felt it was wrong to have Pakistanis standing in dock 'like goats' each week and that something had to be done to protect the community. Their inaugural meeting was advertised through the Indian and Pakistani shops and produced a meeting in the Digbeth Civic Hall of some six hundred Pakistanis and Indians from all parts of Birmingham. The numbers show that many who were not landlords attended because this was not merely a landlord but a community interest.

The C.P.O.A. devoted itself mainly to eliminating the unnecessary exacerbating elements in the conflict. They urged that something more should be done than sending notices of intentions to serve orders through the post and argued that much could be done to improve communications. They were even willing to improve standards themselves by delivering the notices, but would, of course, have been more understanding of the landlords' problems than were the Public Health Inspectors. They believed that the immigrant landlord had a function and that the blanket-condemnation of immigrant landlords was unfair.

The C.P.O.A., however, was not able to maintain the pace of work with which it started and had little success in getting recognition from the Public Health Department, which was of necessity suspicious of a landlords' organization. Its work was continued largely by one or two officers who concerned themselves with promoting better understanding of the landlords' position and took part in a scheme to improve a Sparkbrook street, which had been proposed by one of the more activist white residents.

A small number of Pakistanis thought that their interests could best be protected by carrying the conflict on to an overtly political plane. Contrary to popular impression there is a relatively high level of registration as voters in the Pakistani community, and Pakistanis are easier to organize for voting purposes than West Indians. The group of Pakistanis concerned approached the political parties and asked them to run a coloured candidate. The Liberal and Communist parties were sympathetic but it was felt that their causes were too hopeless and that it was more worthwhile to run a Pakistani candidate for the Council. This occurred in 1963 and its consequences are discussed in the chapter on political organizations. We should note here, however, that this was one possible tactic in the general conflict between the Pakistanis and their hosts. But the candidate himself was regarded with suspicion by other leaders and resigned from the C.P.O.A. when he was not put on the committee. This was all part of the formative stage of an immigrant community structure in which rival leaders and policies are offered to the people as ways of dealing with their problems.

In this struggle for leadership many factors are influential. One, though not necessarily the most important, is the continued discussion of Pakistani domestic politics. There are a variety of different attitudes to the Ayub régime in Pakistan and although our informants were unwilling to discuss these with outsiders, we discovered that there was considerable support for Miss Jinnah's candidacy for the Presidency. Moreover, the Kashmir dispute and the problems of refugees from Indian Kashmir (a term which no Pakistani would ever use) were much in the minds of the Pakistanis of Sparkbrook. Towards the end of our stay it was announced that Sheikh Abdullah would visit Birmingham. He did not come, but he would have had a warm reception there.

The continued awareness of the home culture, and its projection as an element into the Sparkbrook situation, were important in the case of the Pakistani community. The Urdu weeklies were widely read and there were several Pakistani cinemas. To be a Pakistani in Sparkbrook was not to cease to be a Pakistani.

This, however, raises the question of Islam. Nearly all Pakistani residents claimed to be Muslims and most said their prayers regularly. Among the more urbane businessmen, however, we found a distinction drawn between a good Muslim and a good man and a belief that the essentials of religion were universal, while for others shift-work made attendance at the domestic mosque in Balsall Heath difficult. Among community leaders there was a feeling that some more impressive building was necessary which could act both as a mosque and as a spiritual and moral centre for the Pakistani community. To this end the Pakistani leaders had been applying themselves.

A plan had been evolved in about 1962 to collect £400,000 to build 'the biggest mosque in the Western world' in Birmingham and negotiations opened to obtain a site on the edge of Balsall Heath. But the organization was inefficient and when the site was nearly lost, the High Commission stepped in to establish better organization. The local representative of the Commission, a young retired major from the Pakistani army, interviewed a large number of representatives of the Associations and appointed thirty of them to form a fund-raising committee. In late 1964 about £50,000 had been collected and the target figure mentioned above had been reduced to £200,000.

The affairs of the mosque committee occupied a great deal of the time of the community leaders. Their attitudes to the mosque, however, were mixed. They were not on the whole fanatically religious and a group of lay 'Preachers for Islam' who visited Birmingham in 1963 to hold immigrants to the' true faith received only a lukewarm reception. What they did want was a place which could act as a community centre and as the secretary of the Sports and Welfare Association put it, 'stop young students from drinking and going with pro's'. There was the same kind of puritan concern here about the dangers of the city as we found in the case of the Irish missioner.

Although the Pakistani community remains apart socially and culturally from the host society, it should be borne in mind that there are none the less some signs at the margins of lapsing both from Islam and from Pakistani culture. Religious duties are overlooked. An increasing number of Pakistanis drink alcohol. And those few who have wives and families find it difficult to maintain the complete seclusion of women. In this lies the possibility that a minority will begin to be assimilated to English society and this process will be accelerated in the schools where children may develop a positive affiliation to the host culture and to the youth culture symbolized by the Beatles. In this kind of community, the mosque will not necessarily act as an obstacle to assimilation. It may serve only to prevent urban demoralization.

As we have seen in the case of the mosque committee, the High Commission plays some part in the life of immigrants. It is far more evident than is the case with the Jamaican High Commission. But it is none the less far removed from the people, whether landlords or peasant workers. It is staffed by ex-army men and bureaucrats who know little of, and sympathize little with, the interests of the ordinary immigrant. It is an organization of diplomats in a situation where sensitive community leadership and the skills of social work are needed. We found that community leaders found it desirable to work together with the High Commission Office, but regarded it with some measure of suspicion. Attempts by the High Commission to organize and rationalize the associations are likely to produce some measure of political resistance, the more so because there are already political strains on a national level between the associations, which are evident in the work of the National Federation.

* * *

In this chapter we have described three separate immigrations. There are also others, including Indian, Cypriot, Polish, and Arab. But most of these are small and the three which we have mentioned must serve as types. In the case of the Irish, there is no visible colour difference and their institutions are not wholly dissimilar from those of the English. The Irish are well equipped both with a colony structure in the period of transition and with the means to assimilation. The West Indians are marked by their colour, but their culture is less distinctive than that of the Irish. They are lacking in organizations and in commercial influence. They want acceptance into the host society. However, they face discrimination in nearly every sphere of life and have been compelled to organize to deal with this. None the less, their organizations are not militant conflict organizations because there remains the hope that there are advantages in playing down the conflict. The Pakistanis are culturally and racially distinct and are also distinguished by the temporariness of their migration. They form, in a technical sense, a pariah group, being in the society but not of it. They have clear conflicts of interest with the society and have organized themselves to pursue these conflicts and to reach some adjustment compatible with their interests. On many levels of organization they are better equipped than either the Irish or the West Indians. It is out of the interaction of these three groups with an English community in a decaying urban district that Sparkbrook's social system has to be fashioned.

VII. Religion in Sparkbrook

Every Sunday approximately 5,600 people attend church in Sparkbrook. 5,000 of these are Roman Catholics attending Mass. The remaining 600 are spread among the established churches and denominations (275) and the English and West Indian sects (325). The church congregations are predominantly female; just over a half of the Catholics at Mass are women and 62 per cent. of the other congregations on any Sunday are women.

Sociologically the churches are among the more interesting associations in Sparkbrook as they have clearly defined memberships and a definite 'message' which can be related to the status of the group represented by the congregation. A discussion of this and how it relates to the group structure of Sparkbrook will form the main body of the present chapter.[1]

In common with all other associations, the churches fulfil the functions of providing pastoral care, overcoming the individual's isolation, providing a means to individual or group goals and asserting a set of beliefs about the world.

The pastoral work of the churches may be of very great importance when people are experiencing disorientation and other personal and social problems. Yet clearly pastoral work for a church could consist of anything from delivering tracts and evangelizing to ensuring that citizens obtain their rights from the welfare state. Similarly, the variations of aim and motivation implicit in these differing pastoral activities could also influence the nature of the more psychological, individual, case-work by ministers or laity. The exact nature of the pastoral work done by the churches is difficult to study, no case histories are kept as in formal social work agencies, nor does all the work fall into simple case-work categories. We asked the

---

[1] Just as understanding the urban process and the struggle for living space turned us back to the work of the Chicago sociologists, so our attempts to understand the meaning of religion drew us back to Weber, Tawney, Troeltsch, Durkheim, and Niebuhr, and on Niebuhr especially we have leaned very heavily.

ministers of the main parish church and two established
denominations to keep diaries of their pastoral work for a week
which they regarded as typical, classifying the services themselves within simple categories suggested by us.

The clergy of three of the churches made pastoral contacts
with 144 Sparkbrook people in the course of a week, of whom
a little under a half (68) were church members or adherents.
A third (48) were immigrants and a sixth (22) persons of
pensionable age. Just under a third (46) of the services concerned non-religious matters, welfare of children and old people
and housing being the commonest. The remaining contacts
were for routine pastoral visits, friendly calls or evangelism.
Of these 144 clients, 18 were passed on to other voluntary or
statutory bodies and the remainder were dealt with by the
ministers concerned. In addition, all ministers cited the Sparkbrook Association as a 'secular wing' which was carrying out
much necessary pastoral work, with their approval and
assistance.

Thus a small number of inhabitants are helped into the
formal machinery of the welfare services, but many more
receive the direct attention of the church itself. How effective
this assistance is it is impossible to assess, but we can presume
that the availability of sympathetic attention will be important
for those with little or no contact with kin and associations.
The attention itself may produce psychological satisfactions for
the recipients. The ministers in their pastoral work come into
contact not only with their clients, but with their clients'
families, or, in lodging-houses, with other residents. Thus
ministers have a presence evident to the population and are
potentially available for case-work, problem-solving and
advice, and as links between immigrants and either the general
English community or specific agencies. Knowledge of these
services among the immigrant population is indicated by the
fact that nearly a third (11/36) of the immigrant clients calling
on ministers were not members of the ministers' churches.

The Catholic priests, assisted by the Society of St. Vincent
de Paul and the Legion of Mary, engage in extensive pastoral
visitation in Sparkbrook. The priest and the Legion are
hampered by the Irish population's mobility, but their work
consists mainly of keeping in touch with the immigrant Irish,

encouraging them to use only suitable lodgings, to live a life in keeping with the moral expectations of the Church and to maintain religious observances. Housing difficulties are a constant feature of Irish life and to help meet them a specialized agency, the Catholic Housing Aid Society, which in fact serves the whole of Birmingham and is open to non-Catholics, was formed.

The sects do not appear to provide services similar to other churches, as their aims are more specifically religious. Thus the West Indian Pentecostal sects confine their activities to Bible studies and prayer meetings during the week, with occasional evangelization campaigns. The Jehovah's Witnesses concentrate on the distribution of literature and holding classes for members; the Adventists have similar activities, though examination of their record cards for one week (the Adventists are the only group to keep comprehensive records) showed that they had helped forty-seven people throughout Birmingham with food, clothing, and health and welfare services.

While the churches provide potential links with the English community for the immigrants, it is also true that immigrants bring their own religions with them. They may only turn to the ministers of the English churches when they need specific, non-religious services that cannot be provided so effectively by their own religious organizations.

The main immigrant group, the Irish, are overwhelmingly Roman Catholic; thus they are religiously apart from the English who are predominantly Protestant. Catholicism in Sparkbrook is essentially Irish Catholicism and as such creates an atmosphere of worship that the Englishman finds quite alien to an English Catholic service. The Harp Mass Centre is filled at each Mass with men, women, children, and babies; these latter two groups maintain continuous diversions and a level of noise that makes it difficult to follow the service. Sermons are short and the setting of the liturgy on a stage under stage lights with the congregation below and occasionally engulfed by noise and disturbances, separates the people from the ritual and heightening the observer's sense of 'us down here' watching something going on 'up there'. While the conduct of the service may not be peculiarly Irish, it is certainly un-English. Apart from the actual content of the liturgy, the service itself has an essentially Irish content. The announcements concern Irish social events in Birmingham, or trips to Ireland; the faithful are asked to remember in their prayers a list of deceased Irish people; and Irish newspapers are on sale outside after the service. We met a number of West Indian Catholics who had made similar observations to our own, who said they infrequently attended Mass. At home Mass was an intensely religious experience after which one felt 'sanctified', whereas here it is an Irish social event, after which football pools and drink are discussed as the congregation storms the exit doors.

While the presence of English priests on the parish staff does perhaps show the possibility of the Irish moving towards a more English form of religion, it remains true that the substantial Irish colony, with its priest seconded from Clare, constitutes in many respects a parish of the Irish church.

Islam, Hinduism, and Sikhism have no formal priesthood; religion is largely a matter of personal interpretation. For the Hindus, religion in England remains a domestic matter; there are no temples in Birmingham. Islam and Sikhism are organized. The Sikhs have a *Gurdwara* in a converted church in Smethwick and a number of Sparkbrook Sikhs are regular attenders. The services are exactly the same as in India, with music, singing, and scripture readings.

After the service a meal is provided in what used to be the church hall, Punjabi food is cooked by the women and served by the children. This meal must constitute the largest weekly Indian gathering in the area and provides the women with an opportunity for extensive discussion and exchange of news while they sit together at the opposite end of the hall from the men. The *Gurdwara* management committee has set up classes for children so that the home culture, especially language and religion, will not be lost. Clearly, the whole style and content of the religious life of the Sikh community are unknown to the host community. For those Sparkbrook Sikhs who feel the need for a religious expression of their culture and a visible demonstration of the solidarity of a section of the Indian community the Smethwick *Gurdwara* is a vital institution. As our interpreter said at one stage in a service we attended, 'I come here because it reminds me of home.'

Islam is the major non-Christian religion in Sparkbrook. We have seen in Chapter IV that the day-to-day discipline of the religion is not easily maintained by the individual adherent. Nevertheless, the two major Muslim festivals, the Eid prayers, are well attended by some six to seven thousand Muslims drawn from all over Birmingham. These two festivals in fact unite Muslims throughout the world but in Birmingham and Sparkbrook they are essentially occasions when large numbers of Pakistanis come together in the context of religion, thereby giving ritual expression to their sense of difference from the society around them. Islam is itself divided into a number of theological streams but these seem hardly to affect the lives of the working-class Pakistani population of Sparkbrook.

The meetings of the mosque committee do at times show signs of factional disputes as the committee itself represents various property interests in the community. It is intended to build the biggest mosque in the Western world in neighbouring Balsall Heath; it will have a school room and meeting hall besides a prayer hall and will thus be a major cultural centre for the Pakistani community. At present there are only small residential mosques for Pakistanis and Arabs.

Occasionally groups of preachers visit the Muslim communites in England, enjoining them to keep faith and live moral lives in this alien land, but so far there seems to have been little or no proselytization of English or immigrant communities.

When we speak of the sociological functions of religious organizations we are not attempting to assess the truth of any one or all of the faiths, nor do we question the fact that the primary meaning of religious observance and ritual is essentially *religious* for adherents. Most, if not all, of the faithful would be unaware that their religion had any striking sociological meaning or any observable sociological function. We conclude, however, that the observances of the three immigrant groups so far discussed constitute rites of national or ethnic solidarity for the adherents and provide them with psychic and tangible links with their home culture. Further, they ritually recreate the home culture, through religion, thus institutionalizing the differences between the various groups. In our original frame of reference this means that religion helps the individual to dispel any sense of personal isolation and perhaps to assert that the world should (or could) be like *this* when he ritually recreates his home culture and states its religious and most sacred values.

We shall see in considering English and West Indian religious groups that they too have a latent function in tending to maintain not ethnically different cultures but class cultures that in general also set them apart from one another. To understand this we need to move from a fairly simple interpretation of religious rites, as rites of group solidarity, to examine the various types of religious expression possible within Christianity, and why we might expect various social groups to adhere to particular types of religion.

R. H. Tawney[1] suggested that there were four possible types of attitude to social and economic institutions consistent with religious beliefs. These were, firstly, flight from the world, standing 'on one side in ascetic aloofness'. Secondly, 'it may take them for granted and ignore them as matters of indifference belonging to a world with which religion has no concern'. Thirdly, the attitude may be one of throwing oneself 'into an agitation for some particular reform, for the removal of some crying scandal, for the promotion of some final revolution, which will inaugurate the reign of righteousness on earth'. The fourth possible attitude listed by Tawney is that of regarding the institutions of the world, and man's appetites and ambitions, as fallen, but nevertheless potentially material for building the Kingdom and on which we must humbly work.

It will be seen that elements of all these attitudes to 'the world' are present in all the sects and denominations found in Sparkbrook. We felt, however, that the weakness of the revolutionary type in Tawney's analysis is that it would include everything from Christian Socialism to puritan reaction, from millenarianism to pietistic reformism. In fact one then needs to explain how a social and revolutionary doctrine develops historically into one which encourages purely individual piety and even extreme conservatism.

A more important distinction is made by H. Richard Niebuhr. In his *The Social Sources of Denominationalism*, he posits

[1] R. H. Tawney, *Religion and the Rise of Capitalism*, London, John Murray, 1936.

a distinction between two kinds of religion which helps to answer these questions. The first is the 'religion of the disinherited'. The adherents will be drawn from among the lowest social strata, membership will depend on the individual's showing signs of conversion and grace, and there will be no trained ministry but a stress on the individual's ability to interpret the Scriptures through the guidance of the Holy Spirit. The disinherited will look forward to some final reversal of the present order, when the first will be last and the last first. This reversal may be seen as taking place either in this world or the next, with or without the direct action of the adherents. The more they believe that they must be involved in reversing the order in the present world, the more they approach Tawney's revolutionary type.

The 'religion of the middle class' is, as the name suggests, more typical of an economically successful and stable social stratum. The theological and social response is more moderate and 'reformist' (the adherents perhaps having too much to lose in any reversal) and there may be a sense, explicit or implicit, of the adherent's 'election'. Over the generations a trained ministry is created and membership is by birth and inheritance rather than conversion. Middle-class religion, typically, takes on an established denominational structure as opposed to the sectarian structure of religion among the disinherited.

Niebuhr goes on from this static analysis to show how sects develop into denominations. This is not only through the need to incorporate the children into the organization and pass the beliefs on to them but also because in many cases the socio-economic ethics of the sect members is likely to make them more economically successful than the non-religious members of their class.

We found religious groups in Sparkbrook which tend towards these two types. Nevertheless the peculiarities of the Sparkbrook situation stamp on the sects and denominations features which enable us to see them as representing institutionally the conflicts and the distinctive ways of life of groups in the area. Four possible exceptions—Christ Church, the Methodists, the Adventists and Jehovah's Witnesses—variously test Niebuhr's classification and its usefulness in this type of research.

There is no church in Sparkbrook which has drawn its entire membership from the immediately local population; all in some measure rely on outside support. Members of the established denominations may have moved out of the area but maintain active membership of the Sparkbrook church. Some of the West Indian sects draw their congregations from wide areas of Birmingham (as a result of which most of them have acquired small buses). It will be seen that this factor accentuates the ethnic and class differences that are already inherent in the Sparkbrook community.

The West Indian sects have almost entirely lower working-class Jamaican membership. They started from prayer meetings in individuals' rooms but now hold larger Sunday services in local schools, while maintaining two or three week-night prayer meetings and Bible studies in private houses. The Sunday worship is supplemented by a Sunday school for the children which is also attended by a large number of the adults. Thus the sect member will spend two or three evenings a week and Sunday from 2 p.m. until as late as 10 p.m. in religious activities. Formal leadership tends to be in the hands of pastors trained in America, aided by members, mainly women, who display some measure of religious inspiration. The sects tend to split easily; beliefs are held so dogmatically that heresy becomes endemic, and one misplaced word could offend a whole group. We suspect that splits occur over more personal issues, as in the St. Christopher's Football Club, but take on a doctrinal complexion due to the religious context in which they occur. It was not always possible to find out which group split from which, as each group designates the other schismatic. When we first arrived in Sparkbrook two sects met in a school about half a mile outside our area; they met simultaneously and used the same hymn book and claimed no fundamental differences. By the time we left there were three similar sects actually in Sparkbrook and another two within a quarter of a mile.

The evening service congregation of a Pentecostal church[1] we attended consisted of about eighteen women and a dozen men of all ages, and about twenty little children and babies. The services consisted of hymns, sung *vivace* and syncopated to

---

[1] For a general account of these sects see M. Calley, *God's People*, London, O.U.P. for I.R.R., 1965.

the music of piano and guitars; long extempore prayers occasionally with the congregation all praying individually but together building up rhythmic surges punctuated by fervent cries of 'Yeah Lord!' and 'Help me, Lord!' A long Bible-reading is followed by a commentary on it led by a member of the congregation, who frequently calls on other members of the congregation to read other relevant passages, with instructions to 'Stand up, please!' to read. Between the hymns and reading there were testimonies from other church members during which the congregation would murmur, 'Halleluia!' or 'Praise the Lord!' After the sermon there are repeated calls to anyone unconverted to come forward to be prayed for and saved, accompanied by fervid prayer and repeated choruses of evangelical hymns. Finally, half an hour of notices from the church secretary, including such items as the coming week's programme, appeals for money and discussion of the annual national convention of the sect. The atmosphere throughout the service is emotionally highly charged, although this is frequently broken by parents taking noisy children out, taking their babies to be fed and returning to their places. Every service follows a similar pattern, and it is quite evident after a few visits to these churches that there is a very definite pattern of prayer and testimony. There is a formal pattern of behaviour at the service; the services therefore have a liturgy and are not entirely spontaneous or chaotic.

The dispossession of the members is stressed in prayer and testimony, but comes out nowhere more clearly than in the sermon. One such sermon actually said that we are a down-trodden people, bowed down by long and hard labour, but our souls have rest. The preacher pointed out that the congregation was set aside from the world, witnessing. The world is rapidly building up for the day of judgment, which is near. He stressed how it was necessary to eschew the evil things of this world; jewellery (or any bodily adornment), the theatre, the cinema, tobacco and liquor—'You can't get a drink in hell, that's a place burning with fire and brimstone.' It seemed to the observer that these people were rejecting the goods of an affluent society that they were, in fact, denied by their economic position, and rejecting a world which they felt had rejected them.

Great stress was laid on spiritual purity, washing and cleanliness; in spite of the filth of this world the believers are washed in the Blood of the Lamb. The theology is mainly Hebraic, the texts and injunctions coming from the Old Testament. The only New Testament reference in any sermon we heard was to the Sacrifice of the Lamb on Calvary, a reference to another Hebraic idea.

We did not study these sects long enough to elicit all the details of their beliefs and the effects of these on behaviour, but we had hints of the consequences of adhering to such a belief system. Having little opportunity or desire to spend their money the adherents accumulate small sums of capital. For the sect member this opens the possibility of buying a house, and we found numbers of sect members who already owned houses. The possibility of economic and social mobility, and therefore of having a minor stake in the present order, would seem to explain why the adherent's hopes of the final reversal of the social order are projected into the next world. If the members do become predominantly property-owners and thus improve their class position we may see a shift towards 'middle-class religion'. There is evidence in the existence of the Sunday school, some trained pastors, the stress on personal commitment, and the belief in an other-worldly rather than a this-worldly eschatology, that a move in this direction is already under way.

For the present the West Indian sects meet more immediate needs for their members as well as contributing to their longer-range social mobility. The services enable the members to express and release their frustrations and resentments in the present situation in what appears to be a complete and satisfactory manner, in the course of euphoric group activities. The services are something to which the adherents can look forward during the week's hard work and the beliefs provide a meaningful framework within which they can understand and accept their relatively deprived position in society.

There is on the edge of the research area a small, English mission hall where they too were willing to equate the theatre, cinema, tobacco and gambling with sin and death. Here again, extempore prayer and calls for the unconverted to be saved were used, but with considerable restraint and lack of emotional release as compared with the West Indian sects. This is a very small group of working-class English people, the lowest-status group among the English that we found in any religious organization. Their low status and consequent deprivations were reflected in prayer and sermons, both conducted in a mixture of the Authorised Version and modern English. The lay preacher who spoke at our first visit described how he attempted to spread the Gospel among his work-mates; this seemed to consist mainly of keeping his distance from them and 'witnessing'. 'Witnessing' in particular and 'living the Christian life' in general seemed to consist of demonstrating personal piety and asceticism. To these people the world was hostile, the address made reference to 'the seat of Satan's power' (China), 'darkest Congo' and South America beset with 'rampant Roman Catholicism'. The churches were criticized for not taking a stand on certain key issues such as temperance and gambling—'I met a Vicar's wife who was going to a whist drive, she was going to the Devil, I don't know about a whist drive.' Implicit in prayers and sermon was a future, other-worldly reversal of the present order, although '.... it's beautiful, lovely, wonderful to be a Christian here'.

This mission represents a religion transitional between the religion of the disinherited and middle-class religion, the adherents' status lies between the disinheritance of the Jamaican lower working class and the relative economic security of the English upper working class.

Two English denominations, the Baptists and Congregationalists, approach an expression of 'middle-class religion'. The members of these denominations are not disinherited; some have been so economically successful that they have been able to move out of Sparkbrook. These return on Sundays and meet the church members who remain in the area. This weekly return of successful Sparkbrookians must constantly set an ideal of 'success' before the eyes of those who remain. Significantly, these denominations have a *tradition*, they have existed for many years in Sparkbrook through a number of generations; therefore the ties between members are as much affective ties of kin and friendship as of shared religious beliefs or class situation.

The Sunday services display no lack of restraint; they are

the familiar combination of hymns, prayers and sermon. The sermons especially show a stress on personal piety, the virtues of good neighbourliness and fair dealing, and on the importance of the family, this latter being an important characteristic in Niebuhr's classification of middle-class religion. In common with all the predominantly English churches which have a high percentage of elderly members, the prayers and sermons contain much that is intended to comfort and uplift the elderly or the weak.

In following this pattern of worship the congregations are in fact virtually parading the values of the old Sparkbrook when it was a 'respectable area' closely identified with the gentry. The ritual goes beyond this; by drawing in old Sparkbrookians and pulling together members of the old 'respectable' working class, it recreates the old community (as far as this is possible), which corporately asserts its values. For the hour of worship and the time before and after when old friends meet to gossip, it is as if nothing had changed, as if the congregation were still living in the Sparkbrook they remember from their childhood. Nothing in any sermons we heard (one of the authors concentrated much of his church-going in these two churches) suggested that the congregation might be living in a changing society; certainly there were no dark faces in the congregation to demonstrate this change.[1] Standing on the edge of Sparkbrook 1, one church ignored the Pakistani community close at hand, but collected money for missionaries in Pakistan.

Theologically there was a muted predestinarianism running through the worship, a sense of the congregation's election, but this was never made explicit. Thus the total impression conveyed was of a group of people living in a fantasy world of the old Sparkbrook, quietly assured of their place in the next world.

The social ethics of these groups led to little effective social action. They tended more to separate themselves from the wider community. Effective community action for them would involve actually re-creating the old Sparkbrook as their ideal society; as this is impossible they are restricted to asserting the old values, believing that if as a result of this 'witnessing' individuals adopt the same values and beliefs Sparkbrook will

[1] There were occasionally one or two young West Indians in the Baptist Church.

become a better place to live in. The belief of these people
that social ills are a result of individual failure was perhaps best
illustrated at the time of the 1965 municipal elections when a
large notice appeared outside the Baptist church, saying 'Don't
blame your environment; with GOD's help you can change it.'

It is difficult to see how any immigrant would feel 'at home'
in such churches, any more than an Englishman could feel at
home in a West Indian sect meeting. Crucially, there are no,
or few, West Indian Baptists or Congregationalists in the area
with expectations of participation, but if there were it is unlikely that they would be able to participate meaningfully in the
life of the church, just as the West Indian Roman Catholics
felt unable to participate in the life of the Irish church

Three Anglican parishes cover Sparkbrook, roughly coincid-
ing with our three zones. Emmanuel parish covers and extends
beyond Sparkbrook 3, St. Agatha's similarly covers Sparkbrook
2, and Christ Church Sparkbrook 1.

Emmanuel's congregation averages twenty-five older women
and fifteen men plus a young choir some thirty strong. As the
congregation is drawn mainly from Barber Trust housing it is
respectable upper working-class, lower middle-class and this is
reflected in its middle-to-low Anglican tradition. The religion
is simple middle-class religion, exactly what is expected for the
older members of a population drawn from the area described
in Chapter II. Sociologically it is the least interesting of the
Sparkbrook churches.

St. Agatha's has a long Anglo-Catholic tradition. Its services
appear to be attended mainly by middle-class people, a considerable proportion of whom come in from outside Sparkbrook. The services are acts of worship in which the life of
Sparkbrook is remembered in intercession, but the richness,
colour and formality of the architecture, decoration and
liturgy do not lend themselves to the expression of anything
about day-to-day life in the greyness outside. More than any
other church St. Agatha's is able in its ritual to stand aside from
the diversion and conflicts of Sparkbrook, albeit by excluding
them. In keeping with the best Anglo-Catholic tradition, the
vicar engages in intensive pastoral work, though he reported
that he was no longer so welcome in the pubs as in the old days
of an established community when priest and publican allegedly

acknowledged and respected one another as servants of the community. The population changes in Sparkbrook 2 also make it more difficult for him to keep track of families through the generations, as was previously possible.

The presence of immigrants, in large numbers in proportion to the white congregation, with expectations of participation in the life of the church, would redefine the situation for its white membership. This has happened in various ways for four churches in Sparkbrook.

Christ Church parish is almost entirely coincident with Sparkbrook 1. In this area there are large numbers of West Indians. Not only are some of them Anglican, but all of them are, by definition, members of the parish. Therefore they have a right to the pastoral care and other provisions of the parish church and it is the church's duty to draw as many parishioners as possible into the active life of the church.

Thus as a result of pre-existing church membership and the activities of the vicar and his street stewards (who also keep watch for anyone ill or in trouble in their street) Christ Church now has about 30 per cent. of its membership West Indian. The indigenous membership was very similar to that of Emmanuel (with one or two of the ladies active in the Conservative Party). A number of these, it is impossible to say how many, have left as a result of West Indians coming in, and (in their opinion) occupying too much of the vicar's attention. Interestingly enough we found a greater measure of resentment among non-church-going parishioners, who felt that the vicar was *their* vicar and should be doing something about their problems, not fraternizing with coloured people.

Thus because of its constitutional structure the Church of England was able to draw together West Indian immigrants and English, but only at the expense of alienating other English people, whose beliefs clearly did not constrain them to tolerate their coloured co-religionists.

The Methodist church has a similar percentage of West Indian members, but not because of its constitution. There are a large number of Kitticians in Sparkbrook, and in St. Kitts Methodism is both strong and orthodox. Kittician Methodism is so orthodox that those who came to Sparkbrook found the mixture of Wesleyan and Primitive liturgy too free and uninhibited. Thus they instituted their own Order of Morning Worship (based on Anglican matins) once a month. After a time the English members said that this separate service was not a good idea and suggested that they all have the service together once a month. This has continued along with other activities, such as West Indian socials and War on Want suppers laid on for the whole congregation by the West Indians. There seems to be a high degree of mutual acceptance between black and white, which gained great significance through the rituals of baptism and Holy Communion.

The Methodist church, by English standards, is very orthodox, more so than Christ Church, which freely adapted or dispensed with the Book of Common Prayer according to the presumed needs of the congregation. Methodist services were very formal and the intellectual content of the sermons was higher than anywhere else in Sparkbrook, though the content again stressed comfort and support for the weak, in a middle-class Christian context. The congregation consisted of pre-dominantly lower middle-class, smartly dressed people, hatted women, a number of church members coming in cars, one or two from quite far afield. Similarly the West Indians were drawn from among the upper strata of West Indian society, some being skilled or clerical workers. How strongly middle-class the West Indians felt themselves to be was shown by their attitude to Common Law marriages. The previous minister was very strict, telling cohabitants that they were living in sin and using ecclesiastical sanctions to persuade them to marry. The present minister takes a liberal attitude and was criticized for this by every West Indian Methodist we met; our West Indian informants said that this criticism was universal among the West Indian Methodists.

The question is, how far it was the religious beliefs and how far the sharing of either a class culture or specifically Methodist culture that made the two groups so acceptable to one another. Any English person who objected could easily move to another church in a way not possible for Anglicans, yet few appear to have done so. We cannot tell whether the white members find the West Indians acceptable as a matter of religious con-viction or because they conform to common cultural and class standards.

Two other English sects exist in Sparkbrook: the Seventh Day Adventists and the Jehovah's Witnesses. Both these have large West Indian congregations, over 60 per cent. and 30 per cent. respectively. In England we would regard these as fringe sects, adopting a more psycho-sociological frame of reference for explaining membership. In the West Indies, however, these sects have the status of denominations and West Indians arrive here expecting to participate in the same type of church life as they have been accustomed to at home.

Both groups assert that it is the essential rightness of their beliefs that bring black and white together. Logically this cannot be true in both cases, as the beliefs differ, though obviously a sense of the rightness of the beliefs does help to bind people together. The white members of the Adventist church told us that a number of their members had left with the influx of West Indians; they felt that this was due to colour prejudice, and that the leavers were not good Adventists.

The Adventist sect is very strictly puritanical and disciplines members who fall from the high standards required of them. The congregation is drawn from all over the south of Birmingham, this church serving the whole area. It is difficult to imagine what the original white congregation was like, but from discussion with present members it seems it was upper working-class and middle-class. This may have been a sect of the emotionally or psychologically dispossessed rather than the economically deprived. Adventists are required to keep Saturday as the Sabbath; thus there must be a strong desire on the part of English members to set themselves apart from the larger society. Such heterodox religious practices, we were told, offered no problems in the West Indies where Adventism is much more readily accepted and it is much easier to have Saturday off work.

The sect is highly organized; West Indian congregations commend emigrant members to churches here and thus the West Indians have come to predominate in the organization and the English have become a minority group. The pastor is English. We suspect that the beliefs of this sect and its predominant membership are so alien to the ordinary Englishmen that it will not attract any more English members.

We expected to find the Jehovah's Witnesses conforming to

the dispossessed type of religion. In fact, we found it to be a small group of friends (fifty adults, twelve children, including twelve West Indians and six Greek Cypriots) all known to one another. They sat at meetings doing Bible study from leaflets (with highly anti-intellectual biases), and there was little emotion or fervour. Sociologically this sect appears to be a multiracial variant of the Mission church. Again, one might look for a psycho-sociological explanation of English membership.

It seems that what has happened here is that the religious steam had been taken out of ritual occasions by the fact that the group has become a stable, friendly, little group of like-minded people. The West Indians do not disturb this as they come expecting to participate in a fairly respectable, middle-class-oriented denomination. The relative dispossession of the members did not seem very great; this sect's members may have progressed economically beyond the members' of the Mission and the Holiness churches, and this also is reflected in the sobriety of their religious ceremonies.

Evangelism was confined to distributing 'Watchtower' leaflets. The group was highly organized (under lay leadership) so that everybody had a task in the organization and seemed to receive great satisfaction from doing his task. This was borne out by listening to members of the congregation talking to one another about their tasks in a highly specialized jargon; activity within the organization for its own sake seems to produce satisfactions.

This particular sect's pastoral work for the community was nil; they were the only group we encountered who showed pure indifference to social and economic institutions.

In these data on the churches we have a body of material that raises many questions and suggests further research. Niebuhr's classification of types of religious expression and Tawney's account of responses to economic and social institutions seem to hold good, providing we add that in the present context denominations and sects can be multiracial if a cultural as well as a belief system is shared. Where there are differing cultures or expectations multiracialism may not be possible as a permanent, continuing feature of associational life. Where multiracialism is forced upon an association through its structural position and role in the community, then some tensions will result. It remains to be seen whether the shared beliefs will help the various parties to accommodate; it seems unlikely in that the least willing to accommodate will quickly move beyond the influence of (in this case) the churches' belief systems.

The churches have the following positive functions in the Sparkbrook community. First, they provide comfort and security to those of their members who are old or bewildered. Secondly, they operate as welfare and casework agencies in the interstices of the welfare state. The Pentecostal churches and other West Indian sects allow a high degree of tension release among the most deprived section of the community and give meaning to their deprivation. All the immigrant and working-class churches encourage thrift and personal virtue, thus helping to provide part of the economic and moral equipment necessary for full participation in urban life and preventing total moral or economic breakdown in the hazardous urban environment.

In a wider sense, however, the churches represent separate groupings in the community and enable them to assert their identity. This may be useful for immigrants in that it provides a firm associational base (perhaps replacing kin or friends) from which they may operate. Among non-Catholic Christian religions the divisions are essentially *class* divisions such as have always divided sects and denominations; ethnic divisions tend to coincide with this and thus accentuate, institutionalize, and sanctify the differences. Where there is a common class culture mutual acceptance and assimilation are possible.

VIII. The Politics of Sparkbrook

We have often been asked during our research what we think the final outcome for the area will be in terms of race relations, and we have sensed that what is being asked is whether there will be some kind of Notting Hill with race riots going on in the streets. The immediate prospect of this we believe to be slight. But it might still be the case that, even though there is no fighting in the streets, the race relations situation is marked by a high degree of tension. Politically formulated proposals are an index of tension which one would expect in a society with the electoral habits of parliamentary democracy. What we have to do, therefore, in this chapter is to consider the forms of political activity going on in Sparkbrook and to what ends they were directed.

Our research area covers about two-thirds of the Sparkbrook ward, which is, in turn, part of the parliamentary constituency of Sparkbrook. The parliamentary constituency covers two other wards besides Sparkbrook. Its boundaries have varied, but it has been called Sparkbrook for more than twenty-five years and it has always included the Sparkbrook ward. The parliamentary constituency was held by the Conservatives till 1945 and the ward had only once been won by Labour.

In 1945, however, the situation had changed. Middle-class voters had begun to leave and Sparkbrook moved more and more towards being a safe Labour seat. In 1945 the sitting Conservative M.P. for the constituency was Mr. L. S. Amery, Secretary of State for India. He was defeated by the Labour dentist, Dr. Percy Shurmer, who held the seat until 1959. On his death just before the General Election he was succeeded as candidate by Mr. Jack Webster who lost the seat to the Conservative, Mr. Seymour, by 800 votes. Mr. Seymour, however, sat through only one parliamentary session and was then defeated during the period of our research by the Labour candidate, Mr. Roy Hattersley, who won the seat by 1,100 votes.

Before we turn to a more detailed analysis of the 1964 parliamentary election and to the local Council elections which preceded it, it is worth noting what happened and did not happen in the election of 1945, for this points a significant contrast to the present situation. In that election the Conservative Member of Parliament was a Minister with special responsibility for India and he had been in office during the disastrous Bengal famine. He was the target of attack by those sympathetic to the cause of Indian independence and in Birmingham this cause was led by an Indian doctor, Dr. Dhanie Prem. Dr. Prem considered organizing opposition to Mr. Amery, but decided eventually to support the Labour Party. The Communist Party, however, chose to focus attention on the Indian issue by putting up Mr. R. Palme Dutt, the distinguished half-Indian member of its National Executive.

The importance of this, however, is not that the people of Sparkbrook responded to the issue as one of immediate importance to themselves. It is that the discussion of the Indian issue remained a relatively academic political exercise or, at most, a small part of much larger discussions about post-war reconstruction. The poverty of Bengal was not a local issue for the people of Sparkbrook, because there were as yet no Bengali peasants living among them. Moreover, colour meant so little in Birmingham politics that Dr. Prem was shortly afterwards adopted as a Labour candidate for the Council and was elected without special comment as Councillor for Great Barr ward.

It is hardly possible to imagine this detachment from the questions of colonial politics today. Dr. Prem himself has found that not only will the Labour Party not consider running coloured candidates, but that it is extremely reluctant to take active steps to win an immigrant vote. And it is scarcely possible that the problems of India, Pakistan or the West Indies could be discussed in Sparkbrook without their being given local meaning in terms of the problems presented by immigration from these territories.

This is not to say that immigration questions alone decide elections in Sparkbrook. However important they may be, there are other questions which have produced the formal political alignments and machinery of the area, and our problem is to show the way in which these alignments relate to the new problems presented by immigrants. We do not believe that a poll showing, say, that housing was a more important issue than immigration can be taken to mean very much in itself. We can only hope to interpret such findings when we have understood the way in which political discussion is organized in Sparkbrook. What we can do immediately, however, is to note that racial and colonial issues once had little significance for the people of the area. Today they are undoubtedly more important.

The basic political alternatives open to the people of Sparkbrook in the twenty years since 1945 have been to vote Labour or to vote Conservative. With few exceptions, in Sparkbrook they have chosen to vote Labour. What does this mean in terms of the sociology of the local community?

In 1945, of course, the argument was about the welfare state. By that time the overwhelming majority of the residents were manual workers. As such they had had experience of unemployment and voted for the policies of full employment and social security on which Labour fought the General Election. The Conservatives could not have hoped to win this vote as the party of government in the 1930s. It was also the case that a Labour Government devoted to reconstruction seemed more likely to produce a housing programme which would benefit the lower-paid worker who could not afford the deposit to obtain a mortgage.

These national policies had immediate meaning in terms of the large industrial city. As the central areas aged and deteriorated, more and more people, manual and white-collar workers alike, wished to move to better housing in the suburbs. Those who had some hope of buying their own houses were likely to be relatively satisfied with a party which emphasized the idea of a property-owning democracy. But those who had no hope of owning property themselves would look to the party which was prepared to divert the greatest part of available building resources to building subsidized publicly owned rented houses. One party favoured those who saw themselves as being able to find security in private-property-ownership, the other those who found security in the idea of mutual aid and co-operative political action. This need hardly surprise us in view of what we have said about the city in an earlier chapter. But we should note here that this is what the conflict between private enterprise and socialism means to the residents of central areas in the city. What we wish to show, however, is that as time went on it became apparent that neither private enterprise nor local socialism could meet all housing needs, and that the people of Sparkbrook were almost by definition those whom both systems had failed.

From this analysis it follows that there would for local purposes be three classes of people in Sparkbrook; namely, those who had some hope of escape through the accumulation of sufficient money to buy a house, those who had some hope of qualifying for a council house, and those who had neither. But we should wish also to include two other sub-classes; namely, those who were tenants of, or could only aspire to being tenants of, council slum property, and those who had tenancies of privately owned houses or who themselves owned non-slum property in the area. Had there been no political machinery in existence, these groups might each have run their own candidates for the Council and have produced five local political parties. As it was, however, the national political parties were contesting the elections and because of the start which they had in electoral organization the local 'housing classes' had to influence them as best they could.

Seen from national and city offices of the political parties these residents of the deteriorating areas might have appeared as something of an embarrassment. Their candidates had to get support for national and city-wide policies and could only to a limited extent give special consideration to areas whose voters formed a minority of the total. Thus the Labour Party would find itself bound to help established Council tenants and the Conservative Party the owner-occupiers of the commuter areas. Yet they had also to find an electoral organization in Sparkbrook and this depended upon some relationship being established between the aims of the party and those of what became its local cells. This can be seen in both cases.

The local Conservative organization was strongest in the Barber Trust area of Sparkbrook (our Sparkbrook 3) where tenants were particularly anxious about the deterioration of the area as a whole and about the possibility that some of the houses in their own streets might become lodging-houses. To them this was an overriding interest. Rightly or wrongly they say the best hope of preserving their area lies in keeping out coloured people and also, if possible, large Irish families. They therefore had a strong interest in immigration control.

The national and city organizations of the Conservative Party, however, were not immediately responsive to this demand. For purely electoral reasons they were bound to pay more attention to the needs of people in the commuter areas of the city and in the party's rural strongholds. Moreover, they were aware that there was an actual shortage of labour in Birmingham to which immigration provided the most obvious and immediate answer. There was thus bound to be some tension between the local ward leaders on the one hand and the city and national parties on the other.

As far as the local Labour Party was concerned, the main problem lay in accelerating the public housing programme and in the application of the strongest possible measures to stop the deterioration of the area. It was likely to be an organization of working-class people concerned to improve the share of the total public provision falling to the people of Sparkbrook. This did not necessarily fit in with the party's commitment to universalistic standards, which prevented its giving special consideration to particular areas and, if there was a demand for discrimination against immigrants, this would conflict with the liberal racial policies to which the party was historically committed.

These conflicts, then, between national and local organizations seemed to be built into the political system of Sparkbrook. We shall have to see how far they actually showed themselves during the Council and parliamentary elections. Before we do this, however, we must describe the local organizations as we saw them. We begin with the Labour Party, if only because it was the dominant organization in the ward and had all three Council seats.

The centre of Labour activity was the Sparkbrook Labour Club, built, behind the house which served as the Party head-quarters, by the voluntary labour of its members. Here were to be found the key members of the Party organization and here were expressed most strongly the social and political sentiments of the members. To have the support of the club members might not by itself be sufficient to win the ward for Labour, but it was an important asset and no candidate could afford to ignore it.

The main impressions which we had of the club members were that they were predominantly Irish, that they were middle-aged and that they were poor, though not the poorest, members of the community. We also felt very strongly the spirit of *cameraderie* and mutual aid which existed amongst the members. To be a member of the club was not only to have a place to go to at nights. It meant not being isolated and having friends one could trust and turn to in time of trouble.

The impression of Irishness was overwhelming. The list of club members was mostly Irish. The songs that were sung were Irish. The jokes and the names given to numbers in the Bingo sessions had an Irish reference. Although the club did include some pure 'Brummies', they seemed to stand out as foreigners.

On reflection we did not find this surprising. The Irish mmigrants to Sparkbrook, as we have seen, could fairly readily be absorbed into the working-class. As the last-comers amongst the working-class they were bound to be in evidence in Spark-brook, and since few of them had puritanical aspirations to property-ownership, the Labour Party and its policies presented the main hope. Of course, this is not to say that all the Irish were here. Those who identified with the Labour Party were a minority who had become assimilated to the class and political system of English society. But they were there in sufficient numbers to impose their character on the club. 53 per cent. of eligible Irish immigrants in our sample were registered as voters, compared with 89 per cent. of the English sample.

Secondly, as we have seen, those who attended the club were mostly married and middle-aged. Occasionally, they ventured into 'pop-songs', but they were the pop-songs of ten or fifteen years ago and the company was always more at home with sentimental ballads than it was with the violent rhythms of the world of the 'pops'. When one leading member of the club recalled his own best performance we were not surprised to hear that it was a parody of 'Underneath the Arches'. Flanagan and Allan help us to date the spirit and sentiments of the Labour Club.

Thirdly, we were surprised to find how vigorous were the sentiments expressed about the importance of mutual aid. Bingo and other forms of gambling themselves express this sentiment, for if nobody has enough, it is good to think that by giving one's stake to the winner, one ensures that one person at least has an unexpected windfall. But there was also help for old people in the form of outings and, when someone failed to collect his prize, it was put in the benevolent fund; as one of the committee put it, without any sense of being old-fashioned, 'to help people who had fallen on hard times'.

These sentiments, however, are old-fashioned in an affluent society. Working men's clubs as a rule have to adapt their cloth-cap image in order to survive. What we saw here was the working men's club atmosphere of the 1930s, something which only exists today amongst those who are at the tail-end of the queue for affluence and welfare. Yet this in itself is something. For the club was providing social and moral support of some kind to those who joined it. Their morale was high. One has also to note, however, that there were others further back in the queue who did not belong even to this system of mutual aid.

These others included many who did not fit easily into the neighbourly network, the newer arrivals with the foreign English accents of the North, many of the Irish who found themselves more at home in the ordinary pubs, all of the lost and isolated people and, above all, the coloured immigrants. This was an issue of which we were continually aware in the club. There was no formal colour bar. But the only coloured man we ever saw was one of our own assistants from British Honduras, who was admitted after being turned away on a previous night on the ground that the club was too full for the admission of non-members.

We were interested to notice the reaction of our friends amongst the club's leaders to our concern with race relations. Once we were told 'We had a coloured pianist the Saturday before last', and once when we started to discuss our Pakistani friends with a Councillor he immediately came out with the

defensive response, 'We had a Yugoslav here last Tuesday.'
This kind of liberal internationalism is familiar to students of
the American Deep South. Finding it in so pure and naïve a
form in Birmingham served only to remind us how aware
people were of the racial problem and how guilty they were
about their failure to look it in the face.

The club embodied the class sentiments of mutual aid, and
most members would have regarded themselves as socialists.
But the club was none the less not particularly political in
character, at least not in the sense that it was single-mindedly
devoting itself to seeking electoral support for political policies.
The effect of membership was, as much as anything, cathartic.
To have the support of the club made it more possible to live
in the society as it was.

This affected the selection of Councillors. In 1962 the sitting
Councillor retired. The man chosen as her replacement was
one of what sociologists would call the 'sociometric stars' of
the club, that is, the man who would be most chosen as a
friend. If he made only one speech in the Council in two years,
and that to defend the Irish of Sparkbrook against generalized
attacks in connexion with the tinker problem, this in no way
undermined confidence in him. The important thing was that
the man who represented you was a man you could trust, one
of your own kind. As an Irish immigrant who had been through
the mill and now had a good home in Hall Green yet came
back to the Club two or three times a week, he was a man to
be trusted.

Another vacancy occurred in 1965 on the death of the
Councillor who was the least active of the three in club attendance. At the selection conference the candidate who received
the second largest vote put forward a specifically anti-
immigrant programme. He was rejected but claimed that this
was because he had in the past been a Communist. There
may have been some truth in this. The Party members had no
taste for extreme politics of the right or the left. They wanted
someone who would be a good representative.

The other Councillor was the most senior and the most able.
Although himself a Yorkshireman from Doncaster, he had been
for many years in Birmingham and was reckoned an honorary
Irishman. He called himself a left-winger and identified him-

self with the anti-Gaitskell movement in the party. But his main activities were local and he did not talk to his fellow club members in the strange language of left-wing political commitment. He served for a period as Chairman of the Corporation Housing Management Committee and rebelled against the Labour Group's policy of abolishing housing subsidies. This was a gesture of principle and led to the loss of his chairmanship. But he did not seek to carry his local party with him on an issue which was remote from them and in support of a stand which was more in the interests of established council tenants than their own.

This Councillor was an interesting type in terms of the sociology of politics, for he stood somewhere between being a purely local man and being a politician in national terms. He was, in fact, eventually chosen as the parliamentary candidate in 1959 but lost the election. Re-nominated in 1964, he had strong support in his own ward but lost to a more articulate and better-educated young Councillor from Sheffield. Had he been nominated, it is possible that a very different campaign would have been fought. It might not have been as efficiently organized on the formal level and Labour might have failed to gain the seat but the candidate would have spoken with the authentic voice of the working class of Sparkbrook.

The year-by-year Conservative organization in Sparkbrook has nothing like this coherence, partly because the chances of a Conservative victory in Sparkbrook ward are slim. But there is none the less a core of constituency Party workers who have their own distinctive set of attitudes, which are as clear as those of members of the Labour Club.

What surprised us most about the Conservative Party workers were their working-class Birmingham accents. We did not meet Irishmen in their committee rooms, but they were certainly not simply a white-collar group. What distinguished them most was the part of Sparkbrook from which they came. They were, in fact, drawn almost entirely from the Barber Trust area and from the southern boundary of the constituency.

The sentiments which these Conservatives expressed were mostly about their contempt for the idlers whom they saw as being cushioned and protected by the welfare state. They were passionately concerned with respectability and with the defence

of their area and their property, for which they felt the local
Labour Council had very little concern. Above all, they felt
that too little was being done about immigration and blamed
the Labour Party for its evil consequences, even though the
local immigration had occurred entirely during a period of
Conservative rule. The Labour Party was seen as 'soft on
immigration' and it was believed that a Labour Government
would flood the country with thousands more immigrants.
Particular sources of resentment lay in what they saw as the
immigrants' misuse of housing and their ability to draw social
benefits. They favoured stronger health checks, the refusal of
admission to those who had no jobs to come to and the deportation of the criminal and unemployed.

In local elections the Conservative candidate was a housewife
with a Birmingham accent. For Parliament in 1959 they had
supported a local boy made good who, although he lived in
Sutton Coldfield, was thought to have a deep and immediate
understanding of their problems. They saw themselves as better
served in Parliament than the neighbouring Hall Green constituency whose Member of Parliament, Mr. Aubrey Jones,
was accused of not visiting the constituency enough, of being
more concerned with great national issues than with the
problems of his constituents, and of talking over their heads at
meetings.

It so happens that Mr. Aubrey Jones was a deviant in his
party, having his own views on matters of defence, the economy
and race relations. But the same issue would occur with any
Member of Parliament who had not deeply assimilated the
feelings of his constituents. The most illiberal Conservative
would not have been acceptable unless he maintained the
common touch. The common touch, moreover, would certainly
imply an anti-immigrant position even though there might be
some reservation about an overt racialist. In fact, the best hope
of getting liberal-minded Tory Members of Parliament on the
racial question from such areas as this would appear to lie in
the success of carpetbaggers at selection conferences, since the
politician would be rare who gave effective expression to the
sentiments of these constituents and did not include a strong
anti-immigrant plank in his platform.

We found that these tensions were actually reflected in the

committee rooms during election. The ladies who worked for Mr. Seymour had little enthusiasm for their party leader, Sir Alec Douglas-Home. Nor did they particularly enjoy co-operating with the Young Conservatives from Edgbaston who descended on them at election time. On the other hand these imported election workers were openly critical of Mr. Seymour.

We have not discussed the Liberal Party organization at any length, partly because Liberalism is a small force in Sparkbrook, its vote being 673, 444 and 502 in 1963, 1964 and 1965 respectively. But there was usually a Liberal candidate in the local Council election and we did seek to find out whether he represented any special interest. Certainly, we did not find that there were sentiments amongst Sparkbrook's Liberals more favourable to immigrants than those of the Labour and Conservative workers. What we did find was something very like the Conservative Party atmosphere. We need hardly have been surprised, however, for traditional Liberalism in urban areas draws its support precisely from the kind of people we have been describing, 'the better class of artisan', the clerk and the shopkeeper. Such people have so strong a hold on the Conservative organization that they do not need a special organization of their own.

It should not be thought that all the people of Sparkbrook identified themselves with either the Labour or the Conservative ideology. Far from it. In fact we formed the impression that the central identification of many middle-aged men especially was with two great socio-political myths, that of two World Wars and that of the Depression. This produced some strangely confused attitudes as the following research notes indicate:

Conversation between one of the authors and a group of workers (all in their sixties) in The Marlborough

'Britain should have been prepared for the last war. We were only armed with sticks in the L.D.V., but the government was not willing to spend the money.'
R.M.: 'They spend enough now.'
'Got to. Got to be prepared. All these coloured people, the way they breed, the West must stand firm against them—especially Chinese. Indians have got home rule and now they're not much better off than before—worse in fact.'

R.M.: 'If we spend money on them rather than bombs, we wouldn't have to worry.'

'That's right.'

'We kept them poor.'

'The British are the greediest bloody nation on God's earth. Always those in the know who get the most out of it. Kings and Jews, not the workers.'

'But different races and different creeds will never live together. I've got nothing against them. It's not a colour bar, some real gentlemen amongst them. I admire those who come over here to work, but not those that come here and get £5 for nothing. And they live in appalling conditions, crowded and dirty.'

R.M.: 'But so do some of the British working class.'

'Yes, in the old days. What I can't stand are all those profiteers and land-grabbers. It's always the rich that get the most. I'd nationalize everything, then we'd get fair shares for all. Mind you, I wouldn't take anything from someone who'd made a few thousand pounds by his own initiative and enterprise, that's a Communist way of thinking. Mind you, I blame the Labour Government, setting up the welfare state and giving something for nothing.

From attitudes such as these, the political life of Sparkbrook emerges.

Before we turn to a discussion of the General Election, it should be noted that there were three other candidates in Sparkbrook in the Council election of 1963, a Mosleyite, a Communist and a Pakistani standing as an Independent. None of these received 500 votes but they do represent other political possibilities and deserve some special consideration.

It is hard at first to see why an independent racialist candidate should not be successful in Sparkbrook. The relatively high poll attained by such a candidate in Moss Side, Manchester, had been one of the turning points in the debate over immigration control and one would have expected the Union Movement or some other organization to use the racial issue to bring off a similar political victory in Birmingham. The ground seemed to be prepared in Sparkbrook, where the slogan 'House Britons not Blacks' adorns several walls and leaflets in similar vein have been delivered to voters. None the less, the Mosleyite candidate mustered only 68 votes and though this was more than the 50 gained by the Communist candidate, it was far behind the 430 cast for a Pakistani and there has been no attempt to renew the contest.

This should not in our opinion be taken to mean a total rejection of racialist politics by the voters of Sparkbrook, for two reasons. One is that fascism has too many connexions with Nazism and 'foreigners' to be acceptable to the respectable 'Brummy'. The other is that if one wants to press for anti-immigrant and anti-coloured policies there is sufficient hope of success in the Conservative Party and even the Labour Party of getting these policies adopted and an outside organization is unnecessary. In fact, a larger Mosleyite vote might be simply a sign that racialist sentiment was being siphoned out of the other parties and that there was less rather than more institutionalized racialism.

At the opposite end of the local political spectrum is the demand that immigrants should receive better rather than harsher treatment and there have been attempts made in Birmingham to ensure that the immigrant voice is heard politically. Dr. Dhanie Prem, whom we have already mentioned, was concerned to do this early in 1964. Having urged the Labour Party in Balsall Heath to organize the immigrant vote, and having been told that this would damage the Party's chance with the white voter, he threatened to run immigrant candidates in the General Election unless he got assurances from the political parties. He received these assurances from the Labour and Liberal Parties, though not the Conservative Party, and duly withdrew his threat.

Dr. Prem, however, was himself an ex-Labour Councillor and spoke only from the experience of an early professionally qualified immigrant. More significant was the campaign conducted in Sparkbrook by the Pakistani candidate, Mr. Dalal. Mr. Dalal was a young businessman running an estate agency, a textile firm, a finance company and an import-export business. He and his friends had sought the adoption of a coloured candidate by the major political parties, and when they failed in this decided to put forward Mr. Dalal himself.

Mr. Dalal told us that he was a socialist and that his interest in politics had started when he was gaoled by the British for pro-Jinnah activities while at university. His programme, however, had not been in any sense socialist in character. He appealed to coloured immigrants to support him simply on the ground that it would be better to have their own representative and told us that he also sought support from the Irish on the ground that an English-speaking Pakistani could act as a mediator in a difficult racial situation. More specifically he appealed to the Pakistanis on grounds of the need to foster Muslim education in the schools. Curiously, he had not attempted to canvass the West Indians.

Having achieved the modest success of attaining 430 votes in the election of 1963, Dalal decided not to stand in 1964 because, he said, he did not want to embarrass the Labour Party in the election year. It may be that his reluctance was also due to the fact that some of his original sponsors were no longer willing to support him. But he had shown that there were 400 immigrant votes to be sought by the parties and this was of some political importance in a marginal constituency.

Mr. Dalal's candidacy, together with those of two candidates in Bradford, aroused the concern of a socialist Pakistani group in London, who believed that immigrants should identify with the Labour Party as the party of the working class. A member of this group visited Mr. Dalal to dissuade him from standing. He himself had practised what he preached by canvassing on behalf of the Labour candidate in North Kensington despite his anti-immigrant speeches and thought that other politically conscious Pakistanis should do the same. His visit and his failure to achieve its objective serve to symbolize the dilemma in which the immigrants are placed politically.

The Communist vote of only fifty showed that there was little hope of attracting the working class to a left-wing alternative outside the Labour Party. This may seem surprising at first in view of the Communist Party's campaign which was directed at the failure of the Labour Council to solve Birmingham's housing problem. But the strong Irish Roman Catholic vote is unlikely to be won for Communism and the hard political line of the Communists probably has little appeal in the warm and sentimental atmosphere of the Labour Club.

The 1959 election and subsequent Council elections had passed quietly without any concentration on the racial issue. The actual results in the 1963 and 1964 elections were as follows:

TABLE 51: RESULTS OF COUNCIL ELECTIONS,
1963 AND 1964

1963		1964	
J. I. Webster (Lab.)	3,610	W. H. Wiggins (Lab.)	3,000
Mrs. I. E. Winters (Con.)	1,160	Mrs. I. E. Winters (Con.)	1,392
G. C. Strachan (Lib.)	673	H. White (Lib.)	444
A. A. Dalal (Ind.)	430		
H. L. Edwards			
(Union Movement)	68		
J. Reynolds (Comm.)	50		
Majority 2,504		*Majority* 1,608	

But the success of Mr. Peter Griffiths in Smethwick in capturing control of the Smethwick Council for the Conservatives on the basis of a sustained anti-immigrant programme, and his candidacy for Parliament, raised the possibility that the 1964 election could be fought on the immigration issue, if not simply on race. In the six months before the election the parties moved slowly towards deciding whether or not immigration should be an issue. In fact, the Labour Party eventually avoided it entirely, but the Conservatives, through a series of uncertain statements about whether it should be an issue or not, ensured that it was.

We had expected that the Conservatives would be divided, for the reasons outlined above. Many of them would undoubtedly have preferred not to discuss immigration but the pressure from the constituencies had been mounting since the campaign for immigration control had been launched, and some of them at least felt that they should give expression to the party workers' feeling. Eventually a statement was issued by a meeting of all the Birmingham Members of Parliament with the exception of Sir Edward Boyle, the Member for Handsworth and Mr. Aubrey Jones. The meeting was presided over by Mr. Geoffrey Lloyd, Member for Sutton Coldfield.

The statement said that the group were of the opinion that problems arising from immigration and the threat of more nationalization were two points of major importance in Birmingham. It was felt that Harlem must be taken as an advance warning. The statement continued:

The frictions engendered by overcrowded housing, unequal opportunities, and job discrimination, must be sought and rooted out
wherever they may be found. Better, they must be avoided by
forethought.

The good relations which the inhabitants of Britain enjoy, whatever their country of origin, must not blind us to the frictions to be
avoided when different cultures live side by side, or excuse us if we
are not alert to solve them before they harden into ingrained
prejudice.

The size of the problem avoided by the timely passing of the
Immigration Act in 1962 is shown by the fact that at 26 June there
were 315,000 outstanding applications for work vouchers by intending immigrants. Had it not been for the Act, this flood would have
been channelled to a few great cities such as Birmingham, which
though doing what they can to ease the absorption of welcome and
necessary labour reinforcements, cannot but be aware of the in-
separable frictions.[1]

This was hailed in the *Birmingham Planet* in a centrepiece
article under the title 'Common-Sense About Immigrants'. The
author, Mr. Norman Tiptaft, wrote, 'Most people with votes
in Birmingham will rejoice that at long last five Conservative
Members are not only aware of the views of the majority of
Birmingham people on immigration (which the National Conservative Party had ignored for years) they are also trying to
do something about it.'[2]

But the statement's appearance had a double significance.
First, the fact that it was issued represented a clear concession
to party opinion, and meant that the issue was publicly raised
and that people were being invited to vote Conservative if they
were anti-immigrant. But it also sharply drew attention to the
divisons within the party. Not only did two of Birmingham's
most distinguished Tories not sign the statement and four
candidates in Labour seats dissociate themselves from it, but
the very signatories began to disown it or write their personal
glosses upon it. Mr. John Hollingworth in All Saints said that
he would not fight on immigration and insisted that there was
not another secret line being put on the doorstep. Mr. Leslie
Seymour in Sparkbrook said he was in favour of a cessation of
all immigration for a time but told us that this was an expression

[1] *Birmingham Post*, 24 July 1964.   [2] *Birmingham Planet*, 13 August 1964.

of personal opinion and that his actual platform would be fixed by his Constituency Management Committee.

Mr. Seymour had, in fact, already clearly committed himself by his strong advocacy of immigration control before the Act was passed. This had been his response to pressure from the Sparkbrook Association to take action over housing in 1961 and he was sufficiently proud of his work in this direction to quote it in the Press as his main achievement. But after he had met his management committee he began to talk in somewhat different terms, insisting that some immigrants merited consideration. As he said in the Sparkbrook Association's newsletter before the election:

The immigrants that came in the early days were able to settle into society, and have made major contributions to the work of Birmingham including hospitals, transport, gas and electricity undertakings. Their houses are clean and tidy, their children well-dressed, and they made regular attendances at church.

And after this he made very little use of the immigrant issues even if he did not exercise quite the studied care not to which had characterized the election manifesto of Mr. L. Blumenthal, the Conservative candidate in neighbouring Sparkhill in the local elections. Mr. Blumenthal had written:

During my service on the Council I have been determined that Sparkhill must be protected from the deterioration that has occurred in the neighbouring Sparkbrook ward, that our streets must be kept clean and salvage removed quickly and efficiently. I have been active to see that houses let as lodgings must be maintained at a decent standard, so that those who live in them, and just as important, those who live near them are not deprived of decent living standards. . . .

This remarkably precise statement about Sparkbrook's problems clearly avoids what must have been a strong temptation to discuss the issue in racial terms. It is worth mentioning that Mr. Blumenthal lost his seat.

Mr. Seymour does mention immigration in his manifesto, saying: 'Personally, I would ban all immigration, both white and coloured, until such time as families now living here are properly housed', but this comes under the heading 'Housing', there being no separate paragraph in the manifesto on 'Immigration'.

The striking thing about the Conservative campaign as a whole was that the party did not, as once seemed likely, make immigration the central issue in all constituencies in Birmingham. The uncertainty of the August statement, due to the fact that it was not supported by all candidates, and the playing down of the issue by most candidates in their manifestoes do suggest that there were conflicting pressures within the party and this uncertainty was perhaps particularly acute in Sparkbrook where Mr. Seymour shared an agent with his neighbour, Mr. Aubrey Jones.

There were, however, some constituencies in which the issue was not played down. In Yardley Mr. Leonard Cleaver spoke of the influx which could not be checked due to the fact that 'immigrants could bring their wives and children over', and in the Labour-held seat at Perry Barr a leaflet on immigration on the eve of the poll may have won the seat for the Tories. In Sparkbrook a leading Young Conservative told us that the Perry Barr leaflet had been offered to Sparkbrook, but the local association had refused the offer. Perry Barr was a Tory gain, Sparkbrook a Tory loss.

It should be noted that the actual campaigns as they were conducted were not the only factors affecting the voters. The Press had no doubt that immigration was an issue. Neither did the producers of television programmes, and this, coupled with the early Tory statement, must have led many voters to believe that there was a threat from immigration and that some Tories at least were prepared to face up to it. But it was not true, as was sometimes said, that the Conservatives talked liberalism in public and racialism on the doorstep. In most constituencies the doorstep campaign was not directed to immigration. It was the public position of the party which put the issue near the centre of the campaign.

This might appear to contradict what we have said earlier about the conflict within the Conservative organization between a grass-roots anti-immigration movement and 'carpet-bagging' candidates who did not regard the issue as important. What had happened, however, is that the grass-roots pressure in Birmingham had had some effect on the parliamentary party and produced an early anti-immigrant statement from which some candidates tried later to withdraw. In our opinion, the August statement represented the view of most of the constituency party workers. Once it was made it mattered less what their candidates said in their manifestoes.

In the Sparkbrook Labour Party the most significant feature of the election campaign was the by-passing of the local organization based upon the Labour Club. An official of the Birmingham office moved in and established himself as agent and, though he did win the co-operation of the stalwarts of the club, he did not rely on them. The campaign was a national one directed to getting out as many voters as possible and having little regard to specifically local issues or to the informal networks which the experienced would have said were essential to ensure a Labour victory.

Mr. Roy Hattersley, the Labour candidate, coming from Sheffield, won the support of the party by saying that he would live in his constituency but his own interests went far beyond Sparkbrook. He wrote in his manifesto on Housing, Pensions, Health, Prices and Wages, and Schools, and when selected to speak at Mr. Wilson's big meeting in the Rag Market directed himself to the general problems of the economy.

Mr. Hattersley made no mention of immigration in his manifesto, and answered questions on the topic with some reluctance, saying that the present Immigration Act was discriminatory and that Labour would put it on a 'stronger moral basis' by seeking the co-operation of Commonwealth countries. But his main concern and that of his agents with regard to the immigrants was to get their vote out. They established contacts with a few Pakistanis and a few West Indians, who then proceeded to canvass independently. The principal Pakistani involved was the secretary of the Commonwealth Property-Owners' Association. He identified about 800 Pakistani and Indian names and claimed that some 600 voted. The West Indians apparently did less and were less successful.

Our own estimate, based upon a count of immigrant voters at the main polling station in the lodging-house area, was that not more than 500 coloured immigrants could have voted in the whole constituency. But nearly all of these were likely to have voted Labour mainly because of what they regarded as

Labour's good anti-colonial record. Thus, without making any special appeal to coloured immigrants, Labour received a small but perhaps significant bonus of coloured immigrant votes.

In all, there was a swing of 3·6 per cent. to Labour in Sparkbrook as compared with a national swing of 3·2 per cent. and an average swing in Birmingham of 2·5 per cent. Many variables may have affected these figures and they are difficult to interpret. The immigration issue had certainly turned the scales in Smethwick and probably had a good deal to do with the swing in Perry Barr. In Sparkbrook the result might perhaps have been affected to a greater degree than elsewhere by the relative efficiency of the Labour candidate and his organization. But it may also have been the consequence of the deliberate playing down of the immigration issue.

There were, no doubt, a variety of reasons for this, including an unwillingness of many Conservatives to associate themselves with policies which smacked of racialism. But perhaps a major problem for them was that they were defending their own record. A campaign for more immigration control would have been rather curious, since they had already had the opportunity to introduce as much control as they wished. The most that they could do was to attack the Labour Party over its opposition to the Commonwealth Immigrants Bill.

Speaking in sociological terms, what we have seen since the General Election of 1964 is an adjustment of national political conflicts to take account of conflicts existing at grass-roots level. We have shown in this chapter that these conflicts were not yet completely geared in with one another at the beginning of 1964 and that this prevented the use of political sanctions by one group against the other. But the 'contrary swing' in the Midlands has now projected the local conflicts into the national arena and it now seems possible for the first time that they will be played out in political terms.

The debate may still centre on immigration control. But, following the White Paper, coloured immigration may soon become a negligible trickle. The effect of continued debate about control in these circumstances can only be the dissemination of a belief that the immigrants are to blame for all social problems. Once the flow of new immigrants stops, hostility will be transferred to those who are already here. The demand for their segregation might then become explicit. It is in this way rather than through race riots that racial divisions may be widened in Birmingham.

We do not think that this process is completely inevitable. But if it is to be arrested there must be policies adopted which manifestly and clearly offer solutions to the problems of the people of the deteriorating areas in non-racial terms. We think that there is little sign as yet of such problems being pursued and we shall devote our penultimate chapter to suggesting what they are. Meanwhile, noting events rather than recommending alternatives, we see a widening rift opening up between the successful and the beneficiaries of the welfare state and affluence on the one hand and the immigrant standings at the back of the affluence and welfare queues on the other.

To complete the electoral story of Sparkbrook to date, we add the result of the 1965 local election, when there were two vacancies due to the death of Councillor Wiggins. It was as follows:

B. Downey (Lab.)	2,027
A. R. Harvey (Lab.)	1,989
I. Jones (Cons.)	1,870
Mrs. I. E. Winters (Cons.)	1,824
H. White (Lib.)	502

These results do show a dramatic swing to the Conservatives, but one which was nation-wide. It should be noted, moreover, that Mr. Jones was a known liberal on racial questions and an active member of the Sparkbrook Association.

What was perhaps more significant was the dramatic change which occurred in the views of the new Labour Member. Mr. Hattersley made a 'liberal' maiden speech on race relations, but nine months later was willing to defend the Government's policy of strict immigration control,[1] on the grounds that Britain's social services were overstretched. He also argued that race relations would be improved if English families living in crowded conditions were rehoused with as few obstacles and as little competition as possible. We shall discuss the validity of these points in Chapter XI. Here we merely note that Sparkbrook's Labour Member had quickly been forced into an anti-immigrant posture even though he claimed that his proposals were for the ultimate good of the immigrant.

[1] *Spectator*, 20 August 1965.

IX. The Host Community and the Sparkbrook Association

The central problem of race relations in Birmingham in the early 1960s lay not simply in the fact of segregation and discrimination and the consequent concentration of coloured immigrants in certain types of housing. It lay in the reaction of their white neighbours to their presence in that condition. It is this stage of the cumulative cycle of race relations which constitutes the most significant social problem and since we feel that there has been a tendency to ignore this white reaction or write it off as 'mere prejudice' we have decided to give it a central place in our own study.

We have, of course, already considered the white reaction in part in our discussion of political parties and churches. But we have shown that those reactions were to a considerable extent influenced by the history and the other purposes of political and religious organizations. We now have to look at the Englishman's reaction to the presence of immigrants not as a member of a class, a party, or a religious sect, but as someone who identifies himself with a residential community. Here, too, organizational forms affect his reactions and we shall be concerned especially with one such organizational form, namely, that exemplified by the Sparkbrook Association; but we believe, none the less, that in the case of this kind of grouping, the presence of immigrants in certain conditions shapes attitudes far more directly than it does in the case of other groups.

It may be said at the outset that identification with the old community of Sparkbrook is identification with a myth. Relatively few people whom we met actually knew the Sparkbrook with which they identify. But this myth is itself a social fact and one which many people live by. It is the myth of Sparkbrook as it used to be, the best of its history telescoped by memory and including a high-status lord of the manor with

carriages outside his gate, gracious avenues occupied by respectable middle-class professional people and neat terraces and
courts of working-class cottages where, if people lived in
poverty, they lived also with a certain dignity. When houses
for 'the better class of artisan' were attached to the south-east
corner of Sparkbrook this was natural, according to the myth,
since such proud and respectable people could easily be made
to fit into a community as well-balanced and integrated and
as well-led as Sparkbrook.

This picture came through very strongly in our interviews
with the true old Sparkbrookians we did find. Thus Mr. S.
living in Sparkbrook 2 (that is, the slum area) told us that 'the
rot started in 1945 with middle-class people moving out of
Grantham Road and Farm Road [Sparkbrook 1]. In those
days the Councillors and M.P. lived in the area. Now none of
them do'; and Mrs. M. recalled that in her early days in
Sparkbrook 2:

You knew you had neighbours. There were coach parties for the
children every year. The old people stuck together and the whole
street was a club. The children used to band together for tracking in
the streets. They used to go on trips out and attended the church
Youth Club. Now all they're concerned with is what they can
smash up.

According to Miss H., who again lived in one of the slum
streets of Sparkbrook 2, even the smaller houses had a middle-
class population. 'This street', she said, 'had a lot of well-to-do
people. Solicitors, a police inspector, headmistresses, and the
Town Clerk lived in Claremont Road [in Sparkbrook 1]. Of
course, they were working class people, but there was no lower
working class—they were found in the slums nearer the centre.
You had to go quite a long way from Sparkbrook to find a
slum.'

Against this background these residents and others who
identified with the myth of the golden past which they created
saw a steady, disastrous and demoralizing process of degenera-
tion going on. They did not always blame the coloured people
for this. The vandalism of the young was often mentioned.
The Irish were quite often blamed. There was resentment
against those who had left and abandoned them to their fate.

And there was a widespread feeling that the Council no longer cared what happened in Sparkbrook.

Of course, the coloured immigrants were mentioned. But there were some inhibitions about expressing sentiment against coloured people as such and condemnation was often coupled with reference to cases of nice, respectable coloured families. It will be remembered that, in answer to our open-ended question 'What are the main problems of Sparkbrook today?', there were few who responded in purely racialist terms. Only 8·9 per cent. of our sample of 192 English people claimed that there were social groups who constituted a social problem by their mere existence, and another 26·9 per cent. saw certain groups as responsible for certain kinds of problem. 25·9 per cent. identified social problems without attributing them to groups and 30·1 per cent. identified problems which were associated especially with particular groups.[1] In other words, there were far more people giving priority to problems in their answers than there were giving priority to race.

These findings seem to us to be of some significance. Had we merely applied some psychological test of prejudice our results might well have been misleading. What we see here is not simply blind prejudice but the existence of beliefs about coloured people in quite specific action-contexts. In order to understand the 'prejudicial behaviour' of the English it is necessary to understand these action-contexts.

68 out of 102 of those who gave priority to problems over special groups referred to a decline in the physical environment. 30 out of 68 who gave priority to groups mentioned 'coloured' and 14 mentioned immigrants, 5 mentioned the Irish, 8 the tinkers, 3 the Pakistanis, and 2 'the Jamaicans'. Thus it seems that although groups were blamed in a minority of cases, where they were they were blamed as 'coloured' rather than specifically as Pakistanis or West Indians.

The people of Sparkbrook then were conscious of a physical decline in the area and as might be expected they wanted to do something about it. What they did is set out in the narrative account which follows. Obviously the particular story of Sparkbrook depends upon the personalities of individuals and we have tried in this account to do justice to this personal element

[1] See pp. 79–83.

in Sparkbrook's history. None the less it is true that the socio-logical possibilities were not unlimited and we seek also to show what the significance of particular actions was for the changing community structure.

The initiative came from a Labour Councillor, Mrs. Burgess. Mrs. Burgess was herself firmly in favour of immigra-tion control, but saw a danger in the possibility of the debate about control drawing attention away from the problems faced and posed by the immigrants who were already in Birmingham. As she put it, in a letter to the Birmingham *Sunday Mercury* (12 February 1961): 'The focus seems at the moment to be concentrated on control of immigration, but this, desirable as it is, will not cure the problems we already have.'

She went on to call for control of furnished lettings, for increased amenities for immigrants, and for a serious attempt to safeguard the standard of living of the people of Birmingham.

Mrs. Burgess proceeded to call a meeting of the people of Sparkbrook to draw up a petition of grievances. The Vicar of Christ Church, the Rev. Jack Reed, took the chair and the meeting was well attended. It was decided to hold another meeting and at this meeting the Sparkbrook Association was formed. For the first time the people of Sparkbrook could do something more than grumble about their grievances. They now had an association which was non-party-political and non-sectarian. All the people of Sparkbrook could join it and express their grievances through it. But, of course, the way in which these grievances were expressed would depend in part on the perception of Sparkbrook's problems by the people who were the officers and agents of the new association.

The committee members included a number of different types. Some were deeply conservative in their notion of what an ideal community should be like and were inclined to focus attention particularly on the moral failings of some of Spark-brook's residents. Others were more radical and more inclined to demand action by the Council, thus suggesting a political function for the association. Some were business people and some involved in one way or another in social work. Some had lived or worked in the area for many years. Others came from outside, through a general concern with social problems. Some emphasized total community problems, others the problems of family life. One or two from time to time made statements which placed the blame for Sparkbrook's problems on particular ethnic groups.

Speaking in more strictly sociological terms, we would distinguish three social types who were effective in determining the policy of the Association. Firstly, there were those who joined it as a result of their own experience of 'pastoral work' of one kind or another. They were likely to emphasize family problems and moral problems and to draw attention to the dangers of personal demoralization in such an area as this. Secondly, there were those whose experience of social work was more professional. They brought to the analysis of Sparkbrook's problems more objective universalistic attitudes but included the whole range of attitudes to be found amongst social workers, ranging from those whose approach was derived from psychiatrically organized case-work to those who saw problems much more in terms of ensuring that people gained their rights in the welfare state. And thirdly, there were the old community people, ranging from those who were simply deeply identified with the place and wanted to preserve or restore its formerly dignified character to those for whom aggressive racial attitudes were not far below the surface.

The remarkable thing was that all these people could work together. Of course, to some extent, effective decision-making passed to a small in-group and their views prevailed over the others. But there were differences also within this in-group and those who attached themselves more nominally maintained their support of the Association even though they were not involved in its day-to-day administration. They succeeded in uniting behind a rather empty slogan, 'Towards a Fuller and Happier Life', which was about as far as they could go in defining common aims explicitly, but they united de facto behind the more concrete and specific policies pursued by the Association.

The organization did not easily win grass-roots support from the local residents. Although its name was within a year to adorn a building which could easily be seen from the Stratford Road, many residents claimed even by 1964 that they had no knowledge of the Association's work. If support was to be won, it had to be won from outside; from the Council, from trusts and from people of goodwill in the general public. In fact, this effort was not at first very successful and had not a few members of the Association been prepared to give of their own time and resources as an act of faith until public support began to flow, it might well have gone the way of other associations, either becoming a kind of discussion group or going out of existence altogether.

Soon it was apparent, however, that the Association could only carry on with its work if it had a professionally trained and full-time social worker with premises in which to carry on her work. After some uncertainty as to whether it could afford such a step it appointed a new graduate from the Social Administration Department at Birmingham University as a general-purpose social worker. This was a step in the dark but it was the vital step necessary to ensure the Association's continued existence.

It is sociologically important to notice that this appointment could easily have been an unsuccessful one. The training of students in social administration is far from being adapted to problems such as those which Sparkbrook faces. It is not sufficient for a student to have a general grasp of the way in which social services work or to have the orthodox training in practical work. Sparkbrook presents problems of a new kind, although problems which may be typical of modern cities. Its social worker had to be able to understand the problems of a community in conflict, to have a shrewd political sense and great confidence in her own ability to get things done, to be able to act as a representative of the community and to do case-work in this context.

The new organizer's achievement was far from perfect and it should be remembered in all that we say that the Sparkbrook Association represents a weak and inadequate response to Sparkbrook's needs. But no one could have achieved 100 per cent. success in this situation. There would always have been something more to be done. What we do say is that in the organizer's style of work certain lines of action were pursued and others excluded and that in the fight-back of the community against demoralization the lines she chose to pursue were, by and large, the right ones.

The first approach by the Association to the people of

Sparkbrook was an invitation by pamphlet to take their problems to the organizer at her flat in the lodging-house area. After that it was up to her to devise ways 'to a fuller and happier life' for her clients. Problems of housing, of child care, of loneliness and of disputes between neighbours were presented to her in large numbers. Very soon it became essential to acquire premises.

A house was purchased in one of the main lodging-house streets, apparently from the committee's own financial resources, and plans laid for an official opening. The minute-book records that 'Mr. A. Faith' was to be approached to perform the ceremony but the next month it is stated without explanation that 'Mr. H. Lyttelton' had accepted. In due course, with considerable publicity, the new premises were opened by Humphrey Lyttelton.

By this time, however, it was apparent to the organizer that individual case-work by itself was no answer to Sparkbrook's problems and she therefore put forward a number of proposals for the fostering of group activity and improving communal facilities. Among these were proposals for an Adventure Playground and several play-centres where children could be left for half-day sessions. As soon as the Association's building was opened, moreover, a whole range of group activities was started, which came to include an Old People's Lunch Club run by the W.V.S., a Darby and Joan club, a Citizen's Advice Bureau, a Mental Health Club and a Youth Club. Some of these group activities attracted outside support, and soon the Association had established itself as a centre to which all kinds of new voluntary and statutory services could attach themselves.

Probably the work amongst children and adolescents was most successful. The clubs for the old and the handicapped and the social club seemed to be affected by the rather dingy surroundings of the Association's headquarters and it needed all the enthusiasm of the Association's staff to keep them going. None the less, each of these services was important for the small group which it served and none of them would have been there had it not been for the Association's initiative.

The playground was an immense success. Its leader was a young man of very considerable ability who had made the

running of playgrounds his profession, and he showed immediately that more was involved here than 'keeping the children
off the streets'. For a large band principally of Irish children
the playground became the most important if not the only
significant centre of their lives. Street gangs, instead of being a
menace, began to assume a new importance on the playground
as part of the social structure of Sparkbrook. Not that the
children became models of middle-class decorum overnight.
Far from it. An entry in the Association's minutes in mid-
November referring to the burning down of the Glad Tidings
Hall next to the playground indicated the kind of hazard which
the playground leader had to encounter. But the playground
was now part of Sparkbrook and it was there to stay.

It also forced itself on the attention of the City Council, who
were able to provide financial support for the leader's salary
from the Parks Department Fund and a new site in the small
Corporation park around the old Lloyd home. In due course,
the playground leader was appointed to the Parks Department
to organize playgrounds on a city-wide basis and was succeeded
by a graduate woman social worker, who had for some time
been helping by taking the playground children on mountain-
climbing trips in Wales in her motor car. Again, the Association was lucky in its choice and fortunate in finding a leader
so well qualified, for, while the support of the Parks Department was welcome, it was not yet sufficiently realized by the
Council that the organization of constructive play is a skilled
art, which cannot be seen simply as a minor part of the work
of a Parks Department.

The Play Centres supplemented the work of the Local
Authority day nursery. They were essential both as a means
of enabling mothers to do part-time work and as a relief for
mothers and children from the strains of living together all the
time in overcrowded rooms. There were two full-time and one
part-time centres, the full-time centres each holding ten half-
day sessions a week attended by fifty children at a time. The
mothers paid 6d. or 1s. This work, which will be of incalculable
benefit to the children who attend, is partly paid for by the
United Nations Save the Children Fund.

The additional resources which had come the way of Sparkbrook by way of grants from the Local Authority and various

trusts and funds were further increased when the Local Authority assumed responsibility for the organizer's salary. At this point the Association, while remaining a voluntary body under the control of its own committee, had become part of Birmingham's social welfare system.

It is important to notice what exactly had happened, however. In the first instance the structure of local authority services prevented them from meeting the needs of Sparkbrook. Their terms of reference were such that they could not flexibly meet the kinds of problem which Sparkbrook was presenting. But when the Sparkbrook Association took the initiative and defined those needs itself, it was soon possible to show that its work was of a kind which qualified for grant-aid. Resources which would otherwise have been unexploited were used for the first time and Sparkbrook was able to realize a claim on the social services which belonged to it by right but would not have been realized without the Association's work.

Those who are familiar with the social services concerned with personal and family problems will be well aware that they are riddled with problems of demarcation. Moreover, there is no special provision for community services, other than through grants to community centres, which are thought of too often in suburban terms. What is necessary is a restructuring of these services so as to make the kind of services which Sparkbrook has so painfully acquired universal in the twilight zones. But the thinking and the powers of local authority departments are far from making this restructuring likely as yet.

These difficulties became obvious when Dr. Molly Barrow, Vice-Chairman of the Association, promoted a pilot scheme for a Family Centre in Sparkbrook. Representatives of the Local Authority departments participated in the preliminary discussions and attempted to help as best they could. But the fact is that there is no place for 'Family Centres' within the present structure of local authority services.

Because there are so many different social work agencies it has long been recommended that ways should be found of doing case-work with families as a whole. Moreover, the Children's Act of 1963 lays upon the Children's Departments the task of doing preventive work with families. In Birmingham, however, the Family Care Unit of the Health Department has for about twelve or thirteen years done case-work with multi-problem families and it remains unclear whether this work should now pass to the care of the Children's Department. The Children's Department, on the other hand, is not clear as to how wide its mandate under the new Act is and how far it can go with its present resources in fulfilling it.

What Dr. Barrow's committee wanted was a centre where social workers of all kinds could work as a team and pool their resources to do the most effective family case-work, combining this with research work whose results could be fed back into the work. The idea is entirely logical and sensible but it does not fit easily into the existing structure of social services. Particularly, it appears that while an overall Director and Co-ordinator is essential, such an appointment would not be easily compatible with the responsibility of the various kinds of social workers to their Heads of Departments. It is hoped, none the less, that ways will be found empirically of resolving these difficulties and a generous grant from the Gulbenkian Foundation has made a five-year pilot scheme possible.

We have emphasized these details because, important though such schemes are, they are likely to be only a beginning. The Family Centre scheme is not only necessary in Sparkbrook. It is necessary to give an effective service to any part of the city. Moreover, it is itself a scheme limited to families or to mothers with children. It does not touch the problems of the many people who are lost and isolated through their willed or unwilling loss of kin. One could imagine the existence in the future of a comprehensive Personal Service and Rehabilitation Department which worked particularly in the deteriorating urban zones to deal with the whole range of personal problems which are to be found there.

These social work and social group-work activities loom large in the day-to-day life of the Sparkbrook Association. But they are not by any means its only activities. We also wish to mention what we have called the tension-management functions of the Association and its external political function. From a sociological point of view these may be even more important and the social work function may itself be best understood within this wider context.

It should not be thought from what has been said above

that the Association has achieved a great deal by way of integrating the various ethnic groups and breaking down the barriers between them. Though the Adventure Playground has now overcome its original Irish exclusiveness and has a clientele of West Indian and Pakistani children as well, and though West Indian and white children alike use the play centres, the various groups promoted by the Association tend to be ethnically homogeneous. Sparkbrook thus certainly does not have anything like a non-racial community centre. In fact, it seemed to us that such a goal at present would be highly artificial and unreal.

What is important is that members of all communities, though the Pakistani community less than others, use the Association's services as clients and there is in the use of these services in this way an embryonic concept of Sparkbrook citizenship. But such a concept will only gain its full realization as some notion of representative government of the Association's activities develops. At the moment, it is hard to say whether this stage will be reached and whether the untiring middle-class people who have founded and sustained the Association's work will ever be able to hand over to a Community Council.

Certainly this is what they would wish. Efforts have been made increasingly to associate representatives of the various sections and ethnic groups who make up the community with the committee's work, and though sometimes there may be some hesitation on the part of people whose identification is with the old community, there now sit on the Association's Council an Irish priest, the Pakistani secretary of the Commonwealth Property-Owners' Association and the West Indian Secretary of the Commonwealth Welfare Association. Their effective and continued participation could mean that the work of the Sparkbrook Association will enter a new phase. It has not yet entered that phase, however, and will not do so until the advantages of working through the Association for these group representatives outweigh the advantages of separate effort.

None the less, something is achieved already. The presence of these representatives prevents the Association from becoming simply an Old Community Association and demands a different

kind of statement from those who have a sense of grievance
against the immigrants. In this context, we should like to quote
the example of one lady, who sits on the Sparkbrook Council and
who in many ways typifies the attitudes of the old residents.[1]

She feels somewhat ambivalent about the Association's discussion of Sparkbrook as a problem area. When it organized
a photographic exhibition depicting Sparkbrook's slums and
lack of amenities she reacted by complaining that it failed to
show that some Sparkbrook people had the finest gardens in
Birmingham. She was strongly identified with the area and
proposed to 'sit it out' rather than migrate to the suburbs, as
she certainly could. She was profoundly upset by the growth
of lodging-houses in her own street and was particularly bitter
against the tinkers, of whom she had a considerable knowledge
as a result of her forthright complaints to them about their
behaviour.

Three years ago, when the Press was writing up the street
in which she had her home as a street of shame and violence,
she might have become a recruit to racialism. But in the context
of the Association another alternative emerges. She has recently proposed an 'Operation Facelift' for the street and has
won the co-operation of the Pakistani landlords. The Secretary
of the Commonwealth Property-Owners' Association promised
that for every £5 spent by local residents on improvement they
would spend £10, and the Association was intending to ask the
council to make special efforts on behalf of the street as recognition of its plans for self-improvement.

It is hard to say what will become of this scheme and so far
it may be that the various parties see themselves only as calling
each other's bluff. But what matters more is that communication has been established, common interests have been defined
and a co-operative project planned. In this kind of atmosphere
the leaders of various communities may find that it is possible
to state and pursue common interests and wise to inhibit
inflammatory remarks about other groups.

One thing which is clear is that openly racialistic diagnoses
of Sparkbrook's problems have been declared illegitimate by
the Association. This becomes particularly evident at the public
meetings which are held each quarter. If there has been a

[1] See page 61.

particular new scandal, if the tinkers have been fighting or a bad landlord has been exposed, racialism is there under the surface. But in the presence of the Association committee racial responses must be repressed and alternative solutions sought. So long as the Association is able to show that there are other solutions, open racialism will be kept well within bounds. So far it has managed to do this and Sparkbrook, despite its many problems, has not provided a base for any racialist organization.

We have already seen that the Association had succeeded in channelling much local authority aid which might not otherwise have been forthcoming into Sparkbrook. In doing this we might say that it was performing a political function. In a similar way, it acted as a lobby and a pressure group in relation to the disposal of other local authority resources. It continually agitated about street-lighting, pavements, and salvage collection and it claimed that these services had been improved. It had been less successful in its demand for the provision of public baths but was continuing its agitation. It also had the willing support of the Public Health Department in its opposition to some of the lodging-house landlords.

These pressures were, however, pressures on the administration for administrative action. The Association was more successful in this sphere than it was in obtaining political or legislative action in the Council and in Parliament, and this despite the fact that it had made the Member, Mr. Leslie Seymour, its President, and had an able and universally respected spokesman in Alderman Wothers, who had been one of the earliest successful Labour candidates in the Sparkbrook ward. We shall consider three cases in which the Association might have taken action in this sphere and either failed to do so or was ineffective in what it did. These were in relation to successive Housing Acts, in relation to the Birmingham Corporation Bill on multi-occupation and in relation to getting Sparkbrook declared a comprehensive redevelopment area.

In relation to housing, the Association was well aware from its inception of the evils of multi-occupation, and it was in a position to have its views stated clearly in Parliament in the Third Reading Debate on the 1961 Housing Act. Yet it did not or was not able at this time to put forward any clear legislative ideas as to how the problem could be dealt with.

Instead its representatives merely saw the Member and expressed their shock and disquiet at the state of the lodging-houses. Not having been asked to do anything precise, the Member felt that he was carrying out the wishes of the Association when he spoke at a meeting of the Conservative Parliamentary Party in favour of immigration control. The Association never really engaged with him to suggest that it had other and better solutions.

The reasons for this were that many of the leading members of the Association supported control, and a few would not have supported alternative measures. One such alternative measure would have been the widespread use of compulsory purchase as a sanction against the worst landlords, and consequently the takeover and management of the lodging-houses by the local authorities. But when the Council did seek to compulsorily purchase fourteen peculiarly filthy and overcrowded houses, not only the landlords but the ground landlords protested and one of the Association's officers told us that he thought the proposal smacked of Communism.

In fact, when it came to the actual choice of policies a committee bound together only by the slogan 'Towards a Fuller and Happier Life' was bound to find itself in disagreement, and public action in support of a particular line of policy was not possible. This is inevitable since housing issues are political issues and involve some degree of commitment to one or other political philosophy. But even then one wonders whether the failure to try to arrive at an agreed policy was not, in part, due to a lack of incisiveness in the thinking of the Association as well as to potential political disagreement.

Other issues regarding housing also led to little effective action on the part of the Association. In view of the reasonable doubt whether the Housing Department was discriminating against qualified coloured applicants for council houses, one might have expected some action from the Association, but there was none, perhaps because the Association was too English in composition, to want to fight the issue. Or one might have expected a continued and critical scrutiny of the Council's building programme. Here the Association did promote a conference on housing, but apparently lacked the will to carry on the argument after the conference was over.

An organization such as the Sparkbrook Association cannot, of course, be expected to commit itself to a party-political point of view. But it could, none the less, have formulated a non-*party*-political but still political viewpoint. And this it failed to do. Instead, it was inclined to think of the problem of housing in terms of direct action through housing associations. It had worked in close harness with the Birmingham Friendship Housing Association and with its aid had provided about sixteen properly converted flats for families, some of whom were immigrants. And it was also engaged in discussions with representatives of another housing association interested in building new flats in Sparkbrook. The first of these associations had made a contribution to the housing of immigrants which was important in kind but small in quantity. The second, since it was unable to say what its criteria of allocation were likely to be, seemed likely to make little contribution to the needs of the existing population, but rather to initiate a change in land-use in which a different kind of population entirely might invade Sparkbrook.

The important thing to notice, however, about the housing associations was not that they failed or succeeded in their aims but that they were so often discussed as though they alone had the answer to the housing problem, and that, in their eagerness to preserve the goodwill of local authorities, they were inclined to discourage any criticism of the Council. When at a meeting called by a Methodist study group a proposal was put for a 'Crusade on Housing' involving public criticism of the Council's building record, this was opposed by the housing associations, whose representatives praised the Council's record.

In a way, a much more serious issue facing Sparkbrook was whether the Council was treating it as a ghetto. There was a lot of evidence of this during our stay in Sparkbrook and some of this evidence has been referred to in Chapter I. But from the point of view of Sparkbrook one would have thought that this would have been a matter of more serious concern. The Council was clearly opposed to the spread of multi-occupation in the better areas of the city, but had classified Sparkbrook as an area where it had to exist and could, at best only be kept under control. One would have expected the Association in these circumstances to take strong action. But again it failed.

It seemed to accept the inevitability of Sparkbrook's ghetto status and no suggestions were put forward to the Council regarding the dispersal of the lodging-houses and their population.

One reason for this was fear of racialism. To demand that the Council should take steps to reduce multi-occupation might bring the Association close to advocating policies similar to those of Mr. Peter Griffiths in Smethwick and there was some recognition, particularly on the part of the new organizer, that the lodging-house proprietors were serving an essential function. It was not easy, therefore, for the Association or for Sparkbrook by itself to evolve a policy on this issue. Yet the consequence of *not* having a policy was to accept a ghetto-status for Sparkbrook.

The difficulties which the Association faced in this matter were brought to a head over the Birmingham Corporation's Bill on multi-occupation. This Bill, as we have seen, gave the Council powers to refuse to allow particular individuals to run lodging-houses and to declare certain areas as unsuitable for lodging-house development. There were clearly two views on this. One was that these powers might be used to create a more balanced community in Sparkbrook. The other was that they were wholly wrong, both because they would eliminate necessary lodgings in Sparkbrook and because by preventing the spread of the lodging-houses elsewhere they would concentrate them in areas like Sparkbrook. In this atmosphere of uncertainty, no clear and agreed mandate could be given to the new Labour Member, Mr. Hattersley, and the Corporation received all the powers it wished, to be used for good or ill.

A final issue was whether or not Sparkbrook might become a comprehensive development area. On this issue some members of the Association have pressed the Planning Department to make its plans known, but without success. The Association had no idea of Sparkbrook's planning destiny. Again the issue was a difficult one. If Sparkbrook was declared a development area the Council would have to clear the lodging-houses and re-house their population. This would be a solution of nearly all their problems for the people of Sparkbrook. But there was no sign that it was likely to be adopted by the Council, despite vague hints that it might one day declare a second ring of redevelopment. For the moment it thought only in terms of piecemeal development, of knocking down a few houses and, by improving the physical environment, encouraging the old residents to stay. Such proposals appealed to the old community spirit in the Association and took the sting out of their criticisms.

In late July 1964, the Council had discussed plans for the redevelopment of half of what we have called Sparkbrook 1. When the plan came before the Council, however, it was rejected on the ground that '600 immigrant families would have to be rehoused'. The Council, having no alternative plan to discuss, decided to give special support to the 'Facelift' scheme mentioned earlier in this chapter. The Association, however, had failed to put forward precise and practical proposals in a most important matter for the community.

In all these matters one notable fact was the relative absence of communication between the Association and the three Labour Councillors for the ward. Mrs. Burgess had retired from the political scene and her colleagues and successor confined their contacts with the Association to appearances on public occasions. Their view was that while the Association deserved support and encouragement there was much overlapping of function and that they could do a more useful job in their own surgery. Another point was that the Association's non-political position made it difficult for them to contribute solutions, for their solutions were political.

But here we can see why it is important that the Association should take political action of a non-party-political kind. The Labour Councillors were part of a city-wide organization. They were members of a Council Group and subject to its Whip. They could not speak, except in their Labour Group meetings, for Sparkbrook as such. And we found that they did not on the whole press Sparkbrook's special interests on such important matters as multi-occupation and comprehensive redevelopment. Only the Association could do that and up to this point in its history it had not been notably successful.

The Sparkbrook Association was important as a total community organization. It, more than any other organization, was capable of finding some degree of consensus and defining common interests amongst the conflicting sub-groups which made up the community. It could hold in balance the tension between groups and initiate corporate action. For all its weaknesses it mattered that it was there, and other communities which lacked such an organization were more likely to see their problems in purely racial terms. Perhaps its main function in fact was to declare racialism to be an illegitimate response and to offer alternative solutions to the problems which it purported to solve. Moreover, by channelling welfare facilities into the area, it made it a less deprived area than it otherwise would have been and by making available the rights of citizens made possible a kind of entry into Birmingham society, not only for the immigrants but also for its lost and isolated residents. It represented a dignified response by dignified people to a humiliating and demoralizing situation. In subjecting its work to critical examination our main aim has been to show that the potential of such organizations is not yet exhausted. So long as housing policy produces places like Sparkbrook, the kind of work which the Sparkbrook Association does will be important. And it may be that it may yet be able to produce the kind of fight-back which will deal with the causes as well as the consequences of urban deterioration. If it does its greatest reward will be that it is no longer needed. Other areas with similar problems and people in those areas with similar ideals could find much that is instructive in the work of the Sparkbrook Association.

X. The Younger Generation[1]

Community studies undertaken by English sociologists in the past have tended to overlook one important group within society—the children, and one important institution—the school. Occasionally the relationship between school and parents is discussed—as in John Mays' studies in Liverpool.[2] This lack of emphasis upon the next generation stems from a concentration of studies in stable, working-class areas of cities; upon small communities where adult roles are clearly defined and accepted, where, in fact, the role models presented to the children are consistent. The children are likely to remain within the area upon adulthood unless forced to leave by housing need. The schools in this sort of area do not become agents of change except for a very small minority who become socially mobile through the educational system, and then geographic mobility usually accompanies social mobility.[3]

It is immediately obvious from the preceding chapters that Sparkbrook is a very different type of area. Because of its nature as a zone of transition for some families, as an immigrant reception area, and as a residual area for many types of social outcast, there are very few institutional patterns common throughout its social structure. There is, it seems, only one institution which each family, by law, must become part of; namely, the educational system. This compulsory contact and uniform treatment of all groups within the schools is important in understanding the possibilities for change within the social structure.

Neither is Sparkbrook a static area. The continual movement of families in and out means a continual diversification of group

[1] This chapter has been written by Mrs. Jennifer Williams.
[2] J. B. Mays, *Education and the Urban Child*, Liverpool University Press, 1962.
[3] See, for example, M. Young, P. Willmott, *Family and Kinship in East London*, London, Routledge and Kegan Paul, 1957; Willmott, *The Evolution of a Community*, London, Routledge and Kegan Paul, 1963; C. Rosser and C. Harris, *Family and Social Change*, London, International Library of Sociology and Social Reconstruction, 1965.

structures. Because a sociological study can, of necessity, confine itself only to a limited point in time, it is essential to try
to understand the processes of change taking place and to try
to predict future trends. One way of doing this is to study the
children and adolescents. In what ways do they differ from
their parents in their attitudes and aspirations? Are their
parents their role models? If not, who are? To what extent do
the schools present alternative role models and how far are
these accepted by their pupils? Or is school just one of the
conflicting sets of institutions presenting alternative ways of life,
having no more influence than the others—family, peer group,
mass media, etc.? These are the sorts of question which any
study in an area of rapid change must try to answer.

The emphasis, therefore, in this chapter is upon the schools
as an agent of socialization, as the institution through which
society presents certain values and attitudes, in an area where
a considerable section of parents cannot and do not reinforce
the schools' teaching in terms of attitudes and behaviour patterns. This conflict-process is seen most clearly in the study of
the immigrant children—the majority of whom have spent
their formative years in their own country. They are therefore
subject to a double socialization process. The child's and the
whole family's status image and sets of values have to change,
sometimes suddenly and dramatically, and the old pattern is
gradually replaced by one which will enable them to exist in
England.

One of the main agents in this second socialization process
is the school, especially within the Indian and Pakistani communities, where the children do not mix with their English
peers outside school. One unintended consequence of this dual
process of socialization is a conflict of values for the child. He
may well have presented to him three sets of role models—his
family, his school, his peers, within which a workable synthesis
is impossible. We have before us as an example second-generation immigrant delinquency in the United States. In this area
of study the sociologist's aim of understanding and prediction,
and then possibly prevention, ought quickly to be pursued.

Finally, one can justify an emphasis upon education within
a community study from rather a different angle. Racial
prejudice and antagonisms exist among the adults in Spark-

brook. Will the same attitudes be shown by the next generation? Optimists frequently state that the process of being educated together will dissolve racial friction. The teachers in this area repeated this hope. The time has come to test this assumption—to examine carefully the claim that the creation of new and permanent attitudes within school is probable.

So far I have discussed the impetus and justification for this study. The questions raised are large and difficult to answer. The following are the main issues which I shall try to answer in the rest of the chapter. What are the attitudes of the teachers in the schools in Sparkbrook? What aspirations do they have for the children they teach? How do they attempt to guide them into the adult roles they think desirable? How far do the parents' attitudes and aspirations conform or conflict with those of the schools? Do the children absorb the standards asserted by their teachers? How far do the children's attitudes and aspirations differ from those of their parents? How far are the desires of the children realistic? As with so many socio-logical questions which have to be answered with very limited resources of time and money, the methods of study seem in-adequate. All one can offer are clues to the answers which will need further elaboration and checking, here and elsewhere, again and again.

The data on the schools and the teachers was gained by interviewing. Six schools were visited—three Primary schools, one of which was a Church of England school, and three Secondary Modern schools—one boys', one girls', and one Roman Catholic mixed school. The head teachers of all these schools were interviewed, some on several occasions. A few class teachers were seen in the schools; twenty-five attended a conference on education in Sparkbrook, which was held at the Sparkbrook Association.

The data on parental attitudes was obtained as part of the main questionnaire data; the description of the sample and methods used is outlined in the Appendix.

The most comprehensive data gathered concerned the chil-dren themselves. 335 children in five schools wrote short essays as part of their normal school work, on topics set by the researcher, without any knowledge at the time that they were taking part in a survey. The 255 Primary school children wrote on the following topics:

> The story of my life so far
> What I did last week-end
> Where I live

The seventy-eight Secondary Modern pupils wrote on:

> My autobiography
> My leisure time
> Sparkbrook (and how I would rebuild it if a member of the City Council)
> My life from leaving school till retirement

In order to eliminate the need for any special reorganization within the schools, the samples of children chosen could not be random ones, but the work was undertaken by three complete classes. In each school one class was the eldest group. Apart from this no instructions were given, except that where the school streamed, all streams were to be represented. One of the essay topics set within the Secondary Modern school, concerning the future life of the children, was similar to part of the study undertaken by Thelma Veness, and outlined in her study, *The School-Leavers*.[1] Though the particular interests of the two studies are different, some comparisons can be made between them.

Finally, in order to compare the views expressed by adolescents within school and outside, nine youth groups were visited by a group of trainee social work students. In each club the students chatted to members and leaders and discussed their views on Sparkbrook, racial issues, jobs, 'settling down' for one to three hours. Guided group discussions, rather than interviews, summarize the methods used in this section of the study.

A brief mention must be made at this point of the main inadequacies of the methods employed. The interviews with the head teachers were lengthy, and in several instances continued over three or four visits. Much less contact was made, however, with the class teachers. Even at the conference called especially to hear their views, the class teachers allowed their head teachers to monopolize most of the conversation.

[1] Thelma Veness, *The School-Leavers*, London, Methuen, 1962.

The discussion of parental attitudes is limited by the small numbers included in the random sample. Fifty-two immigrant parents were interviewed, but twenty-three of these were Irish. The other groups—West Indian, Indian and Pakistani—were too small for statistical comparisons between the groups to be made.

The sample of school children is inadequate mainly because of the failure of the boys' Secondary Modern school to co-operate in the inquiry. Unfortunately, this unwillingness was not made clear until it was too late to try to find an alternative school. The sample from the mixed Roman Catholic school is also small, owing to their unwillingness to undertake any more work. The class teachers in all schools introduced the work as part of the normal free-writing or English periods. Standardized instructions were given to the teachers, and the researcher can only hope these were followed. Where it was obvious from the essays that some prompting had been given, this was ignored. In most cases, however, I am confident of full co-operation.

There are many disadvantages in relying upon an adolescent sample drawn from youth clubs and similar organizations, especially in this type of area where 'joiners' are not a typical sample of all adolescents. However, a wide variety of clubs was included, including one for 'unclubbables'. The range, therefore, is wider than might have been expected initially.

The main theoretical emphasis of the study lies, as mentioned earlier, in the processes of socialization within the school—'how the school functions to internalize in its pupils both the commitments and capacities for the successful performance of their future adult roles, and how it functions to allocate these human resources within the role structure of adult society.'[1]

This emphasis involves first of all a discussion in general terms of the place of schools in this sort of area. This is because the dilemmas facing the teachers I interviewed stem at least partly from national educational policy and the general processes of social change. The practical problems of schools in 'inner ring' areas were outlined in detail by the Newsom

[1] Talcott Parsons, 'The School Class as a Social System', *Harvard Educational Review*, Vol. XXIX, 1959, pp. 297–318.

Report[1] and are continually being re-emphasized in terms of teacher turnover, class size, inadequate buildings, and so forth.

What need more emphasis are the feelings of bitterness shown by staff—the feelings of being neglected, of envy towards the lavishness of university facilities, of being the very bottom rung as far as educational expenditure is concerned. There is also a feeling of bitterness and frustration among some of the teachers due to their inability to cope with the cultural gap between teacher and pupil—a deficiency both in understanding and in sympathy—and an inability to develop really adequate teaching techniques for this sort of child and area. Bernstein has investigated the communications gaps between English cultural groups,[2] and extension of such work in a cross-cultural context could lead to the development of better teaching techniques for schools such as we find in Sparkbrook.

The feelings of bitterness are marked in all schools, but the frustrations are not so overwhelming in the Primary schools. The aims of these schools are still relatively unambiguous and generally accepted: the development of certain measurable skills in reading, writing and number. Again, it is accepted that this sort of area has fewer Eleven-Plus successes and its tail of slow learners is larger than in middle-class suburbs and new council estates.[3] The Secondary Modern schools have no such acceptable, measurable aims. The current emphasis upon Comprehensive schools is based largely upon the failure of Secondary Modern education to develop its own rationale and methods.

The development of a widespread youth culture in the recent decades seems, in widening the gap between generations, to have widened that between teacher and pupil. This interpretation of recent social changes is supported by Bryan Wilson[4] and Jean Floud[5]. The evidence is somewhat difficult to obtain; but what is important for my argument here is that the teachers felt this is what had happened.

A certain ambivalence has also developed in the general

---

[1] *Half Our Future* (Newsom Report), London, HMSO, 1963.

[2] B. Bernstein, 'Social Class and Linguistic Development', Chapter 24 in *Education, Economy and Society* (ed. A. H. Halsey), Free Press of Glencoe, 1961.

[3] See, for example, J. W. B. Douglas, *Home and School*, London, Macgibbon and Kee, 1964.

[4] B. Wilson, 'The Teacher's Role', *British Journal of Sociology*, Vol. 13, 1962.

[5] J. Floud, 'Teaching in an Affluent Society', *British Journal of Sociology*, Vol. 13, 1962.

reward system and sanction system previously used by the schools. External examinations can be used as a motivational spur in Grammar schools, and for a few pupils in Secondary Modern schools. But the job and status hierarchy can no longer be used easily and in a straightforward manner. When a good school record was the passport to a good, secure and therefore steadily paid job, the school had a reward system ready made. Unemployment was not only an employer's sanction. Now the achievement hierarchy of the school system does not necessarily correspond with the pay structure of the economic world.[1] The 'nice, clean, responsible' job is a bait which the youth culture rejects. The changes in the female labour market are in the same direction as those for the boys, but are not nearly so drastic or clear-cut. For girls, achievement and pay are more nearly related and the secretary still retains her glamour appeal. The great advantage in girls' schools is that skills of the secretarial variety which are very clearly vocational can be taught in old school buildings with a certain minimum of equipment. The boys are not so easily catered for except in new, expensively equipped schools.

The effects upon the schools of these changes in economic conditions and youth behaviour was summed up by the headmaster of a boys' Secondary Modern school in Sparkbrook. When asked what aspirations he had for the boys in his school and what sort of aims he had in mind when organizing his school, he replied that he did not think he had any aims and aspirations at all, but just worked from day to day.

Bearing in mind these general social changes, we can now ask what problems stem more specifically from the situation within Sparkbrook, what local conditions aggravate these national trends and very briefly what sort of schools are the six I visited. They are by national standards small schools— only one, a junior school, having over 400 pupils. The five that are large enough to stream all do so—two or three streams in each year. The boys' Secondary Modern school had about fifteen pupils remaining after the age of fifteen, the girls' Secondary Modern school had at least double this number staying one year, and around fifteen remaining up to a sixth

[1] See for example M. P. Carter, *Home, School and Work*, Oxford, Pergamon Press, 1962.

form. There were no parent-teacher organizations functioning at the time of my visits.

If 'immigrant pupil' is defined widely as any child with at least one parent born outside the British Isles, then the five non-Roman Catholic schools have percentages ranging from 20 per cent. to 40 per cent. If 'immigrant pupil' is defined as 'coloured child', including those born in this country, as it appears to be in the recent Ministry of Education circular,[1] then the percentages are smaller—15 per cent. to 36 per cent. The Roman Catholic school presents a very different picture. Only four pupils are coloured, but of the 360 children, 250 have both parents born in Ireland, and 180 of the children were born in Ireland.

Four of the six head teachers had been at their schools for at least ten years and had seen the composition of the area change. They were nostalgic for the days when three generations of the same family attended the same school. One of their present problems is certainly due to the changing nature of the area—the continual turnover of children as families leave the area and new ones arrive. No head teacher wished to see the percentage of immigrant children rise any higher than at present, and two were actively campaigning for a reduction. All saw themselves as fighting a difficult battle against the social handicaps experienced by their pupils—especially as regards housing facilities and inadequate parents.

Given these general attitudes, how can one translate the role of the school into sociological terms within Parsons's framework? I would summarize it briefly, in the non-Roman Catholic schools, as a socializing, anglicizing, integrating agency. The teachers see their role as putting over a certain set of values (Christian), a code of behaviour (middle-class) and a set of academic and job aspirations in which white-collar jobs have a higher prestige than manual, clean jobs than dirty (shop work is higher on the scale than the factory floor), and interesting, responsible jobs are higher than just 'good money' jobs.

The elements of a middle-class behaviour code manifest themselves in the social training undertaken—cleanliness, tidi-

[1] Department of Education and Science, *The Education of Immigrants*, Circular 7/65, June 1965.

ness, manners, respect for authority, honesty to authority, deferential treatment of adults, punctuality, hard work, and so on, plus a certain emphasis upon standard English. These are elements of a teacher's role which in other areas would be undertaken or at least reinforced by parents. These socialization processes consume a considerable amount of energy and patience. The wider the cultural gap between pupil and teacher, the more the emphasis placed upon this aspect of the teacher's role.[1] When a class includes a sizeable non-English, non-Christian group of children, then even certain basic assumptions about behaviour and attitudes—and humour patterns—can no longer be taken for granted.

The role functions most specific to this type of area are those of anglicization and integration. Immigrants are expected to conform to English behaviour patterns and norms. This is accepted nationally and officially as the schools' task. The Report on Education by the Commonwealth Immigrants Advisory Council states: 'The national system of education cannot be expected to perpetuate the different values of immigrant groups . . . it must aim at producing citizens who can take their place in society properly equipped to exercise their rights and perform their duties which are the same as those of other citizens'.[2] One practical step in this direction has been taken by one Primary school I visited in producing a 'reader' designed to introduce the immigrant child to important aspects of life in his neighbourhood—school, shops, etc.

This process of anglicization is a key factor in the desire of teachers to limit the percentage of immigrants in each school. It is felt that once the percentage of non-English children in any one class reaches a quarter then anglicization becomes much more difficult.

In contrast with the discussion and practical efforts concerning the problems of anglicization, the aim of integration tends to be seen as a by-product of the educational process, not as an integral part of it. There is an assumption current in the educational world, that children do not show racial prejudice, and that even if this develops as they grow older,

---

[1] B. Wilson, op. cit.
[2] Home Office, 'Commonwealth Immigrants Advisory Committee: Second Report', Cmnd. 2266, 1964.

the mixing of races in school will lessen tensions in the next generation. Earlier writings upon this subject have perhaps led to a false optimism which is not justified in present circumstances, especially where large numbers of immigrants are present in one school. However, the feeling that integration would follow from our present educational policy was echoed by Sparkbrook's teachers.

There was very rarely an incident involving racial antagonism within school. But if the same children were interviewed outside school, then a considerable degree of racial antagonism was manifest, particularly among the older pupils. The reason why conflict rarely explodes in school is that the children know this is not the place to show such feelings. Teachers all stressed that they treated the children equally and regarded race as irrelevant in the classroom. Integration is fostered by example. Oscar Tapper, in a paper on *Educating the Immigrant*, summarizes this attitude: 'When the adults in a school refuse to countenance any instances of racial intolerance, then it ceases to be a problem.'[1]

Conflict may cease to be a problem in school, but how far is there a carry-over into other areas of life? How effective in this respect is the teachers' claim to be moulding the attitudes of the next generation? Is it that conflict is suspended during school hours, rather than eliminated altogether? I feel that in fact many are abdicating this particularly vital role because of their own ambivalent feelings about the effects of immigration upon the areas where they teach. Children and parents are sophisticated enough to know what attitudes are appropriate to what situations.

There are many influences stressing antagonism and violence rather than integration. When it was suggested at a conference in the area that schools may have to start positive teaching of, for example, physical anthropology or social studies including race relations, no support was forthcoming for the idea. Many teachers showed their own ambivalence upon the subject and repeated typical stereotypes about racial groups; for instance, that all West Indians are lazy. In this respect, as in several others, some of the teachers have opted out of the conflicts of

[1] O. Tapper, *Educating the Immigrant: A Sample Survey*, London, University House, East London Papers, Vol. VI, No. 2, December 1963, p. 120.

the area and opted out of their claimed role as an important influence upon attitudes. The sharing of a school classroom with a few children from another country does not automatically lessen physical and verbal violence against the whole group.

The social functions of the Roman Catholic school within this survey are slightly different from those of the other schools. The socialization function was stressed in much the same terms. The Christian values, as one would expect, were given a Roman Catholic emphasis, including, for instance, attendance at Mass. This is an emphasis which is necessary as many of the parents of the children, though Roman Catholic, do not themselves attend church. The anglicizing function is not applicable to this school. In fact it may be that the school functions in an entirely different way to emphasize the immigrant's homeland. One unintended consequence, it seems to me, of a provision of Roman Catholic schools in this type of immigration reception area is this emphasis upon Ireland as the homeland, reinforced by the desire to preserve the child's Catholicism in a hostile environment. The end result of this separate provision of schooling is the preservation of the immigrant group and a prevention of its absorption into English society as quickly or as easily as might otherwise have occurred. A parallel example would be the provision of education by a Sikh temple, not to supplement, but to replace state education. Catholic children who did not attend Catholic schools did not live in quite such a closed exclusively immigrant community.

Mention has already been made of the way in which the teachers feel the majority of parents are apathetic about education. What do the parents themselves say? Of the 192 English adults interviewed, 48 had children at school at the time. These were asked:

(1) Are you satisfied with the education your child[ren] is [are] having?
(2) What age would you like your child to leave school?
(3) What schooling would you like your child to have?
(4) What sort of job would you like your child to have?
(5) How often do you visit the school?
(6) When did you last visit school?

Forty-three of the parents stated that they were completely

most replied they would go 'when it was necessary'. This expected finding of lack of parental contact was supported by the teachers. Briefly, it seems that education is seen as the job of the schools, and there is satisfaction, or indifference, over the performance of this job. A considerable proportion of parents appear to have ambitions for their younger children, but once they fail their 'Eleven Plus' this ambition is seen as incapable of realization and indifference follows.

As is shown elsewhere in this book in more detail, certain other adult attitudes and aspirations may well clash with those put forward by the school. Some degree of hostility to coloured immigrants is shown by the analysis of the open-ended questions referred to in Chapter III. This underlines the earlier point that attitude formation in areas of conflict cannot just be left to chance and good example. There is also an expressed wish to live outside the area by at least half the respondents in each group except the Pakistanis. Should the school support this particular ambition or not? This is a difficult decision for the teachers to make. By living outside the area, most teachers show their own preferences, and yet if they encourage the older children to aspire to the suburbs, the composition of their own school intake will more and more be from the residual problem families. The task of changing the nature of the area is so difficult; what alternative to 'getting out' can the school provide? These are questions which some head teachers have thought about deeply and which all teachers in an area such as this need to answer.

Perhaps the biggest conflict between parental and school assumptions is shown among the immigrant groups, especially the Pakistani and Indian adults, who do not support the anglicization aim of the schools. Certain diacritical marks, such as dress, food preferences and so on, are retained by the parents, especially by the mothers. These seem to be abandoned by most children within their first year at an English school. English dress is adopted and many have a school dinner without any direct pressure from the schools to enforce conformity. But certain assumptions concerning the freedom of children to grow away from parents, to choose jobs, choose marriage partners, and so forth, are rejected by these parents. The emphasis upon a return to the home country prevents a commitment to anglicization. As Desai says in his book on the Indians in Britain, in particular concerning the Gujaratis in Birmingham:[1] 'They come not to make a new life but to earn money and accept only those changes which are a minimum condition for making money.' The roles of the child outside school, e.g. of an adolescent boy as housekeeper, may well conflict with the accepted adolescent roles of English boys. The adolescent girls are most certainly presented with a conflict situation, very clearly seen as a conflict between their ascribed status within their own community and the achieved status of their English peers, within their own informal groups and gangs.[2]

The Indian and Pakistani parents wish their children to retain vital elements of their home culture, their language and religion. The Sikh temple in Smethwick provides lessons in Punjabi and the Muslim community is trying to provide a mosque school to supplement the small class at the moment under the supervision of a Pakistani doctor. These provisions mean again that the closely supervised leisure time of the children contrasts sharply with the freedom of their English peers.

The vast majority of West Indian parents do wish their children to become accepted by the English community, but there is again a conflict between generations based upon different emphases upon discipline and control. Harsh physical punishments, and attempts to supervise the leisure of their older children, are resented by the generation aspiring to be like their English peers. It is the West Indian parents who tend to be critical of lax discipline and play in schools. Although the numbers in this survey were too small to bring this out clearly, another study in progress demonstrates this point very sharply.[3]

This last emphasis, upon clashes between parents and children, leads directly to a more detailed analysis of the final group of actors in this situation—the children and adolescents.

---

[1] Desai, *Indian Immigrants in Britain*, op. cit.

[2] The English adolescents have an ascribed status as far as Birmingham society is concerned by the nature of their home locality but within this locality the peer group provides a setting for achieved status.

[3] M. McConnell, unpublished Dissertation, University of Birmingham, Department of Education.

The data in this section are taken from the written work of
355 schoolchildren. Their writing was analysed to see if any
themes recurred, especially to see in what ways school affected
the adolescents' assumption of adult roles. As I stated at the
beginning of this chapter, I was trying to estimate whether
school or home was the more potent force in moulding attitudes, and whether the school was effective as an integrating,
anglicizing force; also to find out whether the views of the children compare with those of their parents on Sparkbrook—the
desire to move out, the dislike of coloured neighbours, etc.

TABLE 52: SAMPLE OF CHILDREN WRITING ESSAYS

	Primary School A	Primary School B: C. of E.	Primary School C	Girls' Secondary Modern	R.C. Mixed Secondary Modern	Totals
Both parents English*	75	47	45	32	2	201
Both parents Irish	11	6	4	2	14	37
Anglo-Irish	10	1	3	2	6	22
European						
Anglo-European	7	2	2	—	1	12
Pakistani†	5	2	—	—	—	7
Indian†	7	2	6	10	—	25
West Indian†	21	13	8	9	—	51
TOTAL	136	73	68	55	23	355

* Including a few Welsh or Scots.
† These totals include a very small number of children of mixed parentage, e.g. Anglo-West
Indian.

Of the 201 children with both parents English, ninety-four
were born in Sparkbrook; ninety-eight were born elsewhere in
Birmingham; and nine were born elsewhere in England.

Of the thirty-seven children with both parents Irish, sixteen
were born in Ireland, and twenty-one were born in Birmingham.

As far as the children are concerned, then, it is a predominantly Birmingham group: 240 out of the 355 were born in
Birmingham. Only a very few of the coloured children, however, were born in England—only one Indian and three West
Indians in this sample.

What are the recurring themes in these children's outline of their own life story? As one would expect, the majority emphasize their own family and their life at school. Two recurring factors, however, must be emphasized: the size of families and the continual movement from one house to another. This movement is not due to geographical mobility contingent upon changing jobs, but is merely a search for better accommodation within the Birmingham area. Of the ninety-four children who had lived in Sparkbrook all their lives, only thirty-seven had remained in the same house. Among the Irish children, movement between Birmingham and Ireland is recorded frequently. Practically all the Pakistani, Indian, and West Indian children mention separation from one or both parents—the West Indian children frequently being left behind with their grandmother.

Apart from family size and perhaps house changes, the most striking differences between the lives of these children and those in non-inner-ring areas of cities concern the conditions in which they live. Among the junior children there is a striking contrast between those who report factually the overcrowded, damp, etc., conditions in which they live, and the large group who assert what a 'nice big house' with a large garden they have. Seventy children comment upon their garden. In contrast there are frequent statements like the following examples:

English girl (aged eight)
'I don't like it very much in my house. There is four rooms my two brothers and my sista all sleep in the same bedroom.'

Indian girl (aged ten)
'Five familys live in my house.'

West Indian boy (aged ten)
'Our house is not a nice one. The landlord is no good. There's a hole in the seeling the landlord said to us I will send some one to fisk it. But no one came to fisk the seeling.'

English boy (aged eight)
'The house is falling to bits and it is damp and we nevr go out into the country and my momy is buse in the shop.'

Problems of another nature can only be guessed at from the following quotations:

West Indian girl (aged ten)

'My mother has three children. We live in one room. My mum works on nights and my Dad works days.'

English girl (aged fifteen)

'When I was about 6½ my mother left us for the first time. She returned about six months later. She left us again in about four months.'

West Indian girl (aged ten)

'When I was six I went to my mothers wedding because my mother wasn't getting marry to my father. When I was 7 my father sended for me to come to England.'

The children also commented upon the district, as opposed to the house, in which they lived. Unfavourable comments upon the whole of Sparkbrook were a feature of the older children's essays. Most of the younger ones make no value judgements at all. Of the 277 Primary schoolchildren, 161 do not express any opinion about Sparkbrook. This is true of only nine of the seventy-eight Secondary pupils. Feelings of dislike of Sparkbrook develop with age. I would also suggest that the child with the more highly developed verbal skills—in the school's terms the brighter child—develops an awareness of other people's attitudes to the area earlier. For instance, two English boys of ten express their dislike of the area in terms of their own needs and frustrations:

'I do not like my Rd. Because the People do not let you play in the Rd. The car park in the Rd. and They get in the way.'

'A lady wount let you play football in the street but we do. She says go to the park but the park is a long way and no buses go up there.'

In contrast, compare the verbal ability and views of the following two quotations:

English boy (aged seven)

'I wish I could live in a nice tidy street where there not very much litter on the ground and the school is just round the corner.'

English girl (aged nine)

'The next door neighbour throws the rubbish out of their house outside the garden. The next door neighbour makes too much noise. My mother does not like it. It gives her headaches.'

The reasons given for disliking the area are almost always in terms of dirt or the people—or a combination of the two.

English girl (aged nine)

'I do not like it around our way. I live next door to some not very clean people.'

West Indian girl (aged eleven)

'The second place we moved to was a road called . . . there we rented a room but didn't stay long because of the mess the Pakistanis and Irish people kept it in.'

English boy (aged ten)

'The street is not very nice and there are coloured people and Irish people living at the bottom of our road.'

The same themes are continued by the older girls:

English girl (aged fifteen)

'The people, some people are alright to speak to, but they are very hard to make friends with but you have to be careful what kind of people you speak to.'

One fifteen-year-old girl had problems of a different nature, partly, I think, due to her imagination: 'If I walk round the streets I get asulted by men or get followed around.'

Though in the Junior school, as I have said, the higher the stream of the child the more likely he or she is to make disparaging references to Sparkbrook, in the Secondary school, the higher the stream the more sympathy and tolerance appears to be shown to other groups. Certainly, the girls staying to the sixth form were markedly more sympathetic than those in '4B'— perhaps because those who are likely to move out of the areas have less need of a scapegoat.

English girl (aged sixteen: sixth form)

'Some parts of Sparkbrook have a family in each room. Many of these families are immigrants from places like India, Africa and Ireland who through lack of money are forced to live in this way.'

English girl (aged fourteen: 4B)

'If I were a member of Birmingham Council I would start by getting rid of all the tinkers out of the houses they are spoiling.'

English girl (aged fifteen: 4B)

'If I were a member of Parliament and were able to rebuild Sparkbrook I would first have the gypsies thrown out, then I would have it all fumigated where they had been living.'

However, one must not give the impression from these quotations that hostile references to immigrant groups were frequent. From the 355 individuals there were ten disparaging references to the Irish community and ten to the 'coloured' or 'the blacks'. To counterbalance these, there were twenty-eight juniors and seven seniors favourably disposed towards the whole area.

English girl (aged nine)

'I have never moved from . . . Street. I like it at Sparkbrook and I would not like to leave.'

English girl (aged eleven)

'I like my house because it is rather large and in my street there are many children to play with.'

English girl (aged fourteen)

'Lots of people say they would like to leave here. I dare say they would but people like Sparkbrook as it is because we know everyone and have made lots of friends.'

The leisure-time occupations of the junior children were predictable—playing out and watching television being almost universal patterns for the under-twelves—with visiting relatives, going out with the family, going to the cinema and attending Sunday school or church as week-end activities of large minorities. Football, judo, skating, swimming, and so on, are much smaller minority hobbies. Among the older girls ten-pin bowling, cinema, listening to records and dancing figure more prominently; very few mention going out with the family.

As compared with other areas of cities, concerning which we have only limited knowledge, two points of contrast seem clear

—more television seems to be watched by the younger age-groups and the adolescents have more freedom to spend their leisure on their own.

Irish girl (aged thirteen)

'I usually go dancing on Saturday night, a lot of Mods and Rockers go there. I like the Mods better than the Rockers because they dress more neatly and dont start fights.'

English girl (aged fourteen)

'I think there are sufficient facilities for young people to use in their spare time although I would like to see more all-night places instead of most places closing down quite early.'

It is from the essays on leisure that I have tried to glean clues as to how much contact there is between the racial groups outside school—supplementing this by a certain amount of observation in the playground, streets, parks and adventure playground. Quite definitely the Indian and Pakistani children keep themselves almost completely separate outside school, and when a child mentioned visiting another in an essay, it was invariably a member of his own community. The pattern is much more mixed as far as West Indian and English children are concerned. Friendships were mentioned and visiting occurred, especially at the junior level but much less frequently among the older age-groups.

The clientele of the adventure playground consisted predominantly of Irish and West Indian children, but the two groups played alongside rather than with each other.

It would have been useful to supplement this somewhat unsatisfactory evidence by a detailed sociometric study.[1] This was not possible with the resources available. Until we have more detailed evidence to the contrary, it appears that school contacts and friendships, and leisure segregation, can exist side by side.

In later adolescence the leisure patterns seem to have separated almost completely. The teachers certainly thought their pupils mixed little. The composition of youth groups, for instance, bore this out.

[1] For a study of this type see L. Silberman and B. Spice (ed. Chapman), *Colour and Class in Six Liverpool Schools*, Liverpool, 1950.

In their final piece of writing, the Secondary Modern group imagined what their life would be like after school—the instructions given by the teachers stressing that they were to be realistic. These essays give the clues to the aspirations of the seventy-eight teenagers. Again, predictably, the girls emphasize marriage and family—only two girls and two boys did not mention this event in their lives. In contrast with their own experience, they are all intending to have small families; usually two children, occasionally three. Thirty of this sample were Roman Catholics, but only five of these intended to have as many as three children. In this area of behaviour, therefore, their norms are not based upon the actual example set by their parents. However, evidence from an earlier fertility survey in this area suggests that the parents hold the norm of small family size but have not managed to achieve it in practice[1] (one boy of thirteen probably gave a clue to the pattern in his street when he wrote: 'I got married and six months later my wife had a baby'). It is difficult to decide how far the school is responsible for this change, and how far it is due to other agencies, such as the mass media. Both Protestant and Catholic children, however, show as great a change in norms. Grand-children assume an important place in the lives of the girls, being mentioned twenty-seven times. In Thelma Veness' study (referred to above) on similar lines an unexpected finding was the number of times a spouse was killed off in, for example, an accident. This occurred thirteen times in the present sample.

The adolescents were certainly realistic in their job aspirations—probably underrating their prospects and abilities rather than the reverse. This has been found to occur in city Secondary Modern schools in previous research.[2] No one aimed at a professional occupation—the highest aim in terms of social status being clerical or skilled manual occupations. A few boys suddenly became managing directors or played for England at football, and a few girls married wealthy businessmen, but for

[1] J. H. Waterhouse and D. Brabham, 'Inquiry into the Fertility of Immigrants', *Eugenics Review*, April 1964.
[2] *Fifteen to Eighteen* (Crowther Report), Central Advisory Council for Education, London, H.M.S.O., Vol. I, 1959; Vol. II, 1960; Thelma Veness, op. cit.; M. P. Wilson, 'Vocational Preferences of Secondary Modern Children' *British Journal of Educational Psychology*, Vol. XXIII, 1953.

the vast majority their future membership of the working class was assumed without comment or question. 'The allocation of human resources within the role structure of adult society'[1] is a function which seems to be performed by the educational system, as far as economic roles are concerned, without too much friction and with a considerable degree of success.

The field in which the future aspirations of the adolescents were completely unrealistic was that of their future housing possibilities. This, I think, is extremely significant for future attitudes. Only one person said she would be living in Sparkbrook, or a similar district. The vast majority plumped for bungalows in the country or by the sea. The most realistic was an English girl (aged fifteen): 'If I live in rooms at first I hope to get a nice modern house in a clean district. I do not mind which district I live in but I would like it to be clean and respectable and not too far away from my mother.' The least realistic was perhaps an English girl of sixteen who owned a ranch-style house in Beverly Hills.

In this area of their life, therefore, the goals of these adolescents are unobtainable by the majority. If as far as their jobs are concerned their membership and reference groups coincide, as far as their home aspirations are concerned their membership and reference groups definitely diverge.

Before turning to a more detailed analysis of some of the issues raised by these essays, it is necessary to try to assess the influence of the school setting upon the views expressed. How different were the comments of the adolescents when interviewed in youth clubs, etc., and to what extent did those who had left school show different attitudes from those still at school? As stated earlier, trainee social workers visited nine clubs, including a uniformed church organization, an adventure playground and a club designed to attract the 'rough' elements which other clubs refuse to admit. Discussions with leaders and members were lengthy but took place upon only one occasion. It was unfortunately impossible to undertake a more systematic survey. Because of these limitations the information gained can be used only to check the consistency of

---

[1] T. Parsons, op. cit.

children's attitudes in a non-school setting, and to make a few comparisons using a slightly older age-group.

The most striking difference between these conversations and the school essays was the more frequent mention of racial issues and, because the subject was pursued in more detail, the differentiation of attitudes to the immigrant groups—the tinker Irish and the Indians being much more disliked than the West Indians. Again and again immigrants were blamed for the deterioration in the area. One observation from the school essays definitely appeared to be corroborated in the clubs—the lower the adolescent's own status—as measured here by their jobs—the more vehement their dislike of outsiders, especially if coloured. Several boys with 'dead-end' or un-skilled jobs claimed to be members of 'Keep Britain White' movements. Most youth clubs had one or two coloured members, but no sizeable group; the West Indian club had no English members present when visited. A wider range of clientele visited the adventure playground—West Indian and Irish children predominating.

One student talked at length to five West Indian boys in their late teens, and found them becoming very belligerent in their attitudes because of the discrimination they were ex-periencing. They were refusing to accept an inferior status and the stereotyping of their group. 'I'm proud of my colour', was repeated several times. And, 'We'll fight to protect our-selves.'

Again confirmed was the desire of the older children to move out of the area because of its dirt, overcrowding, and 'the blacks'. One girl summed up Sparkbrook as a 'rotten, stinking dump'. However, again no realistic ambitions as to where to move to and how to achieve the transition were enlarged upon. For instance, one group of boys, none of whom was earning more than £7 a week, said they would have £500 to £1,000 before they got married at twenty-one or twenty-two.

Most of the themes noticed in the school writing were there-fore continued and reinforced in discussions outside school. The only difference is to be found in the greater frequency of emphasis upon racial issues and the vehemence of the dislike expressed. Those adolescents who have left school also manifest more clearly Merton's classic elaboration of 'anomie'—the gap between the accepted goals of society and the lack of a legal means of achieving these goals.[1]

On the basis of the essays and group discussions, it is now possible to summarize a few areas of conflict, where school and parental role models clash, or where no clear guide is presented by any agency, or, as in this first example, where the ascribed status of the inhabitants of Sparkbrook causes very unpleasant difficulties for those venturing outside the area to make wider social relationships.

English girl (aged fourteen)

'When any friends of mine ask me where I live I am ashamed to tell them in case they think I live in those slums, in fact if I tell anyone I live in . . . Rd, they say, "oh no don't tell me you live there".'

English girl (aged eleven)

'I live at. . . . It is one of the worst roads. So sometimes I am ashamed to tell anybody where I live.'

An older girl at one of the youth clubs complained that her boys friends deserted her when they knew where she lived. The categorization of all people who live in one area as 'slum families' leads to a defensive attitude on the part of children and parents, and often the search for a scapegoat to despise and blame. The feelings of rejection are reflected also in a lowering of the child's self-image. This manifested itself very clearly among the boys at certain youth clubs. One major difficulty in writing this chapter is the lack of essays from the Secondary Modern boys. If these bore any resemblance to the statements of the older boys, then this feeling of being at the bottom of the English social ladder would be a prominent feature.

The scapegoating of certain groups can be seen in the following quotations:

English girl (aged fifteen)

'I would like to send all the immigrants back to where they came from as it is them who have made Sparkbrook what it is now. I

---

[1] R. K. Merton, *Social Theory and Social Structure*, op. cit., Chapters IV and V.

would not like to set up home in Sparkbrook because I should not like my children to live in the same dirty district as I have.'

Not many children, however, were as vehement as the following fifteen-year-old English girl: 'I think all the old houses should be pulled down and flats and masernets should be built and only people who are capable of keeping them clean should go into them. People who live like pigs should be treated like pigs.'

One recipient of this sort of attitude and behaviour, a West Indian boy of eleven, writes: 'I dislike living in . . . because the children tells you to go back to my own country.'

As they grow up then, the English children slowly realize that outsiders have a stereotyped picture of their home area and its inhabitants—they are held in low esteem. To this extent therefore their parents are either seen as unacceptable role models or, even if acceptable, needing justification; or if parental role models are accepted, then the rest of society is rejected—society most forcibly represented in different ways by the teachers and the police. The householder role model put forward by the teachers, largely unconsciously, is unattainable by all but a very small minority. The majority cannot aspire to the middle-class suburbs or even the respectable council estate. They can only dream of the 'country cottage' away from the class configurations of the city.

The process of growing up in this country presents even more complicated problems for the immigrant children. Not only are their parental standards despised either by the community as a whole or at least by their peer groups; these roles are frequently inapplicable in this country. Certain modifications, even if minimal, have therefore to be made by the parents. Either the role models offered by white society may be unattainable through discrimination (for example, the purchase of a single-family house in a better district), or the children may be prevented from following English models by parents who are not willing to allow their children to adopt completely alien behaviour patterns. These types of conflicts are elaborated upon by Sydney Collins in his studies of coloured minorities.[1] The second-generation Muslims he studied had great difficulty

---

[1] S. Collins, *Coloured Minorities in Britain*, London, Lutterworth Press, 1957.

in opting out of the religious activities of their community and in attempting to participate in English recreational activities. The second-generation Chinese, however, appeared to be quite content to remain within their own community and did not struggle for anglicization.

Goode's role bargaining theory may well be applicable in this context.[1] If the economic and social rewards of the immigrant community are great, for example in terms of business ownership, etc., then there are greater sanctions for enforcing conformity. The majority of immigrant parents in Sparkbrook do not possess this sort of sanction. English society offers greater rewards, and so the pressures to move into it will be almost overwhelming for the second generation. Therefore very sharp tensions will be generated if the pattern of social mobility followed by the status-aspiring Irish, Poles, and so on is forbidden to the coloured second generation. Fears have been expressed that the second generation will be allowed to enter only the narrow range of jobs now pursued by the adult immigrant. Desai, in *Indian Immigrants in Britain*, comments that the 'host society is reluctant to recognize internal differentiation in immigrant status, skills and ambitions'.[2] Croward and Ohlin base their theory of delinquency causation primarily upon institutional blockages preventing social mobility.[3] Though this theory was developed with the aid of American evidence, it may well be applicable in this country; its validity could usefully be checked in this sort of area.

What is obvious in Sparkbrook is that the schools inevitably undermine parental authority, especially among the Indian and Pakistani communities. The H.M.S.O. publication, *English for Immigrants*, states: 'The school must be exceedingly careful not to set up or aggravate tensions between the child and his parents.'[4] I think this statement should be rephrased to say that the schools should try to understand and minimize the tensions which will almost invariably arise among certain immigrant groups.

[1] W. J. Goode, 'The Process of Role Bargaining', *Current Sociology*, Vol. XII, No. 3, 1963–4.
[2] Desai, op. cit.
[3] R. Croward and L. Ohlin, *Delinquency and Opportunity*, London, Routledge and Kegan Paul, 1961.
[4] *English for Immigrants*, Ministry of Education Pamphlet No. 43, London, H.M.S.O., 1963.

The following quotations illustrate the problems faced by Indian girls in the areas of occupation, marriage and leisure:

Indian girl (aged sixteen), talking about her future life:

'When I was 21 I became an Air Hostess. I loved my career as an Air Hostess very much.'

In fact, no Indian girl leaving the school so far has been allowed to take a job and it was not likely this girl would be either. Several had stayed on at school to take a commercial course—not with a view to obtaining a job in an office, but to enhance their value in the marriage market.

Another Indian girl (aged sixteen) wrote:

'This Easter I have got engaged to a boy who has been picked for me by my parents, but on my and the boy's decision.'

When talking about her future life, this boy was not mentioned at all. The same girl also wrote: 'My parents do not give me much freedom because it is the custom of our country that a girl should not have too much freedom while she is unmarried. I do not like this custom because I cannot enjoy my leisure time.'

She wished to go to 'pop' concerts with friends.

Marriage patterns and roles may also cause conflict situations for the West Indian second generation. This is an area of study I wanted to pursue further, especially as regards the West Indian boys. As mentioned earlier, in their writing all the girls spoke of getting married early—so at the level of their expressed aspirations they had adopted an English pattern as distinct from the late marriage norms of West Indian society and in spite of the fact that the majority of West Indian children in the sample would be classified as illegitimate here.[1]

I would repeat that I think we ought to take very seriously indeed the problems facing second-generation immigrants. A recent article[2] concerning Cypriot children showed how their

---

[1] See for example R. T. Smith, *The Negro Family in British Guiana*, London, International Library of Sociology and Social Reconstruction, London, 1956; J. Blake, *Family Structure in Jamaica*, Free Press of Glencoe, 1961; M. Kerr, *Personality Conflict in Jamaica*, Liverpool University Press, 1952.

[2] 'The Immigrant Schoolchild and Problems of Adjustment', in CASE Conference, January 1963.

mental health suffered as a result of intergenerational conflict. It was found that the frustration of parental ambitions frequently leads to over-ambitiousness for the child, or the parents themselves were ambivalent towards their adopted country and hindered the child's attempt to become part of it, or they found the meeting of basic needs of such overwhelming difficulty that the needs of the children were temporarily subordinated. All three of these situations exist in Sparkbrook.

Obviously in the foregoing discussion I have not answered categorically any of the questions which were raised at the beginning of the study. I hope, however, that some useful clues have emerged. An understanding of the processes of change in Sparkbrook can best be illuminated in terms of the role conflicts inherent within its social structure. Both English and immigrant children are confronted by a range of possible behavioural norms and goals, presented by teachers, parents, mass media, peer groups, etc. Conflict in a sociological sense—within the social structure—becomes conflict in a psychological sense, within the personality of the individual, and the essential aim for social policy must be to deal with the practical problems posed for the administrators by this situation of conflict. Two points in particular stand out. One is the uncertainty of children, teachers, and parents about the kind of society children are being prepared for. The other is the absence of techniques for dealing with the special problems of different kinds that groups of children face once the desired kind of organization has been defined. Clearer definition is required from teachers and community leaders of the kind of society they live in, which would make a deliberate attempt to prepare children for it possible.

XI. Policy Alternatives

In our final chapter we shall suggest that the nature of the 'zone of transition' and the conflicts within it are explicable in terms of the sociology of the city. But we do not by any means wish to suggest that the processes which we have described are absolutely determinate. In the first place, we wish to emphasize that whenever a sociologist says that social processes are predictable, or that they have a function in terms of some larger social system, it may still be asked whether this larger social system is not one which accords with the goals of a particular group only, and whether the same social situation might not be assessed as 'dysfunctional' from some other point of view. Secondly, even if it were granted that there is only one set of ends which the urban social system had to achieve and that these must be taken as given, we might still ask whether there was one way and one way only in which these ends might be achieved or whether alternative institutional arrangements were not possible. Thirdly, we would ask whether, although certain lines of action seemed logical and necessary from the point of view of those in decision-making positions, these lines of action nonetheless had unintended consequences which were actually harmful to the interests of those whom policies were designed to serve.

All of these questions have relevance to the situations in Sparkbrook, in Birmingham and in England. For, firstly, it must be recognized that even though the housing, planning and public health policies of the Birmingham Corporation appeared necessary from the point of view of old Birmingham residents, they might not be necessary and might be actually harmful from the point of view of newcomers to Birmingham or from the point of view of those wishing to promote Birmingham's long-term prosperity. Secondly, it might be shown that the interests of the old residents were not, in fact, best served by the policies pursued, and that there were other ways in which those interests might be served. And, thirdly, it might be shown that the unintended consequences of protective discriminatory policies were of a kind which, had they known of them in advance, would have caused the policy-makers of Birmingham to think again.

The starting point of our discussion must be the problem which appeared to present itself to the City Council when large-scale coloured immigration began. Birmingham was faced in 1950 with a vast housing shortage and the immediate reaction to the news of a considerable influx of immigrants was fear that the pressure on existing resources would increase and that the housing situation would deteriorate still further. In fact, however, immigration had been going on since the beginning of Birmingham's history and had not of itself made Birmingham's housing problem any worse. In recent times immigration had been accompanied by emigration beyond the city boundaries and the actual population was decreasing. The main difference in the situation was that the new immigrants were more visible because of their colour and that the extent of the problem was greatly overestimated.

Had the Birmingham Council at this stage taken careful note of emigration as well as immigration figures it might have reacted more calmly to the situation. It would then have made its housing plans purely in terms of the number of families requiring housing and given all of its residents, newcomers as well as natives, equal chances of qualifying for a house. This would, of course, have meant that the natives would have lost some of their privileges and many people would have had to suffer the relative hardship of having to share houses with their in-laws. But Birmingham would not have been faced with the totally new problem of the lodging-house areas, which it was ill-equipped to tackle.

There was, moreover, a further and more radical possibility open. This was actually to decrease the demand for houses in the city by doing everything possible to prevent further growth in the number of jobs in the city through the encouragement of *industrial* decentralization. There are, of course, limits to what can be done in this direction if a policy of positive direction in industrial location is rejected at central Government level. But even if this is admitted there is much which could have been done to draw the attention of expanding firms to the advantages of decentralization. What was not at all logical was to permit the continued expansion of Birmingham industry and at the same time exert pressure for the restriction of immigration.

In the event, Birmingham's post-war policy of housing allocation was built around the five-year rule. This meant in effect that the Council accepted that it could make a contribution to housing only part of its population, that the remainder would be left to the mercy of the free market, and that a substantial part of that remainder would consist of immigrants. The policy adopted was in marked contrast to some other cities, for instance Bradford, which had only a six-month waiting period.

In these circumstances the point of major interest in the sociology of housing in Birmingham has been to estimate what kind of housing system would come into being for those at the back of the queue. The answer to this could have been given in advance by anyone who had considered the logic of the situation as it presented itself to those requiring housing and what alternatives were legally possible. No one attempted to work this out, however, and the answer has emerged empirically. The problem today is to decide whether the kind of housing system which has emerged is tolerable in a modern city and, if not, what can be done about it.

We do not wish to repeat here all that has been said in previous chapters about the way in which the lodging-house area develops. The point which needs most emphasis is simply this: that whereas other forms of housing, as in private suburbia or in council houses, were regarded as legitimate, the form of housing in the twilight zones was not. It was left to those who were 'moral outsiders' to work out a form of housing of any kind which would put roofs over people's heads and obviate the necessity of having large numbers of people sleeping on park benches. In some cases the task fell to the most dubious entrepreneurs from the host society. But to a large extent it fell to those who were disadvantaged themselves and had sufficient initiative to do something about their own housing situation.

It is important to emphasize that had there been no discrimination and had the disadvantaged included large numbers of people born in Birmingham, the kind of housing which would have emerged would not have had the 'illegitimate' reputation of the lodging-house zone. More would have been compelled to obtain mortages and, being stable local residents, would not have had great difficulty in getting them. Some would have lived in a not-very-desirable but none the less socially acceptable way with relatives and in-laws. And the Council, faced with pressure from people to whom it had a political obligation, might itself have taken action to convert old houses to flats in a socially responsible way.

In any case, the last-mentioned alternative was open, but was not pursued. A large-scale programme of conversions was regarded as uneconomic and the building resources of the Council were concentrated upon building new houses and flats or on 'patching' slums awaiting demolition. Moreover, even in those cases when through a series of planning accidents the Council found itself in possession of convertible property, it showed little desire to administer such property. Thus, in the case of the compulsory purchase of fourteen houses in Spark-brook, the Council had no plans to use them to provide a new and acceptable model of multi-occupation and would have been glad to have the houses taken off their hands. The only serious attempt which we encountered to provide an alternative and legitimate form of housing in the twilight zones was that of the Birmingham Friendship Housing Association, which had made some good conversions in Sparkbrook in which a small number of immigrant families were satisfactorily housed. But such small-scale operations can only point the way to what might be done. They cannot, of themselves, provide an alternative housing system.

One special problem facing Birmingham or any other large city receiving immigrants is that of housing single men. It is a problem which can be solved in two ways. One is to encourage them to bring wives and families to the city so that they can be housed in the normal way. The other is to provide special accommodation for them. The first alternative was made less feasible as a solution when, because of fear of evasion of immigration controls, the central Government made the entry of dependants more difficult than it had been. The second alternative was not seriously pursued by the Birmingham

Council, which preferred to leave such matters to voluntary bodies such as the Salvation Army.

It should not be thought that the problem of providing acceptable forms of accommodation for single men is an easy one. Bradford had attempted to create small hostels of this kind but found that they were unacceptable because of high rents and because of the desire of single immigrants to live together under their own authority. But there is still room for considerable experiment here and the matter is one in which consultation with the leaders of the various immigrant groups might point the way to a solution.

In fact, in the absence of any provision for their housing, some single men who were temporary migrants, especially those from India and Pakistan, banded together to buy houses to run as lodging-houses, this being the cheapest and most satisfactory way of housing themselves. A few of them might in fact have been good landlords, but as a matter of social policy it should be obvious that a temporary migrant who has no interest in the long-term value of the property will not be the best person to assume responsibility for managing an important part of a city's housing stock. Nor is it likely that a single man working long hours of overtime will be a good manager of a house or a good landlord to his tenants.

The same considerations apply with only slightly less force to any landlord who does not regard property as a capital asset to be maintained against rapid depreciation but rather as a means of housing himself for the moment without regard to whether he has any capital assets at the end. Landlords of this kind present a real problem and the Housing, Planning, and Public Health Departments are bound to take some action to supervise their activities.

The years between 1960 and 1965 have been years in which Birmingham has devoted itself to working out ways of supervising its lodging-houses. It has used its powers to try to ensure that houses are properly managed, that they provide adequate amenities and that they are not overcrowded. But there have been two absolute limits to what they could do. One is that legal pressures alone cannot force a man to be a good landlord. At best they achieve only formal compliance with standards. The other is that it is impossible really to deal with overcrowding unless alternative accommodation is provided for a surplus of tenants.

The first point has in part been met by the provisions of the 1964 Housing Act enabling the local authority itself to assume the management of a house for a period of five years. It remains only for the logic of this situation to be finally accepted and for local authorities to take permanent control of the lodging-houses through compulsory purchase orders. But the second problem remains and it will remain until the Housing Act of 1961 is amended to provide that the serving of an overcrowding order lays upon the local authority the responsibility for providing alternative accommodation for those rendered homeless.

As we have seen, the operation of the five-year rule has thus far ensured that very few of the lodging-house tenants, other than young couples, have qualified for housing by way of the Council list. But some are beginning to qualify and others will gain an entitlement to rehousing through becoming homeless or becoming ill. There is a danger here that local authorities will be afraid of the consequences of rehousing large numbers of immigrants in council estates. The problem will be only more acute in areas like Birmingham where this issue has been postponed by the five-year rule. What is likely to happen, therefore, is that the immigrant population of the lodging-houses will be rehoused in council-owned property awaiting demolition and that in areas where this sort of property predominates secondary ghettoes will develop, and in the long run the problem of rehousing immigrants will appear in an even more overwhelming form. The only way this can be prevented is by an absolute and public insistence by housing departments that their Housing Visitors will not discriminate on racial grounds in the allocation of council houses.

During the period of our research the Birmingham Corporation was not in a position to close down the lodging-houses in the areas where that pattern of housing was firmly established. To have tried to do so would have meant 'spreading the disease' from one area to another. So the first reaction was to try to prevent new areas going over to lodging-house use. In so far as this was the intention of the Council in obtaining special powers to register lodging-houses in advance, it could only result in the division of the city into two parts in which two different laws applied. It would not solve the problems of the twilight zones. It would simply segregate them from the respectable areas. At its worst this policy would lead to the formation of ghettoes.

The suggestion that its new powers would be used in this way was denied by representatives of the Birmingham Council to whom we spoke and at the time of writing our information is that the Council intends to carry out a 'blitz' on the existing lodging-houses. It is by no means clear, however, how it will meet the difficulty which has always stood in the way of such a policy, namely, that of rehousing the lodging-house tenants.

It now feels compelled to act, however, against the twilight zones, and act it undoubtedly must. For the existence of these zones is the leading example of what we called at the outset the unintended consequence of its policy. The policy was evolved as a means of holding back the demand for housing. Its unintended consequence has been the rapid deterioration of an important part of the city's housing stock and the emergence in what were relatively desirable areas of demoralized communities torn by racial dissension and conflict. The people of Birmingham themselves now see the twilight zones as a problem and demand action by the Council to deal with it.

It cannot be too strongly emphasized, however, that the problem has not arisen through an increased pressure of population. The population statistics demonstrate this. It is a problem which has arisen from the discriminatory policies[1] of the Council itself which have had the effect of concentrating new-comers, and many 'problem people' besides, in limited areas of the city.

One alternative which is open to the Council, however, is to declare some of the twilight zones comprehensive redevelopment areas. It has been slow to do this because the twilight zones consist of houses which are still in their twilight. They are not yet slums. But the demand is there for their redevelopment and the Council has been forced to bring forward schemes for at least partial redevelopment.

Even such schemes, however, run into difficulties. A proposal

---

[1] We refer here not to discrimination based on colour but to the five-year qualifying period for all immigrants referred to earlier.

that the main lodging-house streets in Sparkbrook should be cleared to make way for schools and other buildings was rejected. The opposition spokesmen on the Public Works Committee claimed that this was because '600 immigrant families would have to be rehoused'. The Labour Member for Sparkbrook claimed that, faced with a choice between clearing an area where the houses were slums and families living in single-occupation and clearing an area where houses were not slums and houses were in multi-occupation, the Council quite rightly chose the former. Even if this latter interpretation is correct, however, the effect of such decisions is clear. Redevelopment cannot take place in any area where there is a concentration of lodging-houses. And for that reason the likelihood is that nothing effective can be done about the twilight zone.

The effect of this housing and planning situation on race relations is obvious. The account which we have given of the emergence of the lodging-houses is not easy to grasp and the man-in-the-street is easily convinced by an entirely different diagnosis of the problems of the city. This racialist diagnosis would read as follows:

We, in Birmingham, face a tremendous housing problem. Many Birmingham people live in appalling conditions. There was some hope after the War that we might solve the problem. Then there occurred a wave of immigration which placed an unbearable strain on our social services generally, but upon housing in particular. The chances of our own people being housed have been materially reduced. More than this, however. These people from the colonies have a very low standard of life but they have taken over big houses which many British people couldn't afford and turned them into slums. The time has come for a halt in immigration. As to those immigrants who are already here, they must be integrated, that is taught how to live according to British standards.

That this diagnosis is false should be clear from what has already been said. Immigration has not in any way affected the chance of rehousing people of Birmingham. What has happened is that Corporation policy has forced upon immigrants a type of housing and a way of life that is damaging to the city. But it is a superficially plausible diagnosis none the less and one which in some measure informs the thinking of the policy-makers.

It is in this atmosphere that 'integration' of immigrants already in England is discussed. If our diagnosis of immigrant problems of adjustment is correct, then the way to integration lies in reducing discrimination in the sphere of housing and, when the part of the problem which arises specifically from the immigrant's housing situation has been dealt with, applying highly specialized skills of social workers, teachers, and others to dealing with the more subtle problems which beset particular individuals.

Policies for integration which have been advocated, however, are not of this kind and the first point to be noticed here is that the problem has been seen primarily as a problem of colour. This is particularly true in the case of educational policy discussions where, faced with the sudden appearance of large number of coloured children in schools, teachers and parents have feared that the backwardness of such children may retard the education of ordinary English children. This leads to demands for the dispersal of coloured children.

The problems of the schools with high concentrations of coloured children, however, are quite different, as has been shown in Chapter X. The classes in these schools include some children whose English is poor or non-existent, of whom some are Asiatic. They include some who are backward because they have begun their education under a different educational system. They include black and white immigrant children, some of whom have problems due to severance of kinship ties. And they include many English children who are retarded because of the circumstances of their home life.

None of these problems are solved by a policy of dispersing coloured children when their proportion in a class rises above a particular level. There would still be classes in which English- and non-English-speaking children were mixed. There would still be children who were retarded for one reason or another and for whom no kind of remedial education was provided. And there would still be large concentrations of white immigrant children.

It is true that the policy of dispersing coloured children has not won universal acceptance. Unfortunately, however, this opposition occurs for the wrong reasons. It occurs because those who live in the 'respectable' areas of the city do not want coloured children as classmates for their own children any more than they want lodging-houses springing up in their suburbs. So the real problems of the concentration of children with a variety of different educational difficulties in particular schools are never dealt with.

Related problems arise in the local authority's approach to the more diffuse problems of integrating immigrants in general. Apart from drawing attention to the absolute necessity of eliminating discrimination in housing as the precondition of any sort of integration, we have shown that adjustment to a new way of life presents many subtle cultural and personal problems. These problems can be dealt with only by the most sophisticated techniques of a social worker working in close co-operation with those who lead the immigrant communities. Moreover, the problems are problems which face both white and coloured immigrants.

This was not the approach adopted by the Birmingham Corporation. In the first place they appointed an officer who was called plainly a 'Liaison Officer for *Coloured* People'. Secondly, they chose for the task a man whose whole life experience had been in the police, a fact which suggests that they thought of the problem of coloured people as a police problem. And, thirdly, the officer appointed did not work and was not required to work in co-operation with the leaders of the immigrant community.

The Liaison Officer did, it is true, draw attention to the danger of a coloured quarter arising in the city, but as an officer of the Council he could not or did not draw attention to the reasons for this danger. He helped individual immigrants to find jobs and homes, at least during the early years of his appointment, but was forced to accept that this had to be done within a general pattern of segregation and discrimination. And, if he did define his task as one of integrating the immigrants, the major emphasis had to be laid on forcing the immigrant to conform to a British way of life.

In fact, the striking thing about discussions of integration in Birmingham was that it was discussed amongst white people and that it usually finished up with proposals for measures against the immigrants which at best had not been discussed with them and at worst were of a plainly punitive character. Perhaps the most important set of conclusions reached was that relating to housing, and in this sphere Birmingham's policy was to harry immigrant landlords and by parading them each week in court give ritual expression to Birmingham's hostility to them.

Once the process of segregation and discrimination was under way and hostility to the immigrants mounted in consequence, the problems of race relations were bound to be discussed in both national and local politics. There was a period in which there was a real tension of ideas, with some politicians asserting that the problems that Birmingham and other cities were facing were problems of social policy and others claiming that there was no way out but to ban coloured immigration which was at the root of the problem. But this tension disappeared when the new Government elected in 1964 published its White Paper on Immigration from the Commonwealth.

The White Paper accepted as its basic thesis that the social services were overstrained because of the influx of immigrants and proposed measures for restricting working-class coloured immigration to the merest trickle. In so doing it gave the support of its own authority to those who thought that immigration was to blame for the problems of housing shortage and urban deterioration. Those who still sought to argue that these problems had different causes felt they were in a minority while those who called for punitive measures against the immigrants felt that the Government was on their side.

This, however, was not the Government's intention and some of its members genuinely believed that a pause in immigration would create a more favourable climate for the integration of those immigrants already in Britain. To this end, Part 3 of the White Paper was nominally directed. It remains now to be seen whether, if we accept that integration could occur in the atmosphere generated by rigid immigration control, the proposals made in Part 3 would help or hinder the process.

At first the White Paper appears to be taking its stand against discrimination in housing when it says: 'The sole test for action in the housing field is the quality and nature of the housing need without distinctions based upon the origin of those in need.'

This would appear at first to imply a criticism of the policy pursued by the Birmingham Corporation. But this sentence follows an earlier one in which the danger alluded to is that *immigrants* will have special preference and when the section goes on to say: 'As time goes on, immigrants will qualify for rehousing by local authorities either by virtue of residential qualifications or through being displaced by slum clearance and development', it is clear that the authors of the section are misinformed. Immigrants do not qualify by virtue of residence and do not even get on to the Birmingham Council's list for five years. Moreover, it should be clear especially from Chapter II of this book that they will benefit only marginally from slum clearance. Discrimination against newcomers in the system of housing allocation means that it will be a very long time indeed before a significant number of immigrants qualify for council houses.

But these are reasons given for not making proposals. More important is the single positive proposal which the White Paper makes. This is nothing other than that the powers acquired by the Birmingham City Council to restrict lodging-house development should be given to all local authorities. We have already pointed out that these powers can have only a negative influence on the immigrants' housing situation, that they could be used to segregate rather than to integrate immigrants and that they tend to be punitive powers against the immigrants. Coupled with alternative proposals for immigrant housing, such a policy could be useful. By itself it is unlikely to make any contribution to the housing or the integration of immigrants.

On education, the White Paper endorses the circular previously published by the Ministry of Education and Science calling for the dispersal of immigrant schoolchildren. It goes on: 'It is time to urge research into the problems involved in teaching immigrant children', but the issue seems to be prejudged by the adoption of the policy of dispersal.

Related to the White Paper is the Government's Race Relations Bill, which might be thought to be, and in some respects is, concerned with measures which will increase rather than decrease the opportunities open to immigrants. But discrimination in housing and employment are beyond the scope of this Bill and it is to the White Paper alone that one must look for guidance as to the Government's views on these matters.

The White Paper, of course, does not represent the final word on immigration policy or on policies for the integration of immigrants. Immediately, the task of promoting integration must fall to the National Committee for Commonwealth Immigrants and it may be expected to make further recommendations. If this Committee is to take the initiative in revising a trend towards discrimination which appears to be implicit in the White Paper proposals, our study would suggest a number of important recommendations which it should make.

(1) In order that the Government should not appear to be lending its support to those who blame the immigrants for Britain's housing problem, immigration should be permitted at a level which is consistent with the needs of the British economy.

(2) An increase in the amount of rented housing available must have a high priority in the Government's plans.

(3) This increase to be coupled with a variety of provisions including the direction of some available building resources to the conversion of structurally sound old houses.

(4) The enforcement upon local authorities of a 'code of housing allocation' which prevents discrimination between applicants for housing on grounds other than housing need.

(5) Given that proposals 1 to 4 are adopted, a rigorous enforcement of those sections of the Housing Acts relating to management, amenity, and overcrowding coupled with the frequent use of compulsory purchase as a sanction against bad and inefficient landlords.

(6) Suitable financial provision for the adequate conversion of such houses acquired through compulsory purchase and the maximum use of improvements grants to help private landlords convert their property.

(7) Refusal of Government authorization for any development scheme which is designed in any way to discriminate particular classes of tenant.

(8) A government-sponsored investigation into the reasons for the emergence of the lodging-house problem, followed, if necessary, by central Government action to redevelop these areas.

(9) The issuing of an instruction to all Housing Visitors employed by local authorities that the race of an applicant is

not a relevant consideration in deciding his suitability for a particular type of local authority-owned house.

(10) The withdrawal of the circular by the Ministry of Education and Science on the dispersal of immigrant school-children and immediate support for research into remedial teaching methods in deteriorating urban areas.

(11) The setting up of local committees for Commonwealth immigrants which are representative of coloured immigrants as well as of members of the host community with powers to report to local councils.

We do not think that it will be easy, politically speaking, to gain support for these proposals, for, as we have shown in previous chapters, there are built-in reasons in the structure of our society which will make increased racial tension likely. But there are also built-in tendencies the other way and we believe that these would be strengthened if policies such as we have outlined were adopted and problems usually defined in racial terms dealt with in non-racial ways. We should be inclined to say, if we were asked what the future of race relations in Britain's cities is likely to be, that a tendency towards segregation of coloured immigrants in cities will continue and that the inhabitants of these areas will more and more become the target of punitive policies and racial hostility. None the less, we do not yet see this trend to be absolutely inevitable and it is because we, as individuals rather than as sociologists, wish to see it arrested that we have written this book.

XII. The Sociology of the Zone of Transition

It has been our aim in this research to contribute not simply to the sociology of race relations, but also to the sociology of the city. More than this, we believe that the particular aspects of race relations with which we have been concerned are explicable only in terms of the sociology of the city. What we propose, therefore, by way of a sociological conclusion to this book, is to suggest a theoretical model of the city and urban processes as they bear on 'the twilight zones', thus completing the task of theoretical analysis which was begun in the Introduction to this book.

In offering such a theoretical summary, we face a certain dilemma. If we concentrate upon the special features of Birmingham's situation, what we say may turn out to have little general significance. If, on the other hand, we talk in purely general terms, we shall not explain much that is important in the story which we have had to tell. Against this, however, we believe that in large measure what is happening in Birmingham is something which might happen in any West European or North American city and that it will be possible to preserve a balance in this chapter, showing that which is unique, but also indicating what the variables are which have produced it.

Our approach to this study is much influenced, at least on a general level, by that adopted by Park and Burgess in their studies of Chicago in the 1920s.[1] This is by no means to suggest that urban processes in Birmingham exactly reproduced those of Chicago. We do, however, believe that the general processes, which Park and Burgess assumed, were evident in Birmingham and that, although there were substantial modifications due to the operation of additional variables, their framework provides

[1] R. E. Park et al., The City, Chicago, 1923.

us with a useful starting-point. In particular, we recognize the importance of their emphasis upon competitive processes and upon a 'zone of transition' as recurrent urban phenomena.

The competitive process which we observed, however, was considerably more complex than that posited by Park and Burgess. They reduced it to a simple competition for land use. We see it as threefold: (1) as continuing competition for the use of sites; (2) as competition for the use of buildings which have now been abandoned by their original users; and (3) a more general competition for the use of available material resources, which has resulted in limited but significant inter-ference with the rights of property and with pure economic competition, and which has produced a 'welfare' sector in the national economy.

Houses in a modern city are not allocated simply by a process of competition in the market. The notion of a certain style and standard of housing as a right, has meant that, even though private building, sale and purchase of houses continues, a substantial part of house-building is today carried out by local governments and that there is a primary problem of allocation of resources as between this public welfare sector and the private house-owner.

Within the general housing economy, local government, popularly elected, therefore administers its own estate. But this in itself raises two problems: who will benefit from that estate? And how will the specific rights of the individual who does bene-fit be determined? It seems to us that participation in this public estate is a considerable prize in a society where housing is a scarce resource and that such a public estate can bring into being a group whose 'market situation' in the housing market is an especially privileged one.

This brings us to a point which appears to be central to the sociology of the city. Put simply, it is that there is a class struggle over the use of houses and that this class struggle is the central process of the city as a social unit. In saying this we follow Max Weber who saw that class struggle was apt to emerge wherever people in a market situation enjoyed differen-tial access to property and that such class struggles might therefore arise not merely around the use of the means of industrial production, but around the control of domestic property. Of course, it may be argued that a man's market situation in the housing market depends in part upon his income and therefore on his situation in the labour market, but it is also the case that men in the same labour situation may come to have differential degrees of access to housing and it is this which immediately determines the class conflicts of the city as distinct from those of the workplace.

There will therefore be as many potential housing classes in the city as there are kinds of access to the use of housing. Moreover, as in the case of industrial classes, this means more than simply owners and non-owners. As we see it, too much political debate about housing is based upon the assumption that all problems can be discussed simply in terms of the rights of landlords and tenants. The result has been a failure to appreciate the special problems of the people with whom we have been most concerned. Before we can begin to understand what the problems of the zone of transition or the twilight zone are, it will be necessary, therefore, to distinguish the different types of access to housing which are possible in a modern city.

We distinguish the following types of housing situation:

(1) that of the outright owner of a whole house;
(2) that of the owner of a mortgaged whole house;
(3) that of the council tenant—

    (a) in a house with a long life;
    (b) in a house awaiting demolition;

(4) that of the tenant of a whole house owned by a private landlord;
(5) that of the owner of a house bought with short-term loans who is compelled to let rooms in order to meet his repayment obligations;
(6) that of the tenant of rooms in a lodging-house.

It is likely that these types of housing situation will have a definite territorial distribution in the city depending largely on the age and size of the buildings in different zones. If we assume a city as composed of four concentric rings around a central business district, the city itself being surrounded by satellite towns and villages, then the types of housing situation and the housing classes to which they give rise will be distributed as follows, prior to the commencement of major slum-clearance programmes:

(1) The outright owners will be found especially in the third and fourth zones from the centre and outside the city in its satellites.

(2) The owners repaying mortgage loans will be found predominantly in the fourth zone.

(3) The council tenants of houses with a long expectation of life will also be found in this fourth zone. After slum clearance they may also be found in higher-density council houses in the first and second zones.

(4) Property scheduled for slum-clearance will be situated in the first and second zones.

(5) Private tenancies will be found in all zones, but especially in zones one, two, and three.

(6) The lodging-houses, occupied by their owners and tenants, will be in zones one and two, but predominantly in zone two.

The six housing situations mentioned above take the order 1–6 in a scale of desirability according to the status values of British society, except that lack of capital puts the first two situations beyond the means of many urban residents, who can therefore aspire only to a ceiling of situation (3a), and that there will be some overlapping between situations (3) and (4) and particularly between (3b) and (4) (i.e. many private tenancies will be more desirable than some council house tenancies).

Over time there will be a movement of individuals and families from one housing situation to another. Most especially this will be a movement outwards with tenants in situations (4), (5), and (6) moving to situations (2) and (3). Movement to situation (2) requires capital. Movement to situation (3) depends upon the criteria of selection employed by local authorities. We assume that some of those in situation (4) and nearly all of those in situations (5) and (6) desire to make this move.

Situations (1), (2), and (3a) not merely enjoy high prestige. They enjoy legitimation in terms of the value standards of the society as a whole. Situations (1) and (2) are legitimated in terms of the ideal of 'a property-owning democracy'; situation

(3*a*) in terms of the values of 'the welfare state'. Situation (3*b*) is regarded as an unfortunate transitional necessity in terms of welfare state values. Situation (4) is of declining importance because of the gradual disappearance of the private landlord. Situations (5) and (6) are seen as highly undesirable in terms of welfare state standards, and especially in terms of public health standards.

The number of those who can make the transition to situation (3*a*) is limited by the resources available and the standards which operate. Had council building been concentrated on two-room dwellings and families allocated to these regardless of size, all those in situations (3*b*), (4), (5), and (6) could probably have been provided for. But with higher standards and a limited building programme it follows that many will be excluded from this legitimate and high-status provision. Those in situations (5) and (6) will therefore find themselves in a low-status 'illegitimate' situation.

The crucial question then becomes that of the criteria used in selecting tenants for council houses. We have shown what these are in our city in Chapter I. Here we have to point out that local councils are likely to reflect the interests of the long-established residents who form the majority of their electorate. Thus a basic distinction is drawn between local people and immigrants, and between those with normal family situations and isolates and deviants. These will live in the lodging-houses.

The population of the lodging-houses will not consist entirely of immigrants of the same country of origin, nor even entirely of immigrants. Since the basis of the lodging-houses is profit, and neighbourly ethics inhibit the willingness of individual proprietors to exploit their own kin and countrymen, landlords will normally recruit at least some of their tenants from ethnic groups other than their own. And they will also provide for the non-immigrants who do not qualify for council housing, such as newly married couples and those living outside normal family life.

Geographically the lodging-houses may be concentrated in particular areas so that communal facilities are used entirely by lodging-house people. But in our experience this was not the case. We saw that zones 1 and 2 included people in housing situations (3*b*) and (4) as well as (5) and (6) and we would therefore expect the areas where there are lodging-houses to be mixed in their total composition. The areas served by a shopping centre, churches, and schools might include both lodging-houses and scheduled slums, or they might include both of these and houses let to whole families. Thus these zones are more complex in their communal structure than Burgess's account of the 'zone transition' would lead us to suppose. We agree, none the less, that a distinction should be drawn between those communal centres where the lodging-houses are present and those where they are not. To this extent we accept Burgess's distinction between the 'zone of transition' or 'marginal zone' and the 'zone of working-men's houses'.

The people of the 'zone of transition', as we have seen, share certain facilities. To what extent do they constitute a community? The answer to this is complex and has been the main theme of this book. In summary, however, we may make the following points:

(1) There will be a number of different immigrant situations. Some immigrants will maintain strong links with home. Others will not. Some will aspire to assimilation. Some will not. And some will encounter discrimination on grounds of race or culture to a greater extent than others.

(2) For all immigrants, immigration will mean a loss of immediate contact with large numbers of kin and friends. They will therefore face a situation of personal demoralization and anomie from which they will find a way out through affiliation to the host culture or through living in the colony.

(3) The various colonies will have their centres in particular shops, pubs, cafés, clubs, and associations. This will produce ecological changes which can be described in such terms as dominance, invasion, and succession.

(4) The differences of interest among the immigrants and between immigrants and non-immigrant groups will produce a conflict situation in which one group will deploy sanctions against the other, including the sanction of legitimate political power (i.e. by getting the local authority to take action in a particular group interest). Associations may be formed to further these interests or, on the other hand, existing associations with other aims may be used for these purposes.

(5) The extent of conflict may be limited in a number of ways. The associations through which groups pursue their aims may be unsuitable for the purpose and may have multiracial memberships which blur the lines of conflict. Groups may be forced to accept an unsatisfactory position because of the sanctions employed against them. And there may develop institutions within which conflicts may be peacefully resolved or managed.

It will be the case, however, that for most people in the zone of transition, there is a sub-community of some kind in which they feel culturally and socially at home. Social relations within this group will contrast markedly with those of the market place and with relations between any one member of the group and an outsider.

The situation for the lodging-house tenant, however, is more complicated than that which Furnivall suggests with his concept of 'the plural society'.[1] According to Furnivall, in a plural society the members of different ethnic groups meet only in the market place where the absence of shared norms prevents the emergence of a 'common will' and relations tend to be nakedly exploitative. But each of the groups retires at night to its own culture and community where in-group norms do operate. What is different in the lodging-house is that the dwelling-place itself is a market place. Community is found only in the immediate household and beyond that outside the lodging-house in the culture and community of the colony. Intergroup norms within the lodging-house are either commercial or based upon habitual avoidance, backed by an *ad hoc* informal code.

We must now return to the point which we made earlier, that the housing situation of the lodging-houses is illegitimate from the point of view of the public authorities and has a low status in the city's scale of values. The obvious long-term resolution of this tension would lie in rehousing this population in other ways. But the housing shortage precludes this solution and the only alternative is to segregate the lodging-house area from the other areas. That is to say, lodging-house accommodation will be permitted only within certain areas.

[1] J. S. Furnivall, *Netherlands India: A Study of a Plural Economy*, Cambridge, 1944, and *Colonial Policy and Practice*, Cambridge, 1948.

In a strict sense this does not produce a ghetto. A ghetto would appear to imply a segregated ethnic community, and as we have seen the zone of transition includes various ethnic communities, transitional people awaiting rehousing and isolates and deviants of all sorts. What is segregated is a problem area. All those forms of life which are unacceptable according to welfare state standards are confined there. In so far as the system of housing allocation in other areas discriminates against immigrants, the immigrants will not be totally segregated, but they will be compelled to live with other people in an 'illegitimate' problem area.

The kind of housing provision which exists in this area is, however, essential to the city, given its overall housing shortage. Who then will be responsible for its provision? Clearly, the situation demands the existence of a pariah group who do not themselves feel bound by welfare state standards and are culturally distinct enough to be blamed for their departure from such standards.

But it is inherent in this situation that those who provide this kind of housing and those who live in it will be blamed or punished for so doing. Public health standards demand that landlords should be brought before the courts and sometimes forced out of business entirely. There is a limitation on this process in that if it broke down completely there would be no houses available. But the situation demands that the values of the society should be affirmed by ritual and exemplary punishments. At the same time, these punishments may help to ensure that standards are not unnecessarily low.

The same punitive attitudes are likely to be expressed when the public authorities discuss 'integration' of the immigrants. In the sense of facilitating the acceptance of immigrants as citizens with full rights in the host society 'integration' is ruled out, so long as they are discriminated against in the matter of housing. But the maintenance of welfare state standards demands that those practices and customs of immigrants which are offensive to the host society should be suppressed, whether they arise from the home culture of the immigrants or from their housing situation. It is this kind of suppression which is commonly referred to by public authorities when they discuss integration. It is thought of in part as a police function, in part as the business of education. The aims of this sort of integration policy would best be achieved in concentration camps; and the cry 'Put them in camps!' appears from time to time in the correspondence columns of the local Press.

Clearly this situation is not a stable one. It may change in one of two ways. One possibility is that discrimination against immigrants may decrease. In these circumstances those who fail to qualify for houses might find other ways of accommodating themselves, either through house purchase or private tenancies, which are less open to immigrants, or by sharing accommodation with relatives, a form of multi-occupation which does not have the offensive characteristics of the lodging-houses. Alternatively, the punitive policies of the host community and their elected representatives might be checked by the active resistance of the immigrants themselves. This later stage of development in the twilight zones may already have been reached in some American cities where Negro riots have recently had profound political effects.

The punitive policies pursued by the officials of the local authority will reflect and reinforce attitudes of hostility on the part of the host population at large. Amongst these, especially those who live in areas threatened with invasion by the lodging-houses, those whose presence in the lodging-house area itself indicates that the invasion there is not complete, and those tenants of the lodging-houses and scheduled slums who see the immigrants as potential competitors in any plans they may have for a transition to other areas. The fact that the area is a mixed one and the fact that immigrants are slow in acquiring political rights ensure that the legitimate political parties in the area will not reflect immigrants' interests and they will, therefore, be without legitimate political representation.

In these circumstances the political parties find themselves under pressure to adopt a policy of immigration restriction. The adoption of such a policy has several functions for the native residents of the area. Firstly, it appears as a solution of their problems, since they believe that an absolute decrease in numbers will ease the existing pressure on scarce housing resources. The reasoning here is, of course, fallacious, since the numbers demanding housing will be a function of labour demand in the area and overseas immigrants are bound to be replaced by immigrants of other kinds. Secondly, it opens up what appears to be one of the most attractive possibilities for a group in a conflict situation; namely, that the opposing groups will actually be eliminated. Thirdly, the debate about the policy gives opportunities for the open expression of resentment against immigrants, for the expression of this resentment now becomes a theme of legitimate politics. And fourthly, assuming that in terms of local status values, colour and coloured people as such have the lowest status, it helps local people to dissociate themselves from the low-status position in which they find themselves as a result of living in a markedly immigrant area.

In order to understand the structure of community in the zone of transition, it is necessary to answer two questions. Firstly, we must discover what opportunities there are for the residents to leave the area, and secondly we must show how conflicts between the various groups who live there are resolved.

The possibilities of leaving the area differ for the different sub-groups. The simplest situation is that of the newly formed native households. For them residence in the zone of transition and its lodging-houses is a temporary expedient only. In due time they will accumulate enough money or enough 'points' to buy a house or to rent a council house in the suburbs. Their commitment to the local community is therefore minimal. They have no long-term interest in improving its facilities and the main impact upon their thinking which residence there will have is that they may for a while fear that the sheer numbers of residents sharing their plight limits their opportunity of transition to happier circumstances.

The problem facing the native isolates and deviants is different. Many of them will be living in the area because of the positive advantages which it offers, most particularly those which flow from the fact that the landlord asks no questions. But, as Parsons has suggested, it is a common feature of the value systems of deviant groups, that they like to 'have their cake and eat it'. While enjoying the advantages of deviance they may still have some residual commitment to the values of normal society. This commitment can be expressed through the formula 'We live as we do, not out of choice, but because these alien people compel us to do so.' Some of this group may, as time passes, find their way back to family life and to participation in normal society and the aim of social work in the area must be to increase this possibility. But in our experience it would seem that there is a majority for whom this is not a zone of transition, but a zone of stagnation. Their problems are never likely to be resolved and for them the zone of transition provides a niche in an otherwise hostile society.

The most important native group consists of old residents. It has always to be remembered that it takes several generations for a community to abandon an urban area entirely and, although evacuation of the lodging-house area may be virtually complete, there are other houses adjacent to it which are still occupied by local families. These people are distinguished by the fact that they are committed both to the normal values of the host society and to living in the area. The possibility of giving up the struggle and leaving is there, but for them leaving rather than having to stay would be the major cause of resentment. This group will be concerned to maintain the standards of the host community in the area itself and if it does not actively demand the expulsion of the newcomers, will be strongly motivated to demand their conformity with old standards.

The first immigrant group which we must notice consists of single men who regard themselves as temporary migrants from overseas. They are likely to have little interest in conforming to the values of local society or of preserving the facilities of the area. Their aim will be to obtain work and an income which will be used later to improve their living standards in another country. For them the area is at best a dormitory. But the fact that it is also the home of native residents brings them into sharp conflict with those residents, particularly with the third group mentioned above.

Some of this group of immigrants will, of course, come to see their migration as more permanent and show this by bringing dependants to live with them or marrying locally. In this case their position becomes that of the rest of the immigrants who, while they may have some intention of returning to their countries, are at least partially committed to seeking acceptance as members of the host society.

Even if these other immigrants faced no discrimination in the sphere of housing and social life, the process of theirassi milation would not be merely a single-stage one. There would be a period during which they would seek the support of the society and culture of an immigrant colony. This colony would provide an initial sense of personal security and cultural familiarity and, using it as a base, the immigrant would go out to explore the host society and to establish the contacts which would make his eventual assimilation possible.

But in our experience, this was the situation of few immigrants. It was most likely to be found amongst white, English-speaking, or professionally qualified immigrants. The situation of most immigrants desiring assimilation is that they do encounter discrimination and that each step which they take to claim rights in the host society, especially the right to a home, encounters opposition. Hence, the immigrant looks to his colony not just for a temporary home, but as the basis for organizing aggressively or defensively to ensure that he obtains his rights, or he may seek to oppose discrimination by seeking to define a more limited area of rights which his hosts are willing to concede.

Given that discrimination on grounds of colour prevails, it is the latter posture which will be adopted by the majority of coloured immigrants. They will not have a realistic perspective of gradually moving out of the lodging-house zone to the suburbs, but will try to improve their living conditions in the area where they are or try to find some area less desirable than the suburbs as a secondary area of settlement.

There seem to be no studies of these secondary areas of immigrant settlement and little can be said of the possibility of a further move from them. In our experience, however, the transition to such secondary areas seemed possible in two ways. It could come about through house purchase in less desirable areas between the suburbs and the lodging-house zone or through public housing in less desired forms of public housing, for instance, slums awaiting demolition. In so far as the latter transition is made on any scale, one must envisage a further stage in which large concentrations of coloured people have to be moved suddenly to housing estates.

One fact which profoundly affects migration within the city is that the possibility of the lodging-house area itself spreading is limited. Once the problem is identified the residents of the better areas will demand that the area of the lodging-houses is restricted and that the cancer must be stopped from spreading. Thus those who live in the area find that theirs is a distinctive way of life which is not permitted in other parts of the city.

Thus the zone of transition, including lodging-houses and other sorts of accommodation, houses a mixed population of varying degrees of permanence and conflicting interests. The problem of community in such an area is the problem of how, in practice, the conflicts of interest which are present are to be reconciled. The expression of these conflicts and their reconciliation is the work of the associations which exist in the area.

One would expect in such an area that the available associations, whether they be political parties, churches, tenants', immigrants', or community associations, would in part at least provide the means of organizing to advance special groups' interests and that they would ritualize the aggressive and defensive sentiments of the various groups. That they do do this has been amply demonstrated in the previous chapters. But it is also true that some of the organizations in the area are at least partly inhibited from performing these functions by their national and international affiliations and by the universalistic ideas contained in their ideologies and 'charters'.

But individuals must interact with members of outgroups both in the buildings in which they live and in the streets and the market place. These contacts are not regulated as easily as the contacts made between members of an association. They are more likely to be regulated by the police and the courts or by occasional limited use of violence. Again, in our experience the degree to which violence was accepted as inevitable in day-to-day contacts was considerably greater than in other areas of the city, even though this never reached the point at which group was pitted against group in any sort of riot situation.

There is, however, another possibility and it was one which was evident in our area. This is that the leaders of the various ethnic, class, and other groups should meet regularly to define common interests and to find peaceful compromises where there were conflicts of interest. This is the work of community associations in the zone of transition. Some, of course, may be more successful than others. The central problem is that there should be sufficient detached individuals willing to give the necessary time to playing a mediating role.

In whatever degree this task is accomplished, however, it should not be thought that it is possible for the community in the zone of transition to become like any other community. It is a specialized area of the city providing for the needs of special classes of people and, even if there were less intense discrimination, this community would face special problems. What we have sought to do here is to outline the sociology of this sort of area in order that planners and social workers should be better equipped to deal with its distinctive problems. If we succeed in drawing the attention of British planners to the importance of understanding the zone of transition within the context of the sociology of the city, we shall have accomplished one of our main aims in writing this book.

Appendix

(1) *The Sample*

The commonly used sampling frame based on the Electoral Register was unsuitable for our purpose because of the high population mobility in Sparkbrook 1 and the presumed low rate of registration among immigrants. We therefore used the Rating and Valuation lists of 31 March 1963, for Sparkbrook. These gave us not only a list of all the houses in Sparkbrook (a few on the lists had been demolished, in fact) but also some indication of the number and distribution of houses known to be in multi-occupation. There was no sharp cut-off value at which multi-occupation began but the frequency of occurrence of multi-occupation increased rapidly from £55 Rateable Value and upwards.

It was intended that half our sample should be of English people and half of immigrants. As it was obvious from the 1961 Census and from our own observations that immigrants tended to live in multi-occupied houses, the desired result could be achieved by drawing our sample more heavily from the houses with Rateable Value £55 and over.

Since time and resources limited our total sample size to 800 persons, we devised our sampling fractions on the assumption that the £55 and over Rateable Value houses housed an average of 10 persons and the under £55 R.V. houses an average of 2·5 persons. Hence we drew a 1 in 6 random sample of the higher R.V. houses and a 1 in 40 random sample of the lower R.V. houses. Interviewing every adult in each house should have given us a sample of 800 persons. We defined an adult to be any person over sixteen years of age and not in full-time education.

TABLE 53: ORIGINAL SAMPLE

	R.V. £55 and over	R.V. £55 and under	Total
No. of dwellings	135	87	222
No. of persons*	1,350	218	1,568

* Including children.

Our final total sample had to be revised slightly since several houses had been demolished and we were unable to locate others.

(2) *The Incomplete Survey*

One of the major difficulties in interviewing was the problem of finding the interviewees. The first 100 or so were easily found at home but after this interviewers faced the problem of actually locating the people they had to interview. Sometimes interviewers could not be absolutely certain how many people really lived in a given house. In this case, however, estimates were made up using answers to the question, 'Who else lives in this house?' given by those who had been fully interviewed, and re-calling done on the basis of these estimates. In the multi-occupied dwellings, where the composition changed between two visits, we took the earliest known structure in estimating the dwelling and household structure. Interviewers made many re-calls, although more than three only when they had the promise of an interview or believed they were likely to obtain another interview. Shift workers were often either out or asleep; single men used their rooms only for sleeping. At times interviewers could not tell if a man was out, or had moved.

Although we carried out a 100 per cent. scan of the multi-occupied houses in the sample to check on languages spoken,[1] English interviewers sometimes found themselves with non-English-speaking people; this had to be reported back and another interviewer assigned. Interviewees would sometimes make an appointment to be interviewed and then postpone it three or four times. Some were out on the first appointment and had to be re-contacted.

A number of the Indian and Pakistani respondents were suspicious of us, believing us to be from the police or Health Departments, and it took interviewers some time to establish sufficient *rapport* for interviewing to be possible. Many of the Azad Kashmiris spoke a dialect unfamiliar to the interviewers.

With a highly mobile population in Sparkbrook 1, the time-span over which we had to interview, because of the difficulties outlined above, may have introduced some errors into our sample; we took household structure of dwellings for the earliest known date, although in a few cases the people actually interviewed are not the people occurring in the household structure.

When it became clear to us that we were not going to achieve all our interviews in the time available, we visited all the houses in the sample with interviews outstanding and established house-

---

[1] Seventeen languages were spoken normally in Sparkbrook although we only needed to interview in eleven.

hold structure by sex and nationality and, as far as possible, age. In a very few cases this information was obtained from neighbours and not directly. We made use of these data only in population structure tables and as a guide to how far our interviewed sample was comparable in a structure to the total intended sample. The percentage distribution by sex and nationality of these two groups are given later. We also had to re-calculate our actual sampling fractions as distinct from the intended 1 in 6 and 1 in 40. The actual sampling fractions were found to be 10 in 65 and 10 in 386. Also from these data we calculated average dwelling sizes to be 6·51 persons per dwelling for £55 and over R.V. group, and 3·45 persons for the under £55 R.V. group.

TABLE 54: REVISED INTENDED SAMPLE

	R.V. £55 and over	R.V. £55 and under	Total
Dwellings	124	90	214
Persons*	1,240	225	1,465

* Including children.

Of our total sample of 214 dwellings, six were completely un-contacted and seven were empty. Therefore our final achieved sample contained 201 dwellings, 117 in the higher R.V. group and eighty-four in the lower R.V. group. The total number of persons (including children) was 1,052.

TABLE 55: RESPONSE OF SAMPLE

	Total sample	Achieved Sample		% response	
		Outline structure	Complete response	Outline and complete	Complete only
Dwellings	201	79*	122†	100	60·7
Households	382	146*	236	100	61·8
Individuals (adults)	750	346	386	97·6	51·5

* At least dwelling/household size determined and broken down into adults and children.
† A dwelling was taken to be complete if at least one interview was obtained from each household.

The individual responses break down as follows:

TABLE 56: INDIVIDUAL RESPONSES

Complete interviews: English	192	
Immigrant	194	
	—	386
Age, sex and nationality	155	
Sex, and nationality only	191	
No information	18	
	—	364
TOTAL		750

The breakdown by national group of the total numbers of persons in the sample is:

TABLE 57: SAMPLE BY NATIONALITY

	Adults		Children	Total
	Male	Female		
English	161	181	124	466
Irish	88	62	97	247
West Indian	65	53	53	171
Pakistani	69	5	15	89
Indian	11	4	3	18
Other	23	10	10	43
Not known		18	—	18
TOTAL	417	315		
		750	302	1,052

Of the 346 individuals from whom completed interviews were not obtained, seventy (19·2 per cent.) refused to answer and the remaining 294 (80·8 per cent.) were uncontacted. The refusal rate for the total adult sample was 9·3 per cent. and 39·2 per cent. were uncontacted. Reasons for refusals and non-contacts are discussed later.

Most of the tables in the text are based only on completed interviews. The 'complete sample is shown in Table 58.

When we had ceased interviewing we had only thirty-one male Pakistani respondents and since we regarded forty as the absolutely minimum sample size to give our data any statistical significance we obtained nine more interviews by quota sampling. One of the nine was a woman, so our findings are based on a sample of thirty-nine male Pakistanis.

TABLE 58: 'COMPLETE 'SAMPLE

	Male	Female	Total
English	85	107	192
Irish	45	44	89
West Indian	27	21	48
Pakistani	31	1	32
Indian	5	2	7
Other	7	11	18
Total immigrants	115	79	194
TOTAL	200	186	386

These extra eight are not, of course, included in ethnic-comparative and other population tables, but only in those tables which concern Pakistanis alone.

(3) The Questionnaire

To test our questionnaire we carried out a pilot survey in an area adjacent to Sparkbrook. Unfortunately, of the six multi-occupied houses chosen for this, two had been pulled down and two were brothels. Thus we had to carry out a second pilot survey.

Our interviewers were mainly students and members of the Society of Friends. We used these in preference to professional interviewers for the following reasons:

1. A variety of languages was needed for interviewing.[1]
2. High motivation was necessary to achieve accurate results in difficult and at times unpleasant conditions.
3. Tact, initiative and some understanding of the purpose of the work were necessary as we felt that in many cases it might not be possible to administer the questionnaire in a formal, bureaucratic manner.
4. The use of volunteers would keep our costs down.

We are now sure that only volunteers could have achieved our present results; Pakistani and Indian students had the necessary languages and all the interviewers had the motivation and insight necessary for persuading people to be interviewed. This often

[1] Translation of questions by interviewers obviously involves a measure of *interpretation* but we do not believe that this raised any possible sources of error where we were concerned with fairly unambiguous factual answers. Real ambiguities did arise—but not as a result of language problems—e.g., in questions concerning the return home and desire to move from Sparkbrook.

involved long discussions with the interviewees (often faithfully reported, and of interest in themselves), endless tea-drinking, and very many re-calls at given houses. This work was done in the winter of 1964, mainly in the evenings and at week-ends.

(4) The Findings and Reliability of the Survey

Although we did not interview everyone in our sample and given that our final sample was fairly small, we are confident that our findings are not significantly different from those that would have resulted from a larger or more complete sample.

If a comparison is made between the percentage distribution by sex and nationality of the total sample and the sub-sample of those who completed questionnaires, we see that there is no very significant difference between the non-interviewed and the interviewed in these respects.

TABLE 59: PERCENTAGES INTERVIEWED AND NON-INTERVIEWED

	Total sample		Interviewees	
	Male	Female	Male	Female
English	38·7	57·5	42·5	57·6
Irish	21·1	19·7	22·5	23·7
West Indian	15·6	16·8	13·5	11·3
Pakistani	16·5	1·6	15·5	0·5
Indian	2·6	1·3	2·5	1·1
Other	5·5	3·1	3·5	5·9
TOTAL	100·0	100·0	100·0	100·0

Failure to interview was, in general, due to our own lack of time, not to any characteristic of either part of the sample. Exceptions are the seventy people who expressly refused to be interviewed. This group consisted mainly of elderly people who either lived alone and did not want to be bothered or who were 'protected' from us by their kin or neighbours. There were also a number of young couples with children who were too busy to answer (and who said that they would never be free to talk) and one or two others who were quite truculent and even aggressive refusals among the English. However, refusals were about equally divided among English and immigrants.

There was no initial bias in choice of houses by interviewers. Our statistical evidence is used alongside information gathered in other ways. Our three fieldwork techniques may be summarized as:

(i) Participant observation of the routine life and special 'events' of Sparkbrook.

(ii) Informal interviewing of apparently important or interesting members of various groups. This included befriending a number of particular people who became our guides to and commentators on their own community and events. They often provided contacts and introductions for us. We talked frequently with social workers, ministers, and local officials. We spent many hours in pubs, cafés and churches just listening, or talking to chance contacts as well as observing routines or 'events' in progress. Not only did these activities give us running cross-checks on hard data, but a series of points of view of various actors in the situations and their 'logic of the situation'.

(iii) The use of the questionnaire as outlined above.

No one of these methods would have been adequate in itself, but taken together they enabled us to build up various pictures and to cross-check and interrelate them. At no point in our text do we make any statement of our own that is not backed by evidence produced by more than one of the above methods.

Throughout our work we were conscious of how little there was to guide us on matters of technique in the 'zone of transition'; most research of this kind in the United Kingdom seems to have been carried out among ethnically homogeneous groups and often in a single social stratum.

(5) *Population Estimates*

The only method of obtaining a reasonably accurate measure of the population of the survey area would have been to conduct our own census and count everybody in every house. Since the population, especially in Sparkbrook 1, is so mobile this operation would have been hardly worth the effort involved. The estimated population structure given in the tables below is a by-product of the data in our questionnaires and serves to give some indication of the distribution of the different nationalities in our survey area. Since our figures are meant only as a rough guide and cannot be deemed accurate in a statistical sense we have ignored the fact that individuals were, in fact, cluster samples. We have treated the sample as stratified random with a variable sampling fraction.

The following table gives details of the calculation of total population. A rough estimate of the standard error of the mean dwelling size was obtained by dividing the area into five sub-strata and applying the following conventional formula:

$$\text{estimated } SE = \sqrt{\frac{\Sigma\left(\mathcal{N}_i^2 \frac{S_i^2}{\mathcal{N}_i}\right)}{\mathcal{N}^2}} = \sqrt{\frac{\Sigma\left(\mathcal{N}_i^2 \frac{S_i^2}{n_i}\right)}{\mathcal{N}^2}}$$

Where S_i^2 is the variance of the ith sample stratum, $\mathcal{N}_i$ the number of dwellings in the ith stratum of the survey area and n_i the number of dwellings in the ith stratum of the sample.

TABLE 60: TOTAL POPULATION

Rateable Value (in £)	No. of dwellings in sample (1)	No. of persons in sample (2)	Mean persons per dwelling in sample (3)	Variance
Under 35	52	165	3·17	3·01
35–54	32	125	3·91	11·49
55–74	51	261	5·12	8·67
75–94	34	272	8·00	18·82
95 and over	32	229	7·16	24·07
TOTAL	201	1,052	4·324	

The estimated standard error of the mean dwelling size is 0·2543. When account is taken of the finite population correction based on sampling fractions, this estimate becomes 0·2311. The sample mean is 4·324 so with 95 per cent. confidence the population mean lies between 3·871 and 4·777. This means that the estimated population of the survey area is between 15,951 and 19,693 with a best single estimate of 17,823. Since, even at this fairly low level of confidence, we have an error of at least 10·5 per cent., we cannot justifiably make any assumptions about the breakdown by ethnic group of the total population. Also, it must be emphasized that the methods used to obtain the estimate of the population and the standard error of the mean dwelling size are rather rough and ready since the sampling design was never intended to satisfy the criteria necessary for accurate estimation of errors.

Taking 17,823 as the best estimate of the population, and allowing for the weighting of the sample, we derived the following estimates of the percentage distribution by ethnic group:

TABLE 61: PERCENTAGE DISTRIBUTION BY
ETHNIC GROUP

	% of total	Estimated number
English	67·0	11,941
Irish	12·9	2,299
West Indian	8·7	1,551
Pakistani	3·6	642
Indian	2·0	356
Others and not known	5·8	1,034
TOTAL	100	17,823

It is almost impossible to give any measure of the errors associated with these figures, but they will of necessity be large and therefore the numbers must be regarded only as a very rough guide to the ethnic composition of our survey area.

Index